PRAISE FOR *WALMART*

Every brand wants to understand how to sell to Walmart; this book empowers
the reader to understand the strategy behind the giant retailer and gives
the reader a strong foundation to improve their relationship and sales with
all retailers. This is not a book for those who ~~want to sell at the cheapest~~
it is a book that teaches how to build a long-

Phil Lempert, Supermarket t

An insightful, comprehensive and well signp
the investment community's understanding
retailers in general and the implications for consumer staples manufacturers.

**James Amoroso, President, Consumer Analyst Group of Europe
(www.cag.eu.com)**

Walmart is a unique book. It combines a comprehensive history of Walmart's
methodical rise to greatness with a host of scenarios for its future growth.
Must-reading for anyone who wants to know how Walmart did it and
where it could be going – in the US and internationally. Roberts and
Berg have a done a terrific job.

**Brian Sharoff, President of the Private Label
Manufacturers Association (PLMA)**

An incisive assessment of Walmart and its pivotal influence across global retail.

Siemon Scamell-Katz, Founder, TNS Magasin

Library & Media Ctr.
Carroll Community College
1601 Washington Rd.
Westminster, MD 21157

Walmart

Key insights and practical lessons from the world's largest retailer

WITHDRAWN

Bryan Roberts and
Natalie Berg

KoganPage

LONDON PHILADELPHIA NEW DELHI

Publisher's note

Every possible effort has been made to ensure that the information contained in this book is accurate at the time of going to press, and the publishers and authors cannot accept responsibility for any errors or omissions, however caused. No responsibility for loss or damage occasioned to any person acting, or refraining from action, as a result of the material in this publication can be accepted by the editor, the publisher or either of the authors.

First published in Great Britain and the United States in 2012 by Kogan Page Limited
Reprinted 2012

Apart from any fair dealing for the purposes of research or private study, or criticism or review, as permitted under the Copyright, Designs and Patents Act 1988, this publication may only be reproduced, stored or transmitted, in any form or by any means, with the prior permission in writing of the publishers, or in the case of reprographic reproduction in accordance with the terms and licences issued by the CLA. Enquiries concerning reproduction outside these terms should be sent to the publishers at the undermentioned addresses:

120 Pentonville Road	1518 Walnut Street, Suite 1100	4737/23 Ansari Road
London N1 9JN	Philadelphia PA 19102	Daryaganj
United Kingdom	USA	New Delhi 110002
www.koganpage.com		India

© Bryan Roberts and Natalie Berg, 2012

The right of Bryan Roberts and Natalie Berg to be identified as the author of this work has been asserted by them in accordance with the Copyright, Designs and Patents Act 1988.

ISBN   978 0 7494 6273 4
E-ISBN   978 0 7494 6274 1

British Library Cataloguing-in-Publication Data

A CIP record for this book is available from the British Library.

Library of Congress Cataloging-in-Publication Data

Roberts, Bryan R., 1939-
  Walmart : key insights and practical lessons from the world's largest retailer / Bryan Roberts, Natalie Berg.
    p. cm.
  ISBN 978-0-7494-6273-4 – ISBN 978-0-7494-6274-1 (ebook)   1. Wal-Mart (Firm)
2. Discount houses (Retail trade)–United States–Management.   I. Berg, Natalie.   II. Title.
  HF5429.215.U6R63 2012
  658.8'79–dc23

                                                                                          2011043136

Typeset by Graphicraft Ltd, Hong Kong
Printed and bound by Edwards Brothers Inc, Lillington, NC

CONTENTS

10 Facing up to a multi-channel future 159

11 Going global: Walmart's international retail leadership 190

12 Tomorrow's Walmart 215

ACKNOWLEDGEMENTS

Natalie and Bryan wish to thank Joanna Perry for getting the ball rolling and for her invaluable guidance in all matters technological. They also wish to express their gratitude to all past and present Walmart associates who contributed their insights and opinions, both on and off the record. Thanks also to the whole team at Kogan Page for their support.

Bryan wishes to thank Suzy for her support and editorial input and also Luca and Fynn for putting up with countless research trips to Asda.

Natalie wishes to thank Steve for coping with endless dinner chats about EDLP and range rationalization during their first year of marriage, and her Mom who has always been so supportive.

Is Walmart the best-positioned retailer on the globe?

There are some very visible success stories in the globalized economy. Billions of consumers around the world are familiar with names such as McDonald's, Coca-Cola, Heinz, Apple and Nike. Manufacturers, financial services providers and retailers have built up vast multinational empires, seeking to profit from consumers in wealthy developed markets and exploiting the rapid growth potential of less affluent markets. In this book, published in Walmart's 50th year, we will portray one of the biggest and most successful proponents of global growth.

There is a *Fortune* article from January 1989 that hangs in the Visitors Center in Bentonville, Arkansas, titled 'Walmart: Will It Take Over the World?' Some quotes from that article (written by John Huey) include 'In just a couple of years, Walmart Stores will be the largest retailer in the US' and 'You may never have shopped in a Walmart because the company is really just getting started... so sooner or later, there's bound to be a Walmart in your future.' Looking back, the understated prescience of the article is spot on.

The truth of the matter is that, globally, Walmart is only just getting started. CEO Mike Duke told investors at the 2011 Shareholders meeting that 'the same culture that drove our growth during our first 50 years can drive our growth for the next 50 years', adding that 'Walmart is the best-positioned retailer on the globe.'

No disrespect to the good people of Arkansas, but the state is an unlikely home for one of the largest and most technology-driven enterprises on earth. From these humble, and somewhat unlikely, roots has blossomed one of the most impactful organizations in the history of humanity. Not only has the company grown into the largest retail enterprise on earth, with a lead that is unlikely to be challenged by any retailer other than Amazon, but its influence on the broader global retail and fast-moving consumer goods (FMCG) industries has been virtually immeasurable. Walmart's impact has reshaped the world of distribution. The company has directly influenced the technology that is now universally used to make sure that shoppers get the products they desire. Walmart's economic impact, in terms of bringing lower prices to shoppers, runs into billions and billions of dollars. The company accounts for a massive chunk of the annual revenues of many of the world's largest consumer goods suppliers. Walmart has perhaps caused, or undoubtedly accelerated, the demise of many competing retailers. Simply put, it is one of the most important commercial organizations in the world.

There are many facts and figures that are testimony to the sheer scale of the business:

- Walmart's annual sales in 2010 stood at $419 billion: if it were a country, it would be the world's 25th largest in terms of gross domestic product (GDP), ahead of Norway.

- It is the world's largest commercial employer, and the second-largest employer in the world behind the Chinese military.

- Procter & Gamble's sales to Walmart amount to some $13 billion, bigger than the total sales of many leading retailers and FMCG suppliers around the world.

- Walmart now sells more groceries than Kroger and Safeway combined – it is salient to remember here that Walmart only started selling groceries in a meaningful fashion a little over 20 years ago.

- Over the same period, over 30 sizeable supermarket chains in the United States have entered Chapter 11 bankruptcy protection.

- Four of the top ten richest people in the United States are from the Walton family.

- As a standalone retailer, Walmart International will be the world's second-largest retailer by 2012, trailing only Walmart US. Its rapid growth has been juxtaposed with former number two Carrefour's divestments and stagnant trading.

We are assessing the world's largest retailer at an intriguing time. We cannot refute Mr Duke's claim that Walmart is currently the best-positioned retailer in the world. Owing to their scale, they are best positioned to absorb inflation, to drive efficiencies in the supply chain, to leverage power over their suppliers, to influence the millions of consumers who shop at a Walmart every week. They have achieved unprecedented levels of growth in their 50-year history.

But the question is – just how much is left? Walmart got to where it is today because of ruthless efficiency. Very simply, focusing on driving costs out of the business has enabled them to offer consistently low prices on a wide assortment of branded goods. Price and assortment, price and assortment.

But is this enough for today's demanding, tech-savvy shoppers? It's no secret that when Walmart veers away from its core business model of price and assortment, it fails. This is why we witnessed over two years' worth of declining comparable store sales in its domestic business. 'We recognized we needed to improve in certain areas and we are working hard to do that. We must increase customer traffic, uphold our price leadership and make sure that we have the broadest assortment and the right products in every store', Bill Simon, President and CEO of Walmart, told the authors in an exclusive interview for this book.

But the challenge facing Walmart is that today price and assortment are simply prerequisites for many consumers, and increasingly they are finding another one-stop shop that delivers even greater price transparency – the internet.

Another hurdle will be the imminent saturation of the Supercenter format in the United States, necessitating the need for Walmart to unleash new growth channels and tap into markets previously deemed too challenging, whether that's the bright lights of New York City or the vast plains of sub-Saharan Africa.

Walmart International continues to be a key growth vehicle; in fact, 2010 was the first year when Walmart's overseas stores outnumbered stores in the United States. It is its International division that will most likely enable Walmart to become the first retailer in the world to break the trillion-dollar mark. Yet, having learnt from previous blunders in Germany and Korea, Walmart today is taking a much more cautious and increasingly flexible approach to international development. It's no longer about planting flags. It's no longer about exporting big boxes around the globe, and crucially, it's no longer about broadcasting from Bentonville. Instead, Walmart is sharing best practices and drawing on local expertise, whether that is using the UK team to help launch grocery e-commerce in the United States or creating a new concept in China based on a Latin American bodega. It is exploring new, underpenetrated geographies such as Africa and the Middle East, while backfilling its most promising existing markets in Latin America and Asia. Private label development, supply chain efficiencies and ongoing investment in systems are also central planks of Walmart's global growth strategy.

Throughout this book, we will assess how the changing strategies of Walmart will impact competitors, suppliers and shoppers. Walmart is at an interesting point in its evolution, and we firmly believe that the strategic reconfiguration that is under way in Bentonville will continue to reshape the world of production, distribution and consumption.

As independent retail analysts, we have immense respect for what Walmart achieves as a commercial entity. In our opinion, it is certainly one of the best and by far the most efficient retailers – in the world. That said, Walmart is not perfect – it can certainly do much better in certain areas like labour relations, ethical sourcing and vendor relationships, to name just a few. In many respects it is no better or no worse than many of the retailers it competes with. Walmart is neither the down-home rustic innocent it would like to think it is occasionally, nor is it the source of all of the world's evils that its detractors would suggest. Yet one thing is for sure – no other company has had a greater influence on the world of consumption over the past 50 years.

Rise of consumerism

In 1919, a 21-year-old demobbed soldier was returning to England after the First World War. Using his £30 stipend, the young Jack Cohen set up a market stall in London's East End. His business model was simple: buy surplus groceries from the armed services and sell them cheaply to his budget-conscious customers. His business soon flourished and expanded to additional market stalls and a wholesale unit. However, this wasn't enough for the ambitious Cohen. In 1924, he signed a deal with a tea supplier, TE Stockwell, to sell their unmarked tea under his own brand. Cohen took the first three letters of his supplier's name and the first two of his own and the very first Tesco private label item was launched.

Tesco today is one of Walmart's fiercest competitors in the multinational food-retailing arena. In stark contrast to Walmart, whose 'house of brands' model initially left little room for private label, Tesco made private label a core component of its business strategy from day one. Today, it is arguably the world's most successful private label retailer, with Tesco-branded goods accounting for approximately half of all products that go through the till. It was the first retailer to establish a three-tiered 'good, better, best' private label portfolio, a strategy that has since been admired and replicated by leading retailers across North America, Europe and Asia. Its Value range was launched in 1993 as a means of fending off competition from new entrants to the UK market: discounters Aldi and Lidl. Five years later, through the analysis of shopper data, Tesco recognized that there was a gap in the market for premium private label items and launched its Finest range. Today, Tesco Value and Finest are both £1 billion+ brands, making them larger than national brands such as Walkers or Coca-Cola in the UK. The company has found equal success in non-food private labelling. Its Florence & Fred apparel line has been turned into a standalone clothing store in the Czech Republic, competing with fast-fashion chains such as H&M. Meanwhile, Tesco has extended its brand into financial services, letting its shoppers decide whether their car insurance requirements fall into the Tesco Value, Standard or Finest bracket.

The company's unparalleled success with its private label portfolio helped it to drive shopper loyalty, differentiate from competition, increase profit margins and cement its status as the world's third-largest grocery retailer.

Yet in spite of Tesco's accolades, its turnover is equal to just one-fourth of Walmart's. While Tesco looked to private label to drive loyalty, Walmart's notion of attracting shoppers was based on the premise of stocking national brands, albeit at the lowest price around. In fact, its first major private label launch didn't take place until 1983, nearly 60 years after Tesco introduced its branded tea to London shoppers.

Despite the fact that today Walmart and Tesco are major competitors on a global front, it's important to look at their domestic markets to understand how each strategy evolved. Market conditions have played a major role in the global development of private label. In Western Europe, a combination of retail concentration and the presence of hard discounters paved the way for private label development at an early stage. In fact, according to Nielsen, Switzerland, the UK and Germany are the global leaders, with private label accounting for more than half of all products sold in Switzerland alone. Meanwhile, in Walmart's home territory, private label today continues to lag behind Europe, with a modest share of 22 per cent of the US market. Despite bouts of retail consolidation over the past several decades, the US grocery sector remains extremely regional in structure. This, combined with the fact that the United States is a vast, sparsely populated country, means that private label has not had the opportunity to build up the same level of scale as it has done in the more concentrated European markets. As a result, US retailers have historically put minimal effort into their private label items, leaving it to be perceived for many years among shoppers as the ugly sister to the national brand, a generic alternative that historically lacked in quality.

But let's also not forget that Walmart used to be a self-proclaimed 'discount department store' and it wasn't until the late 1980s that they began adding groceries to the assortment. Prior to that, Walmart's merchandising efforts were centred on home wares, apparel, sporting goods, toys, electronics, health and beauty care (HBC), garden supplies, automotive and pharmaceuticals. When Walmart was starting out in the 1960s, these general merchandise categories featured influential brands such as GE and Whirlpool which continued to gain momentum as post-Second World War prosperity led to increased consumer demand for household products.

Therefore, in order to get a better understanding of how Walmart's branding strategy has evolved, we have to go back to the beginning. In fact, we have to go back to post-war America, well before the first Walmart store even opened.

Arrival of the boom times

'In the fifties and sixties, everything about America was changing rapidly' SAM WALTON

The end of the Second World War resulted in newfound economic and individual prosperity. This happened much quicker in the United States where, unlike in Europe, consumers did not experience the war on their own soil.

In his autobiography, Walmart's founder Sam Walton writes: 'During the Depression, few of us had enough money to shop very often, and during World War II, everything – meat, butter, tires, shoes, gasoline, sugar – was rationed. But by the time I started out, the shortages were pretty much over, and the economy was growing. Compared to the Depression we had been used to, boom times had arrived.'

Brands suddenly became a symbol of status and convenience. They transitioned the whole notion of consuming from functional to fulfilling, enabling consumers to lead easier and more fruitful lives. In the mid-1950s, economist and retail analyst Victor Lebow described how consumption drastically changed in post-war America. In his essay 'Price Competition' in 1955, Lebow writes:

> Our enormously productive economy demands that we make consumption our way of life, that we convert the buying and use of goods into rituals, that we seek our spiritual satisfactions, our ego satisfactions, in consumption. The measure of social status, of social acceptance, of prestige, is now to be found in our consumptive patterns. The very meaning and significance of our lives today expressed in consumptive terms... We need things consumed, burned up, worn out, replaced, and discarded at an ever increasing pace. We need to have people eat, drink, dress, ride, live, with ever more complicated and, therefore, constantly more expensive consumption.

So what were the factors behind America's newfound appetite for consumption?

1 Democratization of education and home ownership

In the United States, the induction of the GI Bill entitled returning soldiers to higher education, something that was previously exclusive to wealthier families. In fact, prior to the war, only about 10–15 per cent of Americans went on to college. Many looked to capitalize on this new opportunity laid out by the government and by the peak year of 1947, veterans comprised half of college admissions. This democratization of the education system led to a more skilful workforce, with many veterans soon equipped with higher-paying jobs.

At the same time, the GI Bill was providing millions of veterans with new home ownership opportunities. Loans administered by the Veterans Administration (VA) were co-signed by the government for about half of one's mortgage. These low-interest loans, which in many cases did not even require a down-payment, meant that returning soldiers could get a head start on life. By 1950, the VA backed over two million home loans for World War II veterans.

As a result, residential construction increased nearly 1,400 per cent, from 114,000 in 1944 to 1.7 million in 1950. Families headed to the suburbs in droves, looking to achieve the American dream. They were empowered, optimistic, educated and, most importantly for retailers, full of pent-up demand.

'Retailers must face the fact that the urban population is shifting in massive proportions', Lebow wrote back in 1955. 'The middle- and upper-income groups are moving to the suburbs, where they not only have higher rent or property maintenance charges, but are also changing many of their habits in eating, dressing, transportation, recreation and social contacts.'

This societal shift created opportunities to build new schools, highways, churches and eventually strip malls to service the growing consumer demand. Like television, car ownership transitioned from luxury to necessity and the large department stores began to build branches in the suburbs. 'Traditional diners and cafes suffered because of the new car-oriented chains like McDonald's and Burger King, and the old city variety stores like Woolworth's and McCrory's just got smashed by Kmart and some other big discounters', Walton noted in his autobiography.

2 More women in the workplace

In his book *Paradox of Plenty*, Harvey Levenstein writes: 'Virtually unnoticed behind the idealized image of men "bringing home the bacon" for full-time housewives tending efficiently to their homes was the fact that many men could not pay for the new homes, cars and appliances without a financial contribution from their wives.'

Prior to the United States entering the Second World War in 1941, many US companies had secured contracts to produce war equipment for the Allies. At this time, most women were either housewives or employed in typical pink-collar jobs such as clerical work, nursing and waitressing. Having received the right to vote only 20 years earlier, women were still a long way off from true emancipation.

In fact, many employed women, particularly those of a middle class, were looked upon negatively for working as it was viewed as stealing jobs from men who became unemployed during the Depression. However, the mass mobilization of men during the Second World War resulted in severe labour shortages during the 1940s. For the first time, women began to fill these roles, working in what were predominantly 'male' roles such as welding and building planes. Many women saw this as an opportunity both to support their country and to supplement their household income owing to husbands being at war. Rosie the Riveter, a fictional character created by the government, helped to recruit more than two million women into the workforce.

For the first time, it became socially acceptable for women to work outside the home and, although many returned to their roles as housewives once the war ended, the number of working women never again fell to pre-war levels. By 1960, there were twice as many working wives as there had been a decade earlier. The number of working mothers increased by 400 per cent, a large number of whom were middle class, whereas prior to the war most had been working-class women. Such a massive socio-demographic shift became a goldmine for marketers who could promise convenience to these new cash-rich, time-pressured consumers.

3 Access to credit

At the same time, the introduction of credit created a whole new sense of affordability among consumers. Unlike their parents and grandparents, who were used to buying only the essentials, consumers of the 1950s were quickly embracing the notion of buying on time.

In 1949, businessman Frank X McNamara was dining at New York City restaurant Major's Cabin Grill when he realized that he didn't have enough cash to pay. His wife had to come to the restaurant to pay the bill, and his embarrassment ignited a new business idea – to create a charge card that could be used at multiple locations. Up until this point, consumer credit was primarily based on instalments (as opposed to the revolving consumer credit which is commonplace today) and offered by individual companies as a means of driving loyalty. In 1950, McNamara launched the Diners Club in partnership with his attorney Ralph Schneider and Alfred Bloomingdale, grandson of the founder of Bloomingdale's. The world's first charge card was originally aimed at travelling salesmen who needed to dine at various restaurants entertaining clients. In its first year of operation, the cards were issued to 200 people and honoured by 27 restaurants. By the end of the following year, 42,000 people were holding a Diners Club credit card, with more than 300 businesses accepting them as a form of payment.

However, this was only the beginning. While Diners Club restricted cardholders to select restaurants, the emergence of the general-purpose bank card created a whole new set of shopping opportunities for consumers. In 1951, the first bank-card programme was launched by Franklin National Bank. Seven years later, American Express and Bank of America's BankAmericard (which would eventually become Visa) also emerged. Initially, large retailers were reluctant to accept this new form of payment. Not only did it compete with their store cards, but it also came with a fee. What was the incentive? Retailers came round once they recognized the soon to be monumental shift in how US shoppers paid for their goods. Accepting credit cards could result in increased sales and not accepting them would drive shoppers elsewhere. By 1962, American Express alone boasted 900,000 cardholders who could swipe their cards at 82,000 merchant locations.

For better or worse, easy access to credit has helped to create an entire nation of consumers. Back in 1950, outstanding revolving credit as a percentage of total consumer credit was zero. Fast-forward 50 years to 2000 and 40 per cent of consumer credit was related to outstanding balances on credit cards and other unsecured revolving lines of credit.

Today, in the face of economic uncertainty, consumers have reined in their swiping. Revolving outstanding consumer credit has dropped to approximately one-third of total outstanding consumer credit. Yet the economy is still hugely reliant on us to shop: consumer spending accounts for more than two-thirds of economic output in the United States. It's no surprise, therefore, that even when the going gets tough, the government continues to encourage consumers to spend, spend, spend. 'Take the kids to the park, buy a pizza, see a show.' This was the advice of then mayor Rudy Giuliani to the people of New York following the 9/11 terrorist attacks. Several years later, President George W Bush broadcast a similar message during a 2006 press conference. During a time of heightened global uncertainty, Bush told Americans that they can play their own part in growing the US economy. In his words, 'I encourage you all to go shopping more.' Today, consumers around the world are faced with a number of economic uncertainties that have impeded their ability and desire to spend. Unemployment concerns, inflationary pressures and, in many countries, rising taxes have dented spending. Such consumer retrenchment results in a decline in tax revenues for governments. In the United States particularly, where the average household spends about $50,000 each year, this can have a drastic effect on the overall economy.

4 Technology reshaping the kitchen

But back in the 1950s, consumerism was very much on the rise. New brands, products and even categories were emerging owing to technological advances and new scientific findings. For example, in 1955 the Crest toothpaste brand was launched after it was discovered that the use of fluoride could help protect against tooth decay, which was the second most prevalent disease at that time. In 1960, it became the first toothpaste brand to receive an endorsement from the American Dental Association, thereby establishing credibility and trust among consumers. Crest went on to dominate the US toothpaste market for the next 30 years.

Brands were synonymous with innovation during this time of social and economic reform. A growing fascination with television led to the launch of another new product: the TV dinner. In September 1953, Swanson's launch of the cleverly named product struck a chord with consumers who could now eat dinner while engaging in their new favourite pastime. Swanson had forecast selling 5,000 meals priced at 98 cents in its first year. It sold more than 10 million. Future endorsements by Howdy Doody and President Eisenhower made the brand all the more powerful.

The rise of TV dinners and other frozen foods had a knock-on effect in another area of the kitchen: the fridge freezer. Before the war, many household refrigerators lacked significant freezer space (and similarly it was too expensive for most supermarkets to feature them in stores). However, the rising popularity of frozen foods, combined with the introduction of open-top 'coffin' freezers, allowed retailers to make more space available for these products. Meanwhile, manufacturers quickly worked to develop a larger fridge freezer for consumer use.

In the kitchen, brands were quick to innovate, capitalizing on the new house-proud female consumer. In 1955, Lebow wrote: 'Where clothes were formerly the measure of the man, or woman, today the hostess may entertain in the most casual dress, but her table settings, her decorations, her recipes, and her manner of serving become her claims to social status and prestige.'

Changes in technology were reshaping the way people prepared, consumed and stored food. The 1950s and 60s saw the launch of household microwaves, non-stick Teflon pans, coloured kitchen appliances (no more white, thanks to General Electric), automatic can openers and toaster ovens, as well as enhanced features for refrigerators and stoves. Brands were so influential that some product launches from this era are still known today by their branded name. Tupperware and Saran Wrap are classic examples.

5 The television – an advertiser's dream

Known as the Golden Age of Television, the 1950s saw TV ownership sky-rocket in the United States, representing one of the most significant social and technological changes of the century. In 1950, a mere 9 per cent of the US population owned a television set. Within five years, this jumped to 65 per cent and, by the end of the decade, 86 per cent of US households were watching television in their own homes.

Many popular brands found on supermarket shelves today were brought to market during these two decades. Dove soap was introduced in 1955, Cornetto ice cream in 1963, Diet Pepsi in 1964 and Doritos in 1966, just to name a few. New product launches supported by powerful marketing campaigns forever changed US lives. For example, 1956 saw the debut of Miss Clairol, the first at-home hair colouring kit, supported by the advertising slogan: 'Does she or doesn't she? Only her hairdresser knows for sure.' From Miss Clairol's launch in the 1950s to the 1970s, the number of US women dying their hair soared from 7 per cent to more than 40 per cent.

TV therefore changed the rules of the game for a vast number of consumer brands emerging at this time. This was an entirely new form of communication and entertainment, and quickly became a mass-marketing vehicle that enabled brand manufacturers to bring their products to life. In 1960, Wrigley used its first set of twins in a TV spot to tempt viewers to double their pleasure and double their fun. A few years later, the giggling Pillsbury Doughboy introduced himself to US viewers, followed by Oscar Mayer spelling out bologna's first name to America. Manufacturers could now reach consumers directly in their own homes and were quick to invest in

TV advertising. In 1952 alone, commercial airtime advertising increased 38 per cent over the prior year to $288 million.

At this time, television in the United States was limited to just three networks: ABC, CBS and NBC. To put this into perspective, the average household today has more than 100 channels available, not to mention various new forms of media such as blogs and social networking sites. In the 1950s, the concentration of media created a captive audience and therefore TV advertising was hugely effective, unlike today where, owing to a fragmentation of the media, only 18 per cent of TV advertising generates a positive return on investment. Today, according to Socialnomics, 90 per cent of people skip television ads via TiVo/DVR, effectively making television advertising redundant. Consumers today have much more control over what messages reach them. The rise of social media and consequent product recommendations is quickly becoming a far more relevant and effective tool for reaching consumers.

Yet back in the 1950s, television advertising ruled the roost. As Lebow put it in 1955, 'Probably the most powerful weapon of the dominant producers lies in their use of television. To a greater degree than ever before a relative handful of products will share a monopoly of most of the leisure time of the American family.' This was the golden age for brands.

Mr. Clean, now owned by Procter & Gamble (P&G), debuted in 1958 with its first all-purpose cleaner. The launch was supported by the brand's first television commercial, which aired on WDTV/KDKA in Pittsburgh. Within six months, Mr. Clean had become the number-one household cleaner in the United States, and to this day it holds the title of the longest-running advertising jingle in television history. In his book *Brought to You By: Postwar Television Advertising and the American Dream*, Lawrence R Samuel said: 'After the Depression and the war, television advertising took on the important responsibility of assuring Americans that it was acceptable, even beneficial to be consumers. A vigorous consumer culture, largely suspended for the previous decade and a half, was about to be primed by the biggest things to hit advertising since the commercialization of radio in the 1920s.'

The promotion of consumerism wasn't just limited to television ads. The 1950s also saw the emergence of television game shows such as *The $64,000 Question* (1955) and *The Price is Right* (1956). In their book *Consumed*, Andrew Benett and Ann O'Reilly note: '... TV game shows contributed to the consumerist mind-set by giving "ordinary" people the chance to win the latest exciting products, thereby alerting viewers to what was especially desirable in the way of toasters, washing machines, and automobiles.'

By the time Walmart opened its doors on 2 July 1962, consumerism was in full force.

03

House of (Walmart) brands

> *Quality, name-brand merchandise offered at everyday low prices is the merchandising/pricing format around which we have constructed the Wal-Mart store.* (WALMART)

Walmart's initial merchandising strategy was centred almost entirely on selling national brands. Harvard Business School Professor John A Quelch and Katherine E Jocz define a brand as:

> a promise, an assurance of consistent quality from one purchase to the next. Brands make decision-making easier for consumers; instead of inspecting myriad unbranded options at market stalls every time they shop for an item, consumers can conveniently buy the same trusted brand on each purchase occasion. They may pay a little more for the branded item, but the time saved and the peace of mind make the trade-off worthwhile.[1]

Brands therefore formed an integral part of Walmart's merchandising strategy. The idea was to give shoppers greater access to these brands in the form of lower prices, bearing in mind that Walmart got its start by opening in rural areas of the United States targeting lower-income shoppers. Many of these smaller towns had been abandoned in the 1960s as retailers followed the millions of – in retailers' eyes – more lucrative consumers who were moving to the suburbs in pursuit of the American dream. The suburbs soon witnessed the emergence of neon lights, big-box discounters such as Kmart, convenience stores and fast-food chains. Meanwhile, the smaller, more rural areas of America were left neglected as many retailers deemed them insignificant in comparison to the more profitable and densely populated suburbs. This is where Walmart came in.

In his book, Sam Walton describes how small-town commercial centres began to shrivel up:

A lot of our customer base had moved on, and the ones who remained behind weren't stupid consumers. If they had something big to buy – say a riding lawnmower – they wouldn't hesitate to drive fifty miles to get it if they thought they could save $100... It was this kind of strong customer demand in the small towns that made it possible for Wal-Mart to get started in the first place, that enabled our stores to thrive immediately, and that eventually made it possible to spread the idea pretty much all over the country.[2]

Selling for less, buying for less

Low prices, a wide assortment of popular brands and to a certain degree limited competition were Walmart's initial recipe for success. In that respect, not a whole lot has changed over the past 50 years. Walmart eventually expanded beyond Northwest Arkansas to more established markets with fiercer competition. But that didn't prove to be a problem; in fact Walmart's winning formula of offering extreme value on popular brands resulted in a number of companies filing for bankruptcy protection or going out of business altogether, particularly when they began selling groceries, as we will discuss later in the chapter.

Its massive scale has enabled Walmart to shift the power successfully from the hands of manufacturers to the hands of consumers. It has become the advocate for the consumer in the form of offering low prices for nationally branded goods. And this is something that has been happening for quite some time:

> When we opened Wal-Mart No. 3 in Springdale, Sam wanted a red-hot price on anti-freeze. So he got two or three truckloads of Prestone and priced it as $1.00 a gallon. Then he priced Crest toothpaste at 27 cents a tube. Well, we had people come from as far as Tulsa to buy toothpaste and anti-freeze. The crowd was so big that the fire department made us open the doors for five minutes, then lock them until shoppers left. (Clarence Leis, one of Walmart's first store managers[3])

Walmart's former motto, 'We sell for less... always', would perhaps have been more accurate if it read: 'We sell for less because we buy for less... always'. Walmart was then and is now able to offer such deep discounts on national brands thanks to its ruthless efficiency and cost-cutting measures. Walmart has stripped out middlemen, eliminated redundancies, reduced packaging, invested in technology, consolidated buying and pressurized suppliers, all in the name of offering nationally branded items at a low price. These brands already stood for quality, so selling them cheaper than the competition allowed Walmart to gain market share as a discount retailer without the worry of its customers questioning product quality.

In his book, *The Wal-Mart Way*, Don Soderquist, former Senior Vice Chairman and Chief Operating officer (COO) at Walmart, writes:

> Wal-Mart has been, and most likely will remain, a retailer that supports national and international brand merchandise. In the minds of many consumers,

brands are synonymous with quality. Therefore, our strategy was to offer primarily name brands at everyday low discount prices, thereby providing our customers with genuine value and with a direct comparison to our competitors.[4]

Brand dilution makes private label more attractive

Today, national brands remain a vital component of Walmart's merchandising strategy. However, the distinction held by these brands has become diluted in today's prolific retail environment. National brands can now be bought across a wide spectrum of retailers, channels and geographies and therefore they no longer drive loyalty to a particular bricks-and-mortar retailer. Well ahead of his time, Victor Lebow recognized the need for merchandising differentiation back in the 1950s, a time when national brands ruled the roost. In 1955, Lebow wrote:

> Quite a few studies have shown that a large proportion of shoppers, when questioned, cannot tell which of several competing variety chain stores, or supermarkets, they have just left. But this sameness of their merchandise, in stores that look like twins, provides the opportunity for different merchandise in stores that look different, individual, with a character of their own.[5]

Today, such brand dilution, in food categories particularly, is even more evident as alternative retailers look to cash in on selling grocery products. For example, leading US drugstore chains Walgreens, CVS and Rite Aid are all adding fresh foods to their assortment in a bid to cash in on their extensive geographic reach, a topic we will discuss in further detail later in this book. Meanwhile, Target is looking to replicate Walmart's success by transitioning away from being a pure mass discounter and adding perishable groceries to its mix. Its Pfresh format, which features a 50 to 200 per cent increase in food, is being rolled out across hundreds of stores nationwide. From a shopper's perspective, pricing of national brands is becoming ever more transparent and there is of course the convenience factor as shoppers no longer need to make a special trip to Kroger to pick up their Tropicana orange juice or Yoplait yogurt. From a retailer's perspective, such channel blurring in the food, drug and mass sector puts pressure on pricing and further commoditizes brands, reinforcing the need to differentiate through exclusive, private label items.[6]

This is not to say that consumers don't want brands. In fact, according to Interbrand's 2010 ranking of the most valuable global brands, nine out of the top ten are US-based, proof that brand affinity is still very much alive and well among US consumers.[7] The quickest way to confirm this is by taking those brands off your shelves. Walmart's attempt to rationalize its assortment, although clearly effective in terms of reducing inventory and labour costs, was by no means the smoothest of the company's initiatives. We will discuss this topic in further detail in the next chapter, but the general idea was to cull those secondary and tertiary brands that were collecting dust on the shelves and costing Walmart money in the process. In addition to improving profitability, rationalizing stock-keeping units (SKUs) would free up employee time to do more customer-facing tasks, as opposed to restocking shelves, create more visibility for private label (more on that to come) and simplify the shopping experience. Surely it must be a win–win, provided you're not that tertiary peanut butter brand.

However, Walmart got it wrong here. They soon found out that even though Brand Y wasn't a top seller, it was still an important item to an important shopper. The result? Some of Walmart's most loyal and profitable customers took their entire shopping basket to competitors where they perhaps paid a little bit more, but at least they found what they were after. In financial terms, the elimination of a slow-moving $1 item could result in the loss of a shopping basket worth $60–80. Walmart has since added back nearly 9,000 of those items that were originally delisted. Its top two priorities are now restoring Everyday Low Prices (EDLP) and offering the 'broadest assortment possible'[8] – clearly quite a contrast to its original goal of range culling:

> The running joke used to be if we didn't have it you didn't need it. And all too often what we were finding was people came with 20 items on their list and left with 16 in recent years and that's not who we are.'
>
> (Bill Simon)[9]

Despite initial setbacks, Walmart persevered with its SKU rationalization efforts in a bid to strip out inefficiencies and improve the shopping experience. Like the barcode scanner and various other industry-changing initiatives, Walmart looked to do business in a more efficient way, so much so in fact that others would follow suit, thereby improving the overall health of the industry.

In his book *The Wal-Mart Effect*, Charles Fishman describes a similar situation where Walmart's ruthless drive for efficiency resulted in improvements in the greater sector. In the early 1990s, deodorant was packaged in a cardboard box. Despite being the norm among consumers, Walmart saw this as an unnecessary cost. Fishman writes:

> [The box] added nothing to the customer's deodorant experience. The product already came in a can or a plastic container that was at least as tough as the box, if not tougher. The box took up shelf space. It wasted cardboard. Shipping the weight of the cardboard wasted fuel. The box itself cost money to design, to produce – it even cost money to put the deodorant inside the box, just so the customer could take it out.[10]

Needless to say, Walmart went back to its suppliers and asked that they begin selling deodorant without the box. Doing so, according to Fishman, saved about five cents for each product sold, which enabled Walmart to pass the savings on to manufacturers and, more importantly, customers. The move had a knock-on effect within the industry as suppliers and other retailers recognized the cost savings, and it soon became the normal way in which customers purchased deodorant.

Shifting away from national brands

As we have already touched on, brands today are struggling to retain their influence over shoppers. A combination of media fragmentation and retail consolidation has resulted in a shift in power away from the brand manufacturers. Gone are the glory days when a brand had a captive audience by advertising on one of the United States' three TV networks. Gone are the glory days when a new product launch was a guaranteed success. Today, consumers are savvy and empowered. Product and pricing information is at their fingertips, and in a time of economic uncertainty many have begun to question the premium paid for a branded product. At the same time, retailers have merged, expanded and evolved, resulting in greater buying power when dealing with their suppliers. Retailers have transitioned beyond the physical box that sells the goods, and are now viewed as the gatekeeper to shoppers. They decide what products make it onto their shelves, and which ones should be delisted. They control the messaging both in the store and increasingly out of the store through loyalty schemes and social media. But what is perhaps most worrying for brands in today's era of retailing is the fact that their retail customers are increasingly becoming the competition. Today, private label is a key strategic focus for virtually all US grocery retailers.

Walmart's endless strive for efficiency has enabled them to undercut rivals with national brands. The idea sounds so simple now, but it's important to remember that when Walmart began, retailing was a hugely inefficient industry and many companies included phenomenal mark-ups in their prices. Nevertheless, Walmart recognized that low prices resulted in volume. And volume made up for the margin investment. Of course, none of this would have happened if the right merchandise wasn't on the shelves, and this is an area to which Sam Walton dedicated his entire life. 'There hasn't been a day in my adult life when I haven't spent some time thinking about merchandising', he writes in his autobiography.[11]

Merchant roots

Walmart certainly gets a lot of media attention for being the world's largest retailer. For its cut-throat distribution, for embracing technology, squeezing suppliers and attempting to open stores from Brooklyn to Johannesburg. Where Walmart doesn't get enough credit is in its merchandising, particularly in the early days when Walton himself scoured the country looking for hot bargains which we knew would fly off the shelves. As David Glass said: '... your stores are full of items that can explode into big volume and big profits if you are just smart enough to identify them and take the trouble to promote them'.[12]

Today, Walmart's principle of retailing is still very much centred on offering those popular brands at the lowest possible price. Of course, there is one major difference today – Walmart's own private labels are now included in the mix. Despite a growing focus on private label over the past couple of decades, Walmart has vehemently defended itself as a 'house of brands'.

The basis of our business is still built upon and will continue to be built on national brands. They will continue to be the base of all our operations. There's a danger of overemphasizing private label.

(1993, then Vice Chairman Don Soderquist)[13]

We are a brand-oriented company first. We became the largest retailer in the world by offering quality, well-known brands at everyday low prices. But we also use private labels to fill a value or pricing void that, for whatever reason, the brands have left behind.

(2000, Bob Connolly, then Executive Vice President (EVP) of Merchandising)[14]

We've always been a house of brands – it used to say 'brands for less' on the side of the building – and we believe selling national-branded product is a very important driver that communicates value to our customer.

(2009, Bill Simon)[15]

That may be so, but there is no denying that private label has become an essential ingredient in Walmart's merchandising strategy. In North America, Walmart's private label grocery items generate revenues in excess of $30 billion.[16] Sales of the Great Value line alone in the United States reached $12.5 billion in 2009, making it the country's largest food brand in terms of both sales and volume.[17] As a percentage of overall sales, food private label remains quite low at 16 per cent; however, if we factor in general merchandise, approximately 35–40 per cent of Walmart's sales come from private label products.[18] A house of brands Walmart may be, but only if we are including their own brands.

Don't spend a penny on marketing

When it came to developing private label, a senior Walmart executive confirmed that there was a fair degree of resistance from the top in the early days. 'Obviously, national brands spent a lot of money on marketing and innovation, and you always had to show your value relationship.' But back in the early 1980s, a significant change took place that would open Walmart's eyes to the lucrative world of private labelling.

At the time, the pet food sector was fragmented and lacked a national brand. Walmart saw this as an opportunity to launch its first major private label line. Named after Sam Walton's hunting dog, the Ol' Roy dog food line was designed to fill the gap for an opening price point, while still placing an emphasis on quality. So how could Walmart create a private label that was equal to, or better than, comparable national brands in terms of quality while undercutting them on price? The answer was simple: there would be no marketing budget, no television commercials, no circulars. All the marketing needed would take place at the shelf and, considering that there are quite a lot of Walmart shelves across the country, this wouldn't be an issue. Walmart's scale, combined with its focus on quality and price, enabled Ol' Roy to surpass Nestlé's Purina to become the number-one-selling dog food brand in the United States.

It's no surprise then to learn that the US operations of Doane Pet Care, the company which manufactured the Ol' Roy line for Walmart, were acquired by Mars in 2006. Mars, of course, is the parent company of Pedigree, a brand that competed with Ol' Roy since its launch in the early 1980s. At the time of acquisition, Bob Gamgort, former North American president for Mars, commented: 'The acquisition of Doane by Mars is an important part of our strategy to strengthen and grow our pet care business in North America.'[19] In other words, if you can't beat 'em, you might as well join 'em.

Driving loyalty with exclusive products

The success of Ol' Roy showed Walmart that shoppers would view private label as a brand in its own right, provided the quality was there. In fact, good-quality private label actually drives shopper loyalty and differentiates retailers from competitors. In its 2000 annual report, referring to its successful Equate health and beauty care line, Walmart notes that 'the products are so popular, in fact, that suppliers get letters from customers asking why they can't buy Equate [private label] products at other retail chains'.

Exclusivity is becoming more and more important in today's competitive retail market. However, that is not the only incentive for launching private label – in the majority of cases, stocking private label is far more profitable than stocking national brands. As mentioned, the lack of marketing expenditure allows for increased investment based either on price or on margin. For many grocery retailers, the investment is primarily based on profit margin. In other words, they price their products based on what the market will bear, whereas Walmart, owing to its focus on offering everyday low prices, aims to sell private label for as low as it possibly can. That is not to say that private label isn't profitable for Walmart. In fact, a senior Walmart executive confirmed that while private label is sometimes used as a loss leader among other grocery operators, at the very worst it is used to break even at Walmart and in many cases it is a profit-generating tool. For example, the Equate line is 40 per cent more profitable than national brands, while dry grocery private label items are between 10 and 15 per cent more profitable than leading national brands. Let's not forget that price/margin investment is always made up for in volume at Walmart. It all goes back to scale.

Sam's Choice: making a big play for food

By 1990, Walmart had surpassed Sears and Kmart to become the largest retailer in the United States.[20] Its discount store division had grown to nearly 1,600 outlets trading in 34 states.[21] But Walmart has never been one to rest on its laurels. The discount retail sector may have been close to saturation, but the grocery sector was still hugely fragmented. It was time for Walmart to shift its focus to a new avenue for growth: food retailing. Walmart had spent the previous decade growing not only its core discount store operation, but its Sam's Club business as well. By 1990, there were nearly 150 Sam's Club outlets, including several prototypes with fresh departments for produce, meat and bakery.[22] Walmart was also trading through a handful of Supercenters and Hypermarts (which would go on to be converted to Supercenters, Walmart's secret weapon that would eventually enable it to become the largest food retailer in the world).

It's important to remember that Walmart was under relatively new leadership at this time. David Glass took the helm in 1988.[23] Glass joined Walmart in the mid-1970s but he previously served as an executive with Consumers Market, a major Ozarks grocery chain. His food background was instrumental in shaping Walmart's strategy throughout the late 1980s and 90s. By the early 90s, under Glass's leadership, Walmart had acquired McLane, a large grocery distributor with over 26,000 retail customers,[24] and the lesser-known Phillips Companies, a 20-store grocery retailer also based in Bentonville.[25] Food retailing was beginning to take shape.

Around the same time, national brands were increasing their prices 'beyond levels [Walmart] believed to be reasonable', according to Soderquist.[26] After its profound success with Ol' Roy, Walmart decided it was time to give private label food a chance. Once again named after Mr Walton, the Sam's American Choice line hit the shelves in 1991.[27] At that time, a number of supermarket chains were already offering private label food items, often priced lower than the national brands. However, in many cases, little effort went into the quality or packaging of these items. In other words, they were cheap for a reason.

Walmart, however, aimed to change shoppers' perception of private label by placing a strong emphasis on quality while maintaining the low prices.

'This was a major departure from the historical practice of private label merchandise in retailing. The standard at that time for private label merchandise was definitely lower price, but also significantly lower quality sold in attractive packaging', said Don Soderquist.[28] Chocolate chip cookies from the Sam's American Choice range featured over 39 per cent chocolate chips while the packaging claimed that many competitors featured less than 20 per cent chocolate chips.[29] This premium line helped to dispel the myth that private label had to be of poor quality. It also aimed to tap into shoppers' patriotic side with its red, white and blue packaging and domestic sourcing claims.

It's interesting to look back on how the Sam's American Choice brand began. Inspiration for the line – as well as initial supplying – came from what is now one of Walmart's largest North American competitors: Canadian grocer Loblaw. Sam's American Choice was based on Loblaw's President's Choice range, which was launched in the mid-1980s and had grown to be a phenomenal success within just a few years. This was particularly true in Canada[30] where retail concentration is much higher than in the United States (today President's Choice is the largest consumer packaged goods (CPG) brand in Canada), but the brand also became a household name internationally as Loblaw licensed the brand to overseas retailers looking to differentiate with an exclusive line.

Walmart, however, wasn't looking to license the President's Choice brand. Instead, Dave Nichol, Loblaw President and the driving force behind the brand, helped Walmart to develop its own premium line. Nichol provided Walmart with the initial guidance and support needed for the Sam's American Choice line, and Loblaw even supplied some products within the range for the first couple of years. Loblaw also played a key role by introducing Walmart to some of its own private label producers such as the Toronto-based beverage manufacturer Cott Corporation. As with Doane Pet Care, Cott was a fairly small vendor at the time. Prior to the deal with Walmart, Cott had little luck in the United States as US supermarkets just weren't ready to go up against Pepsi and Coca-Cola with a private label line. The deal with Walmart was a breakthrough for Cott, as it spurred private label development across the entire grocery industry sector. Today, Cott produces 60 per cent of all private label carbonated soft drinks sold in North America and 56 per cent of those sold in the UK. However, the world's largest private label non-alcoholic beverage manufacturer is still heavily dependent on its retail customer in Bentonville. Walmart accounts for almost one-third of Cott's total revenues globally, including 39 per cent in North America, 17 per cent in the UK and 39 per cent in Mexico.[31]

The launch of Sam's American Choice was a real turning point for Walmart. Although today the range is overshadowed by the more successful Great Value and Equate lines, the launch of Sam's American Choice sent a very clear message to the industry – Walmart had its sights set on grocery and there would be no stopping them.

US private label market still lags behind ROW

Sam's American Choice was instrumental in igniting a change in shopper perception of private label. It began very slowly to transition from commodity to a brand in its own right. In the 1990s, some industry observers[32] believed that Walmart's foray into the sector would result in US private label penetration reaching 40 per cent by the year 2000. But here we are in 2012 and private label penetration is still less than 25 per cent of the overall market. So why, despite the United States being the largest and one of the most sophisticated grocery markets in the world, does it lag behind the rest of the world when it comes to private labelling?

There are a few explanations for this. Firstly, despite bouts of consolidation over the past few decades (think Safeway and Kroger), the grocery sector is still very regional in structure. Ahold is one of the leading chains in the Northeast while Publix continues to hold the title of Florida's largest grocery retailer. Walmart itself only accounts for 15 per cent of the entire US grocery market, a statistic that continues to shock even the most experienced of observers. In contrast, Tesco controls approximately one-third of the UK grocery sector and in Switzerland, where private label penetration is highest, there are essentially two retailers – Migros and Coop – controlling the market.

Secondly, in relation to the previous point, the United States is a vast and sparsely populated country, making it difficult to achieve economies of scale through private label production. It is generally more efficient to rely on branded manufacturers, although some retailers such as Kroger have built a strong private label programme owing to its vertically integrated structure. Kroger has 40 manufacturing plants that produce 40 per cent of its private label items.[33] As a result, the retailer has one of the highest private label shares in the country, with own brands accounting for more than one-third of units sold.[34] However, very few grocery retailers – Walmart included – have gone down the route of vertical integration, which has inhibited the greater sector from growing private label share to Kroger levels.

Thirdly, the lack of a major hard-discounter presence means that there was traditionally little incentive for the supermarkets to launch private label. In contrast, when Aldi and Lidl entered the UK in the early 1990s, Tesco immediately launched its Value line, which today is the second-largest food brand in the country.[35] Similarly, in Germany, the birthplace of the hard discounters, private label penetration is among the highest in the world. Outside Europe, the Aldi effect has also impacted the Australian grocery market, which, despite Australia being a vast and sparsely populated country, is dominated by just two grocery chains: Coles and Woolworths. In 2000, prior to Aldi's entry, private label accounted for 10 per cent of supermarket revenues. By 2010, that figure had jumped to 23 per cent as Aldi's presence sparked private label investment by the country's domestic retailers.[36]

Meanwhile, in the United States, Aldi is beginning to gather momentum having opened over 1,000 stores, but it has yet to have a major impact on the grocery sector, mainly owing to its secondary locations which do not place it in direct competition with the supermarkets.[37] That said, Aldi – like the dollar stores – tends to do very well when located within close proximity of a Walmart as they benefit from the traffic of a similar shopper demographic. In the future, a combination of better sites and increased shopper acceptance of European-style discounting could spur further private label development.

Finally, private label growth has been stunted in the United States because, relative to other markets, there is still a strong shopper affinity for national brands. This goes back to the fact that the consumer packaged goods industry is still more consolidated than the grocery retail sector, thereby limiting retailers' influence over consumers.

Historically, such affinity for national brands quickly softened during times of economic uncertainty. Retailers have used past recessions as an opportunity to tap into the consumer's newfound, and often temporary, quest for value. As such, there has always been a very strong correlation between recessions and private label growth; and, in the past, at the first sign of an upturn, shoppers quickly abandoned private labels and returned to national brands.

However, things are different today. Retailers have come a long way over the past decade, improving the quality and brand attributes of their own brands, which has resulted in annual private label sales increasing by 40 per cent at supermarkets and by 96 per cent in drugstores.[38] By the time the most recent recession struck in 2008, retailers were extremely well positioned – not to provide shoppers temporarily with better value but to showcase their own brands in a bid to drive long-term loyalty to both the brand and retailer. Private label is sticking today.

Looking ahead, brands will have a much harder time competing for share of wallet owing to a number of factors: the continued rise of a savvier shopper, fragmentation of media, mergers and acquisitions (M&A) in the retail sector, ongoing improvements in private label quality and innovation, SKU rationalization efforts which have created more visibility for private labels, and the emergence of alternative formats such as Tesco's Fresh & Easy or Sobeys' FreshCo which place private label at the heart of their strategy.

Great values

Private label exists when national brands fail to fill the void for the customer in terms of quality, price and innovation.
(BOB ANDERSON, FORMER WALMART VICE PRESIDENT RESPONSIBLE FOR THE LAUNCH OF GREAT VALUE)

On 2 April 1993 – a day that is now known as Marlboro Friday – tobacco company Phillip Morris finally succumbed to the pressures of private label cigarettes which were continuing to eat into its market share. Phillip Morris slashed the price of its Marlboro branded cigarettes by 20 per cent, causing its stock price to decline by a similar figure.[39] This led to a ripple effect among other consumer packaged goods companies that relied heavily on advertising their products, and the shares of Coca-Cola, P&G and many others suffered. Rather poetically, within one week of Marlboro Friday, Walmart announced plans for a new private label food line called Great Value – the range would eventually go on to become the largest food brand in the United States.[40]

At that time, some Walmart executives felt that its existing Sam's Choice line was becoming too stretched. It was sold across categories ranging from soft drinks to batteries, and Walmart rightfully felt that it needed to maintain its premium positioning. The Great Value line was the answer. Unlike Sam's Choice which was designed always to be superior to the national brand, Great Value was intended to be equal to, or better than, the national brand, thereby creating a clear distinction between the two lines. It's interesting to note here that while most US supermarkets' foray into private label was through cheap, copycat versions, Walmart recognized that sustained success with private label required quality and innovation.[41] 'Walmart has skipped that stage – that stupid process – and gone to a premium private label', Loblaw's Dave Nichol said back in the 1990s. And this was no different when it came to the Great Value launch.

Great Value was originally designed to compete with other supermarkets' private labels, or generics as they were known as then. For a short time, Walmart tested about 50 generic SKUs as it looked to reduce its dependence on Fleming, the food wholesaler that was supplying private label for them at the time. When they saw that the products were met with limited acceptability among shoppers, they knew it was time to cut ties with Fleming and go it alone. But Walmart's aim for this new line would be for it to become a quality brand in itself rather than the generic alternative to the brand. 'In my mind, all generics did was reinforce that you knew how to cut quality', Anderson said.

Led by Anderson, the Great Value line initially comprised 350 product lines, primarily in dry grocery categories such as coffee, cereals and potato chips. Walmart originally relied on the 'vital few', maintaining a focus on the 20 per cent of products that made up 80 per cent of sales. The first group of '80/20' items were those that were high volume, although not necessarily the most profitable as a result. The second and third groups of products consequently saw more profitability but less volume, and in the end Walmart was left with a private label SKU base that was substantially smaller than the average supermarket. The idea was to supplement – rather than replace – national brands while being able to compete with other supermarkets' private labels.

Recession revamp

The Great Value line was overhauled in 2009 in a bid to capture more bargain-hunting shoppers in the midst of a recession. Products were repackaged and recipes re-engineered in the timely and well-executed re-launch. In the end,

Walmart tested more than 5,000 products to ensure that the quality was equal to, or better than, national brands, conducted more than 2,700 consumer tests to compare flavour, aroma, texture, colour and appearance of Great Value versus the national brand, and changed the formulas of 750 items, including cereals, yogurt, laundry detergent and paper towels, in a bid to improve quality. And at a time when brand suppliers were reining in new product development (NPD) owing to a combination of SKU rationalization and general austerity measures, Walmart introduced more than 80 new Great Value items, including organic cage-free eggs and fat-free caramel swirl ice cream.[42] Walmart has always been known for low prices; this re-launch was about establishing a quality perception at a time when consumers were shunning brands in favour of lower-priced private label items. However, Walmart doesn't always like to admit this:

> For Great Value, many people misinterpreted the package redesign of Great Value as a shift in focus towards a private brand strategy that some of our competitors follow. We are a house of brands. We prefer to sell national brands because that's how we can differentiate ourselves in price better. When we sell Oreos and our competitor sells Oreos, and our Oreos are cheaper than their Oreos, the customer knows that we have a better price. When we sell cream-filled chocolate sandwich cookies and they sell cream-filled chocolate sandwich cookies, and you're not sure whether the quality is the same, the size is the same, it's very hard to differentiate yourself. We like to sell national brands. The Great Value program for us has been a program designed to bring a more uniform look to the product and to provide alternatives to the customers who were buying those in other places.
>
> (Bill Simon)[43]

Today the Great Value brand is larger than the likes of Coca-Cola, Heinz, Campbell's and Kelloggs. These national brands have spent more than a century in some cases building up strong equity amongst consumers, yet Walmart's Great Value brand has pushed them from their leading spots in a short space of a couple decades. Walmart achieved this not because Great Value is necessarily the best-tasting or the cheapest product on the market, but once again because of Walmart's scale. Today, Great Value is found not only in Walmart's 4,000+ North American stores but also internationally in Asia and Latin America, where it has had particular success in Mexico ($30+ million in sales) and Chile ($7 million in sales).[44] It is sold in every Walmart market except for the UK. It's important to mention here that the Great Value line today spans over 100 product categories ranging from oatmeal to light bulbs.[45] This is more than any national brand portfolio.

Private label allows for supplier leverage

This is another example of how the power shift has transitioned from the hands of manufacturers and into the hands of retailers. Manufacturers have spent the past two decades rationalizing their brand portfolios in order to create a leaner structure from which to trade with the retailers. For example,

Unilever went from owning 1,600 brands in the mid-1990s to just 200 in 2003.[46] And this is a process that continues today as retailers – Walmart in particular – embark on SKU rationalization programmes, which have a knock-on effect among the supplier community. If Walmart is reducing shelf space, then it's far more efficient for manufacturers to cull their tail brands in order to free up financial resources to plough into those power brands.

That is, of course, unless Walmart decides to purchase one of those tail brands and turn it into one of its own. That is exactly what it did in the 1990s when P&G discontinued its White Cloud brand, then the leading two-ply bath tissue brand.[47] P&G wanted to focus its efforts on its more promising single-ply Charmin brand, which was a wise move at the time, given the increased pressure suppliers were beginning to feel from retailers. Little did they know that several years on Walmart would buy and register the trademark to turn it into a private label. White Cloud continues to sit on Walmart shelves today.

Private label has enabled Walmart to gain better leverage and control over their suppliers, and not only through the sheer battle for shelf space. For example, food price inflation has been an ongoing source of contention between retailers and suppliers in recent years. In today's competitive market-place, retailers will do anything to avoid passing the cost on to their shoppers. However, given that margins in the grocery sector are razor thin and the fact that retailers often have the upper hand, nine times out of ten it is the supplier who is left to absorb the cost. So where does private label come in? 'We know the formulas of our private labels so when a national brand manufacturer comes to us and says "hey, Walmart, the price we pay for sugar has gone up so we'll need to raise our prices", well then we have something to bench-mark them against', a Walmart executive told the authors.

Driving innovation

Despite the many challenges that manufacturers continue to face with private label, there is a silver lining to every cloud. 'I made sure we didn't become a piñata brand', said Bob Anderson, having been interviewed exclusively for this book, referring to the fact that private label wasn't designed to bully national brands but to act as an alternative for shoppers. Private labels have helped to nudge brands away from complacency, and the Great Value line in particular helped to bring quality to the industry. Quality assurance was a major focus for Great Value, and Bob Anderson confessed that product recalls were the one thing that kept him awake at night. Great Value has a presence in more product categories than any national brand, which means that Walmart deals with hundreds of suppliers at one time. It's no surprise that Anderson became obsessed with quality and it was for this reason that Walmart avoided high-risk categories such as eggs (where product traceability was difficult to manage) or baby formula (where one product recall could have ruined Walmart's entire reputation).

However, when we talk about private label innovation in the United States, it is typically retailers like Kroger, Safeway, Publix and Whole Foods that spring to mind. Walmart often gets overlooked in this regard, despite some fantastic achievements. It was the first major US retailer to feature bilingual packaging on private label products, catering to a fast-growing Hispanic population. It launched the industry's first-ever fat-free coffee creamer, now a staple product in the dairy section, and was among the first to identify which products were gluten-free, which were Kosher and which featured 100 calories or fewer.

Supplier metamorphosis

Although the company can boast about such innovations, it's important to remember that any additional costs always had to be justified. Bob Anderson recalls a time when ketchup packaging began to transition from the old opaque milk-carton-style packs to the clear bottles that we find on supermarket shelves today. At the time, the clear bottles cost five cents more than the traditional packs, yet this particular ketchup supplier was keen on the transition owing to rising consumer demand for the new pack. Walmart, although aware of the fact that the clear bottle was an improvement aesthetically, was still unconvinced that its shoppers would pay more for new packaging without any improvements to the product itself. During a meeting with this particular ketchup supplier, Mr Anderson went out into the hallway and called in a few passing members of the sales team:

> I stopped them and said: 'Which bottle do you like better?' 99 per cent of them chose the clear bottle. So then I asked: 'Now if I charged you a nickel more, would you still buy it?' They all said no. 'Would you pay anything more for it?' They all said no.

What happened next was no great surprise. Walmart went back into that meeting in their Bentonville headquarters and told the manufacturer that although they appreciated the improved design, the product would not make it onto shelves until it was cost-effective to do so. 'We went through quite a big metamorphosis of educating our manufacturers', said Mr Anderson.

The globalization of private label

As discussed in the last chapter, private label opportunities are often more lucrative in international markets. Walmart has consequently adapted its business model in markets such as the UK, where half of its Asda division's sales come through private label, and emerging economies where private label allows Walmart to deliver on its core promise of saving people money so that they can live better.[48]

International, as we will discuss later in the book, will be a key component to Walmart's future growth. It is already a substantial business; in fact, if it were a standalone company, Walmart International would currently be the one of the largest retailers in the world with sales in excess of $100 billion.[49]

Walmart's acquisitive market entry mode into many countries and its desire to preserve local brand equity have seen it hang onto many local private brands around the world. Walmart has, however, deployed a number of its flagship global private label brands in a variety of its operating markets in categories including non-food, food and drink, apparel, and health and beauty. In Table 3.1 we provide an international matrix and overview of some of these flagship brands.

A key challenge for Walmart with regard to its global private label strategy, and broader format strategy as we discuss in the multi-channel chapter, is balancing scale with customization. On the one hand, leveraging a particular brand such as Great Value internationally enables Walmart to achieve greater economies of scale, which results in lower prices at the shelf. However, one

TABLE 3.1 Walmart: global private brand portfolio by market, 2011

Brand/country	AR	BR	CA	CL	CN	CEN	IN	JP	MX	PR	UK
725 Originals	X	X			X	X				X	
Athletic Works	X	X	X		X	X	X		X	X	
Bakers & Chefs		X			X				X	X	
Durabrand	X	X	X		X	X				X	
Equate	X	X	X	X	X	X			X	X	
Extra Special		X						X	X		X
Faded Glory	X	X					X		X	X	
George	X	X	X				X	X	X	X	X
Great Value	X	X	X	X	X	X	X	X	X	X	
Kid Connection	X	X	X		X	X	X	X	X	X	X
Mainstays		X			X	X	X	X	X	X	
Member's Mark		X			X				X	X	
Ol' Roy	X	X	X		X	X			X	X	
Select Edition	X	X	X		X	X		X	X	X	
Simply Basic	X	X	X		X	X	X	X	X	X	

SOURCE: Walmart, Authors

size doesn't always fit all, and Walmart must be able to sacrifice scale and offer local brands where necessary. For example, in Brazil the Great Value line was phased out almost in its entirety in 2010 and replaced with a new line called Bom Preço (Good Price in Portuguese), which has far greater resonance with local shoppers. Similarly, in India, the retailer balances global brands such as Great Value and George with local lines such as Astitva which is used solely for Indian ethnic products.

Global brands

The George range was the product of a partnership between Asda and Next founder George Davies which saw the introduction of George clothing into 65 Asda stores in February 1989. George is now a global brand stocked in more than 3,000 stores in eight different countries. Walmart Canada recently stripped out Walmart brands such as 725 Originals and Faded Glory, replacing them with an expanded and overhauled range of George clothing.

Equate is a brand used for health and beauty items, such as shaving cream, skin lotion, over-the-counter medications, and pregnancy tests. In mid-2010, the brand underwent a logo redesign, as well as packaging changes similar to the Great Value brand. It is so far limited to Walmart's operations in the Americas.

Simply Basic was previously a brand used for health and beauty items, but is now used primarily for sleepwear and underwear.

Mainstays products include curtains, bedding, some small home furnishings, and various other products, including office supplies and kitchen utensils.

Member's Mark and Bakers & Chefs are brands designed for commercial clients through the Sam's Club chain.

Kid Connection is a global brand for toys used throughout Walmart's operations.

Recent moves have seen Asda's Extra Special range introduced to Canada, Japan & Mexico. Extra Special wine is a best seller in Japan, while Extra Special groceries are sold in Walmart Canada and through the Superama chain in Mexico.

Alongside these global brands, Walmart has retained pre-existing local private label ranges in a good number of its overseas operations.

Mexico and the Caribbean

In Mexico, the company markets over 1,000 own labels under banners such as ATVIO, Extra Special, Equate, Great Value, Aurrera, Marca Libre, Sam's Choice, Color Place and Vips. It imports some own label products from Walmart USA and Walmart Canada, and is looking to introduce generic pharmaceutical products at a cost 40 per cent cheaper than leading brands. In the Suburbia clothing stores, over 35 per cent of sales come from own label clothing.

Walmart Mexico's private label sales have been growing at a higher rate than total sales for many years, and have accelerated over recent years. This expansion also varies quite a lot depending on the product category, as customers are more loyal to leading brands in certain categories. As of 2010, share of private label sales is still fairly low (less than 5 per cent of turnover), although, for certain categories, own-brand share has reached 10 per cent and is growing. At the Superama chain, Extra Special, a 105-strong line of Asda private label products, is sold. Among the list of categories introduced in 2008 are varieties of tea, olive oil, European bread, canned fish and seafood, and gourmet sauces. As of 2010, Wal-Mart Mexico works with more than 180 suppliers of private labels, of which 120 are domestic and most are medium-sized enterprises.

In Puerto Rico, Walmart sells the usual range of Walmart and Sam's Club private labels, augmented by the Amigo brand for that chain.

The UK

In the UK, private label products, which represent around 50 per cent of total sales and 45 per cent of food sales, have traditionally been used by Asda in the UK as a means of offering low-priced alternatives to national brands, acting as a strategic weapon to counter competitive price offensives and as a way of breaking restrictive pricing practices, such as on over-the-counter medicines. The company notes in its accounts that 'essential to the company's success is the delivery of fresh, innovative, good value products, which are unique to Asda. Our buying teams, food technologists and marketeers are continually searching to improve the quality of the company's products and to develop new ideas, many of which are sold under the Asda, SmartPrice, Extra Special and George labels.'

Asda attempts to shift consumers away from brands and towards its private label ranges, given that these tend to be more profitable and of higher quality than manufacturers' brands. Recently, the company has placed more emphasis on developing higher-quality ranges (Extra Special, Fresh, Go Cook and Good for You!), pushing up average basket size and helping the chain to capture a broader market. These new lines are designed to move the chain away from price promotional activity to constant low prices.

Asda's private label food range comprises the following main lines:

- SmartPrice – food and general merchandise essentials, from baked beans and potatoes through to dishcloths and tea towels, all offered at opening prices point with no compromise on quality.
- Asda Chosen By You – the Asda food and drink range was re-launched in 2010 as Asda Chosen By You. The range has sales of between £8

and £9 billion and was redesigned, reformulated and re-launched after extensive customer testing.

- Extra Special – premium food and drink brand that 'offers the best food delivered through authentic ingredients, provenance and the way the product is made. For customers wishing to treat themselves, Extra Special allows them to do this at affordable prices.'
- Asda Organics – a range of 'affordable, accessible' organic food and drink.
- Good for you! – meals and foods with a lower fat content than the standard Asda brand.
- Asda Great stuff – a healthy range of kids' favourite meals, snacks and drinks.

Central and South America

Regarding the recently acquired business in Chile, D&S's private label programme was launched in 1992. D&S has revealed in 2010 that it had rolled out over 600 new and reformulated private label products, including the debut of Walmart's Great Value private label range. According to D&S, the Walmart private label range is imported 'in order to have a better range of products at a great price' in the food and household categories. D&S states that its private label penetration in consumer products (including health and beauty care (HBC) and food) reached 14.5 per cent, well above the Chilean supermarket industry average of only 2.2 per cent. The D&S private label portfolio now encompasses nearly 2,000 SKUs, comprising Líder (around 1,200), Body+ (20), BGOOD (180), Acuenta (250), Selección (100) and Great Value (120). Walmart's Equate range is also sold in Chile.

In Brazil – where Walmart bulked up through two multi-chain acquisitions – it is little surprise that there is an extremely fragmented assortment of private label ranges. Although many banners sell common global Walmart brands such as Equate, Durabrand, Kid Connection, George, Ol' Roy and Great Value, there are a number of banner-specific PL ranges, including Big, Bom Preço, Mercadorama and Nacional. In addition, there are company-wide private label ranges unique to Brazil, such as Bom Preço (the 150-strong range was made available in the Walmart, BIG, Mercadorama, National and Bompreço chains in 2010, and comprises food and cleaning items). The lines – many of which feature sustainable packaging – are priced at between 10 and 30 per cent lower than manufacturers' brands and include Sentir Bem (a healthy-eating range launched in July 2009), Mais por Menos (an economy range of household and HBC items) and +ekonimico (an economy range exclusive to its Todo Dia discount stores). As usual, Sam's Club in Brazil sells the Member's Mark and Chefs & Bakers ranges.

A similar situation prevails in Central America. While we might expect to see greater alignment in private label terms with Walmart Mexico going forward, for the time being Walmart Centroamérica's private label offer comprises pre-existing lines with a sprinkling of Walmart global brands. Private label ranges are produced by Desarrolladora Comercial Internacional (DCI), with the products being distributed throughout Walmart Centroamérica's stores in Guatemala, Honduras, El Salvador, Costa Rica and Nicaragua. The three main brands are: Sabemás (food and drink); SuperMax (household and drugstore); and Suli (economy ranges). Together, the three main brands account for over 500 SKUs. Walmart's Equate, Simply Basic and Great Value brands are also available in certain chains.

Asia

In Asia, private label is showing signs of traction in general (private label penetration has historically been at much lower levels in Asia than it is in Europe and even in North America owing to consumer concerns over food safety and traceability in the supply chain), and Walmart is no exception to this overall trend.

In India, 2009 saw Bharti Retail introduce eight Walmart private labels, including Great Value (flour, dry fruits, spices, cereal and tea) and George (clothing) in its supermarket chain Easyday and in its cash & carry wholesale store. Other Walmart private labels introduced in India include Home Trends (home furnishing), Mainstays (plastic containers, kitchen accessories), Kid Connection (toys), Faded Glory (footwear) and Athletic Works (athletic shoes, equipment).

In China, a comprehensive range of Walmart global private labels are available, although these are often manufactured locally and heavily tailored to meet local tastes.

Seiyu in Japan has a mix of Walmart and brands and legacy Seiyu private labels. Private label development is one of Seiyu's core merchandising strategies, and it has been enhanced since Seiyu announced plans to revamp its private label offering in 2005. Despite recent efforts, the private label penetration rate in 2011 is thought to have remained at slightly over 10 per cent. The effort to drive up private label sales is likely to be bolstered by Walmart initiatives such as its partnership with Li & Fung and the development of Global Merchandise Centers.

A number of Walmart private label ranges from around the world have been introduced to Seiyu since the retailer first took a stake in the Japanese company. In August 2004, Seiyu launched a modified version of the George brand developed by Asda. Other ranges introduced have included Great Value for groceries, Simply Basic clothing ranges and Kid Connection as a key strength in the toy category. Extra Special cookies were introduced in 2008, with wine introduced in 2009. Both ranges are sourced from Asda in the UK and the Extra Special wine range has become a phenomenal success in the Japanese market.

However, from late 2005, Seiyu has modified Great Value to be better suited to Japanese tastes. Currently some 100 Great Value products are sold, but these are mostly Japanese traditional food items and produced in Japan. Great Value lines are at the core of Seiyu's private label strategy and therefore they replaced the legacy range Seiyu Fine Select. Similarly, George product specifications and materials are customized for the Japanese market, while Asda's influence remains only as a design source.

Besides the above, there are several private label brands that Seiyu developed before becoming a part of Walmart. The Shoku-no-Sachi range (the name translates as Food Delights) was launched to 'meet the demands of consumers concerned about food safety'. The company states that 'this house brand is based on the concept of providing safe, delicious foods from the best producing regions and producers, using methods that bring out the best in the ingredients'. The range is sourced directly from suppliers (which enables higher quality control) and is to be expanded from the current ranges of fruit and vegetable produce, meat and seafood to include categories such as processed foods, dairy products and prepared foods. Other Seiyu private label ranges include Clothing everyday fashion lines and Kankyo Yusen environmentally friendly health and beauty and stationery products.

The brands behind the private labels

Up until now, we've generally been focusing on the growth of private label at the expense of national brands. However, it's important that we take a step back to examine the increasingly complex relationship between the two. While both are very much competing for a share of the shopper's wallet, increasingly it's the national brand manufacturers who are supplying the very same private labels that they compete with at the shelf. This explains why today we hear more and more consumers recommending private label – 'oh, that store brand is just as good as the name brand – and it's cheaper!' – and also why retailers are becoming ever more confident in the quality of their private labels, often offering consumers a money-back guarantee and in some cases giving away their private label product when shoppers buy a comparable national brand.

So who is doing it? Many people would be surprised at some of the big names behind the retailers' brands. ConAgra, for example, produces Walmart's Great Value frozen potatoes from its Lamb Wesson facility and also supplies the company with private label granola bars.[50] Kimberly-Clark, Del Monte and Sara Lee also contribute to the behind-the-scenes production of Great Value foods. Ralcorp, the maker of Post cereals, also produces Great Value breakfast cereals while Kelloggs makes Walmart's frozen pie shells. McCormick, Hormel and McCain also dabble with private label, and it's not only Walmart they are producing for. '[ConAgra's] Chef Boyardee packs our canned pasta products. They wouldn't want you to know that', said Bill Moran, founder and former CEO of SuperValu's

Save-A-Lot chain, back in 2003. The company looks to private label for 85 per cent of its assortment.[51]

So why would a large consumer packaged goods company help to create a private label product, only to find themselves competing with that very item once it reaches the shelf?

There are a few reasons. Initially, many national brand manufacturers viewed supplying private label as an opportunity to make use of surplus plant capacity, thereby improving operational efficiencies. In that sense, supplying private label was more of an afterthought than a strategic imperative. However, in the United States today, sales growth of private label has outpaced that of national brands in recent years, a reflection of increased retail investment and consumer acceptance of these items, particularly in a down economy, as discussed previously. In dollar terms, private label grew 2.9 per cent in 2009, compared to the 0.1 per cent growth achieved by national brands. The gap in unit terms is even more staggering: private label grew by 6.4 per cent while national brands declined −1.7 per cent.[52] This, of course, is a reflection of the fact that low-priced, high-velocity items such as milk and bread are increasingly being bought as private label. National brands have since fought back, slashing prices and running temporary promotions in a bid to regain some ground. As a result, the following year, in 2010, national brands in supermarkets gained 1 per cent while private labels were essentially flat.[53] However, it's important to point out that ongoing price-cutting by brands is not a sustainable strategy – private labels will continue to gain momentum and national brand manufacturers can no longer ignore them.

Therefore, for many, producing private label is necessary to regain some of that share lost to those very items. If you can't beat 'em, you might as well join 'em. Consumers will continue to buy private label and therefore the national brands are now acknowledging and capitalizing on this trend. If they don't, surely one of their competitors will.

CASE STUDY

In the past several years, we have even seen the emergence of new consumer packaged goods companies built to address this very trend. Sun Products, for example, was formed in 2008 through the merger of Huish Detergents – the leading manufacturer of private label laundry and dish products – and Unilever's North American fabric care business. Unilever was losing share to competitors such as Procter & Gamble in this category and, like many other suppliers, looking to divest non-core assets. Meanwhile, Huish had a 90 per cent share of the private label detergent category with customers that included Walmart, Costco and Aldi. The combined company is now able to continue servicing those legacy retail customers from a private label perspective while also offering well-known brands such as all, Snuggle, Wisk and Surf. At the time of the merger, the CEO of Sun Products Neil DeFeo said: 'We're taking a business out of Unilever without its overhead structure, without a sales organization, without back-office operations and putting it right on top, selling to the same buyers, in the same category, buying the same raw materials, talking about the same issues with the trade as we had always done.' Further consolidation on the CPG side is likely as these companies look for more efficient ways to service their retail customers' changing needs.

In the case of Walmart, scale is always an enticing factor for suppliers to engage in private label production – let's not forget that Great Value is the largest food brand in the United States so there is a clear revenue opportunity. Yet, supplying private label is also beneficial from a buying perspective. 'I am sure our volume helps [our suppliers] be more efficient in leveraging purchases', a senior Walmart executive told us. The scale associated with supplying Walmart's private label has almost certainly provided the likes of ConAgra, Ralcorp and Del Monte with the ability to leverage better terms with their own producers. Once again, this is a classic example of how Walmart drives efficiencies throughout the value chain, whether intentional or not. However, the flip side for these companies is further dependence on the retail giant – producing Walmart's private label cereal means that Ralcorp relies on the retailer for nearly 20 per cent of its annual revenues.[54]

Therefore, not everyone is ready to pack it in and become a private label supplier. While it makes sense for secondary and tertiary brands – particularly those that may face the cut as part of a SKU rationalization process – many leading brands find it far more valuable to focus on their core. For example, Procter & Gamble's portfolio consists of leading brands in low private label share categories so there is little incentive to help retailers develop private label. (It's important to point out here that P&G has also been one of the more aggressive CPGs when it comes to filing patent infringement lawsuits against private label.) Nestlé and PepsiCo have also done well to strengthen their brands, with both focusing on innovation and PepsiCo on NPD as a means of defending market share. Meanwhile, some leading brands have dabbled in private label only soon to recognize that it's far more powerful to focus on the national brand. Birds Eye, for example, used to be a leading supplier in the private label frozen vegetable category; however, the company exited that business in 2006. At the time, the fragmented nature of this category – there were over 15 competing producers – made it unattractive for a leading brand such as Birds Eye to turn to private label production. Profit margins and return on invested capital were low. According to Brian Ratzan, a managing director at Vestar Capital Partners which invested in Birds Eye at the time, the private label business required $100 million of working capital, which only generated $1–2 million of earnings before interest, taxes, depreciation and amortization (EBITDA). Once the company divested the business, its SKU count was reduced from a whopping 4,500 to 480, enabling Birds Eye to refocus its efforts as number-one branded frozen vegetable manufacturer in the United States.[55]

While these leading brands often have the clout to reject private label production, it is a very different story for the number two and three brands. As part of its SKU rationalization programme, Walmart removed the Hefty and Glad brands from its food storage category at the beginning of 2010. The end result was a shelf reminiscent of that of a warehouse club – one leading national brand (SC Johnson's Ziploc) and, you guessed it, Walmart's Great Value brand.[56] The idea was to reduce clutter and make the decision-making process at the shelf easier for shoppers, not a terrible idea for a proliferated and not particularly brand-loyal category such as food storage bags. Doing so would also lower inventory and labour costs while giving greater visibility to the private label product. All in all, it made sense for Walmart from both a shopper satisfaction and financial perspective. But for the brand being delisted, it was catastrophic: Walmart accounts for 21 per cent of Hefty parent company Pactiv's annual revenues.[57] Are you sensing a pattern here?

Pactiv CEO Richard Wambold commented at the time: 'At the end of the day, we think that's not a real good decision for [Walmart]. And we think that [they're] going to find that that category performs very poorly without Hefty OneZip which is the leading brand.'[58]

Pactiv also supplies Walmart in the waste bag category, where it managed to retain a presence on the shelf despite that category also undergoing a brand consolidation process. Hefty's assortment was reduced in the waste bag category but they were still present nonetheless. Surely, it's no coincidence that, while this was taking place, Pactiv signed a multi-year agreement with Walmart to become its sole supplier of private label waste bags under the Great Value brand, going on to become Walmart's Supplier of the Year. Could Hefty have preserved its position by succumbing to private label production?

After four months, Hefty slider bags were added back to the food storage category.[59] Sure, it could have been down to the fact that there was genuine consumer demand for the item (Hefty claims they have 65 per cent share in category). In fact, Walmart made several hundred so-called 'corrections' almost immediately after removing brands that turned out to be quite important for their shoppers. However, we can't help but wonder whether Pactiv's sudden importance as a private label supplier has helped them to get back on the shelves and avoid further culling.

In any case, the Hefty example brings us on to a much broader topic. For a company that prides itself on its roots as a merchant, the removal of thousands of well-known products from its shelves certainly raised a lot of eyebrows. Now let's explore the motives behind what has been one of the largest-ever merchandising blunders in Walmart's history – SKU rationalization.

Notes

1 http://www.american.com/archive/2008/november-december-magazine/for-the-greater-goods/article_print

2 Walton, S with Huey, J (1992) *Sam Walton: Made in America*, Doubleday, New York, p 224

3 Walton, p 64

4 Soderquist, D (2005) *The Wal-Mart Way: The inside story of the success of the world's largest company*, Thomas Nelson, Nashville, TN, p 85

5 *Journey of Retailing*, Spring 1955, Victor Lebow

6 http://pressroom.target.com/pr/news/target-offers-a-handpicked-selection.aspx

7 http://www.interbrand.com/en/best-global-brands/best-global-brands-2008/best-global-brands-2010.aspx

8 walmartstores.com

9 Transcript – Wal-Mart Stores, Inc. at Bank of America Merrill Lynch Consumer Conference – Final, March 2010

10 Charles Fishman, *The Wal-Mart Effect*, 2006, Allen Lane, London, p 1

11 Walton, p 72

12 Walton, p 79

13 *Discount Store News*, Private label goods on rise throughout all formats, 7 June 1993

14 Walmart 2000 Annual Report. http://walmartstores.com/Media/Investors/2000_annualreport.pdf, p 14

15 *Supermarket News*, April 3, 2009 http://supermarketnews.com/news/great_value_0403/

16 Planet Retail report, Private labelling in North America: Fertile ground for growth

17 http://walmartstores.com/pressroom/news/9028.aspx

18 FT and author estimates. http://www.ft.com/cms/s/0/762b1f80-1259-11de-b816-0000779fd2ac.html

19 http://www.marketwire.com/press-release/mars-incorporated-announces-agreement-acquire-us-operations-doane-pet-care-company-591041.htm

20 http://walmartstores.com/AboutUs/7603.aspx

21 1991 Annual Report, p 4. http://media.corporate-ir.net/media_files/irol/11/112761/ARs/1991AR.pdf

22 1991 Annual Report, p 5. http://media.corporate-ir.net/media_files/irol/11/112761/ARs/1991AR.pdf

23 http://investors.walmartstores.com/phoenix.zhtml?c=112761&p=irol-newsArticle&ID=1278353&highlight=

24 1991 Annual Report, p 2. **http://media.corporate-ir.net/media_files/irol/ 11/112761/ARs/1991AR.pdf**

25 *New York Times*, Wal-Mart is making supermarkets edgy, Eben Shapiro, 30 December 1991

26 Soderquist, p 86

27 **http://walmartstores.com/aboutus/7603.aspx**

28 Soderquist, p 86

29 *Fortune*, What intelligent consumers want – Quality is still important, but these folks now expect to get it at the lowest possible price. Manufacturers and retailers had better watch out. Bargain buying is likely to last, Faye Rice with Sally Solo, 28 December 1992

30 Loblaw 2010 Annual Report. **http://www.loblaw.ca/Theme/Loblaw/files/ doc_financials/2010_Annual_Report_complete_report.pdf**

31 Cott 2010 Annual Report, p 7

32 Planet Retail

33 Kroger 2010 Annual Report. **http://www.sec.gov/Archives/edgar/data/ 56873/000110465911017372/a11-2299_110k.htm**, p 3

34 Kroger 2009 Fact Book

35 Tesco, 2011. **http://ar2011.tescoplc.com/pdfs/business_review/ building_brands.pdf**

36 Blair Speedy, The Australian In-house labels are proving a big hit for Coles, 18 September 2010. **http://www.theaustralian.com.au/business/ in-house-labels-are-proving-a-big-hit-for-coles/story- e6frg8zx-1225925610532**

37 **http://aldi.us/us/html/company/3503_ENU_HTML.htm**

38 PLMA **http://plma.com/storeBrands/sbt11.html**

39 The Motley Fool, How Marlboro Friday changed the world. **http://www.fool.com/investing/general/2008/01/15/how- marlboro-friday-changed-the-world.aspx**

40 *The Wall Street Journal*, Wal-Mart develops new private label for packaged food, Bob Ortega, 6 April 1993

41 **http://walmartstores.com/pressroom/news/9028.aspx**

42 As above

43 Transcript – Wal-Mart Stores, Inc. at Bank of America Merrill Lynch Consumer Conference – Final, March 2010

44 Walmart insider

45 **http://walmartstores.com/pressroom/news/9028.aspx**

46 *Fortune*, Brand Killers Store brands aren't for losers anymore. In fact, they're downright sizzling. And that scares the soap out of the folks who bring us Tide and Minute Maid and Alpo and..., Matthew Boyle, 11 August 2003.

http://money.cnn.com/magazines/fortune/fortune_archive/2003/08/11/346850/index.htm

47 *Advertising Age*, White Cloud Returns to haunt P&G: Wal-Mart resurrects paper brand for premium bath tissue, diapers, Jack Neff, 11 October 1999

48 *Marketing Week*, Asda own brand is Chosen by You, Rosie Baker, 21 September 2010. **http://www.marketingweek.co.uk/sectors/retail/asda-own-brand-is-chosen-by-you/3018416.article**

49 Walmart, Authors

50 Anonymous Walmart executive

51 *Fortune*, Matthew Boyle, 11 August 2003, as note 46

52 PLMA/Nielsen. **http://mypbrand.com/2010/06/28/plma-publishes-the-2010-private-label-yearbook/**

53 PLMA/Nielsen. **http://plma.com/pressupdate/pressupdate.asp#ID42**

54 Ralcorp 2010 10-K. **http://www.sec.gov/Archives/edgar/data/1029506/000095012310109405/c60605e10vk.htm**

55 Buyouts Yearbook 2010, Vestar Capital leads Birds Eye through double-digit growth, *Buyouts Magazine*'s 'Large Market Deal of the Year', New York, 14 April 2010. **http://www.vestarcapital.com/en/news/141/**

56 *Advertising Age*, Walmart food-bag consolidation wipes Glad, Hefty from shelves, Jack Neff, 4 February 2010

57 Pactiv 2009 10k. **http://www.sec.gov/Archives/edgar/data/1089976/000095012310017882/c55895e10vk.htm**

58 Pactiv at Longbow Research Annual Paper & Packaging Investor Conference – Final, 22 June 2010

59 As above

Don't aggravate the customer

04

I can't believe it's not on shelves

Removing 20 per cent of a range from a business of our size can have quite a dramatic knock-on effect.
(DARREN BLACKHURST, FORMER CHIEF MERCHANDISING OFFICER AT ASDA)[1]

I Can't Believe It's Not Butter (ICBINB). In the early 1990s, the quirky US butter substitute brand was introduced to UK supermarket shelves by owner Unilever.[2] Despite some initial setbacks, the tongue-in-cheek brand opened up a new and innovative product market to British consumers. Within several years, ICBINB had captured 6 per cent of the market with retail sales of £37 million.[3]

However, it wouldn't be long before competitors followed suit. In 1995, the Utterly Butterly brand, now owned by Dairy Crest, was launched as direct competition to ICBINB. In its first year, Utterly Butterly captured almost 20 per cent of the market.[4] Retailers were also quick to capitalize on this segment in the 1990s and today copycat private labels can be found at most major grocers, including Asda (You'd Butter Believe It), Tesco (Butter Me Up) and Sainsbury's (Butterlicious). Inevitably, ICBINB continued to lose market share and soon became a classic example of a non-core brand in a high private label share category.[5] I think you can sense what happens next.

Despite Unilever's best efforts to revive the brand in terms of both advertising and price investment, by 2007 Asda had its mind made up: it was time for a cull. That year, Asda delisted ICBINB as part of the company's aim to remove 'unnecessary duplication' from its shelves.[6] It was the first step towards SKU rationalization, a cleansing process that eventually saw Walmart remove nearly one-third of SKUs from its UK shelves and approximately 10 per cent of products in the United States[7] (although the reductions ranged from 2 to 26 per cent depending on the category). The knock-on effect was incredible. The strategy, in varying forms, has since been pursued in some way by virtually all major grocery chains around the world, from Carrefour in France to SuperValu in Minnesota. According to Nielsen, 40 per cent of US grocery retailers reduced their product assortments in 2009 by an average of about 5 per cent.[8] Once again, Walmart ignited change in the industry, driving further efficiencies, acting as the consumer advocate and, as a result, keeping its suppliers and competitors as far away from complacency as possible.

But let's go back to ICBINB, because the story doesn't end there. Back in 2007, when Asda was just testing the rationalization waters, it had also delisted the Princes Tuna brand in favour of John West. In an interview with trade magazine *The Grocer*, Darren Blackhurst, then Chief Merchandising Officer at Asda, commented:

> We are challenging whether certain brands have brand equity. We took Princes out. The tuna don't swim past and say "bugger me, I don't want to go in that can, I want to go in this one". So we said we'll go with one can or the other, and chose John West. And have we had a single complaint from customers? Not one. Why? Because it wasn't a brand. We did the same with Utterly Butterly and I Can't Believe It's Not Butter. It's just margarine. I can't even remember which one stayed in, to be honest. And again, not a single complaint.[9]

Those are quite powerful words considering that if you go into an Asda today, Princes Tuna and I Can't Believe It's Not Butter are back on the shelves. Turns out they were brands after all.

Asda began restocking ICBINB two years after delisting it, primarily succumbing to customer demand.[10] It may not have been the number-one brand in the category, but clearly it was important to some of Asda's most loyal shoppers. As discussed earlier in the book, the biggest risk associated with range rationalization is the removal of an item that, although perhaps not top-selling, may be important to a retailer's most loyal and therefore most profitable shoppers.

We didn't add back 3,000... no it was more like 9,000

Walmart has had no choice but to be very open about the merchandising errors it made during this process, which were certainly a contributing factor to Walmart reporting its first comparable sales decline in history (in Q1 2009). This was followed by more than two years' worth of quarterly contractions.[11] Of course, there were other factors at play here, but its less than seamless SKU rationalization initiative can certainly be held accountable for a large part of that decline.

'We had done some things that lost a trip,' said Bill Simon, '... and we did discontinue some things that people didn't buy very often, but were aggravating to a customer to lose. And, you know, Lee Scott told us recently, rule number one in retail, don't aggravate your customer.'[12]

Walmart reduced its overall SKU count by 9 per cent in 2010. However, up to a quarter of the range was removed in some key non-food categories such as hardlines, clothing and hardware, quickly leading to shopper dissatisfaction. In 2010, Mr Simon noted: 'We added back, I said about 300 SKUs, but we didn't add back 3,000. We added back a small percentage of what was removed. The vast majority of what was removed was done for the right reasons in the right way, and have actually improved the category sales in those categories.'[13] Fast-forward one year and Walmart did in fact add back thousands of SKUs: 8,500 to be precise, or 11 per cent of the range.[14]

It all goes back to being able to offer the right products to the right shoppers at the right time. A study by Nielsen showed that more than half of US consumers are likely to shop somewhere else if they notice a reduced product assortment.[15] Customers have the ability to vote with their feet and take their entire basket to the competition. Therefore, while SKU rationalization is necessary for the overall health of the industry, retailers are still a long way off from perfecting this trend. It's no surprise that Walmart's focus today – to offer the 'broadest assortment possible' – is in complete and utter contrast to SKU rationalization.

SKU rationalization: far from perfection but a vital process

However, back in 2007, delisting those few brands gave Asda the confidence to embark on a much bigger programme known internally as 'Less is More'. It was time for a widespread cull, time to put its brands under the microscope and, consequently, time for suppliers to start shaking in their boots. In its quest for cost and complexity reduction, Asda went on to remove between 20 and 30 per cent of SKUs from an additional 10 categories.[16] Products that used to enjoy a comfortable spot on Asda's shelves simply disappeared. Now we already know the customer backlash that could result when this is done incorrectly, but let's spend some time thinking about the immediate results.

Firstly, you have a much cleaner shelf. While SKU rationalization is tragic for those secondary and tertiary brands, in many ways it actually benefits the brand leader who is suddenly afforded the luxury of more prominent shelf space, not to mention reduced competition. 'I continue to believe that the biggest casualties of the weakened economy will ultimately be tertiary brands with poor consumer equities. Strong brands or category leaders like Heinz that leverage consumer insights to drive innovative and successful new product development should win', said Heinz Chairman, President and CEO, William R Johnson, in 2010.[17] However, the extra shelf space doesn't always come without expectations. In the case of John West tuna – the brand that was kept over Princes – Asda consequently received better terms and was therefore able to offer shoppers a better price on a major brand of tuna.

This brings us to the second point. If you're a shopper, you are likely to benefit from lower prices on leading brands. This is in part true because of the potentially better terms agreed between retailer and supplier, but also because SKU rationalization results in lower inventory and labour costs – imagine the time and money saved on having to restock only three varieties of ketchup instead of 15! And it's not just replenishment costs but the indirect costs involved with negotiating, ordering, processing, sorting, delivering, pricing, scanning and bagging that very item. Let's not forget that this is the heart of Walmart's strategy – its unrelenting drive to streamline costs has enabled them to lower prices on well-known brands in the most sustainable, powerful and profitable way.

But let's go back to the shopper, because price isn't the only benefit when we talk about SKU rationalization. Shoppers also have the benefit of improved stock availability, resulting in greater shopper satisfaction (presuming the brand you're after hasn't been culled in the first place!). In the United States, out-of-stocks at competitor Kroger were cut by 38 per cent after reducing its SKU count.

SKU rationalization also enables retailers to carve out more shelf space for private label items. It's no surprise that the re-launch of Great Value coincided with Walmart's brand consolidation initiative. And Walmart isn't alone. According to a study by Nielsen, 48 per cent of US retailers confirmed that an incentive for SKU rationalization is the ability to make room for more profitable private labels.[18] In the United States, this wasn't possible in the past because private labels on the whole were never strong enough in terms of quality, packaging, marketing and so on. However, as we have seen thus far, consumers are increasingly warming to retailers' efforts to turn these products into brands in their own right. Could we one day reach a point where we have only the brand leader and private label on the shelf? Surely, that is a discount model just waiting to happen – particularly given the forecast growth in e-commerce which is where shoppers will go for broad assortment, an area we will discuss in further detail later in the book.

Yet perhaps the most important benefit for the shopper is getting rid of the tyranny of choice: reducing complexities, improving the shopper's decision-making process. Over the past two decades, retailers and manufacturers on both sides of the pond filled their shelves with choice, choice, choice. More flavours, more variants, more pack sizes, more brands. The irony is that they were doing this because this is what the shopper wanted. 'All that go-go 1990s where we were adding items in and adding items in, and people wanted more, more, more choice just didn't pay off', Catherine Lindner, Walgreen's divisional vice president for marketing development, said in 2009.[19] Lindner's comments are confirmed in the figures – the Food Marketing Institute states that the average food retailer in 2008 stocked 47,000 SKUs, up more than 50 per cent from 1996. New products were quickly coming to market to satisfy the consumer's desire for variety. In 2008, according to Mintel, there were 47,113 new products launched, more than double the number introduced a decade earlier.[20]

What is perhaps more astonishing is that shoppers weren't taking much notice. According to AMR Research, at any one time in the United States there is a pool of over 1 million items available to shoppers, of which the average shopper uses approximately 340 unique items per year.[21]

One of the main impacts of product proliferation was that Walmart shoppers were increasingly faced with a bewildering array of choices when attempting to navigate a store, a department and a category. A Walmart Supercenter carrying roughly 100,000 SKUs would be shopped for 22 minutes by an average shopper, implying that a thorough evaluation of each product carried would require an investigation of 75 items per second!

Certain categories have become proliferated and are truly in desperate need of a cull. Take the bottled water category, for example. SuperValu CEO and ex-Walmart executive Craig Herkert commented on how one of his stores was stocking eight different varieties of 24-pack water. 'It's water. We have eight different brands of water. And I just find it hard to imagine that our customer is demanding of us that I need eight different brands of H_2O.' It's no surprise then to learn that in 2009 US grocers reduced the bottled water category by an average of 6 per cent, according to Nielsen. 'I'll name a category, cereal, where we'll carry four sizes of the exact same box of cereal that might be ranked number 72 in the category', Herkert added. 'I'm not sure our customer's telling us that's real variety.'[22]

While SKU rationalization was spurred on by the recession as a cost-savings initiative, it's important to remember the overall benefits it brings to the industry and most importantly the shopper. It is a healthy – and many would argue vital – exercise that allows both retailers and suppliers to get rid of the tail. Let's not forget that suppliers themselves will not benefit by holding on to underperforming SKUs.

Doing more with less

With too many choices, they actually don't buy.
(DUNCAN MAC NAUGHTON, CHIEF MERCHANDISING OFFICER, UNITED STATES)

Above all, the shopper benefits from clarity. P&G estimates that the average shopper spends a mere 2.5 seconds looking for an item but notices only half the items at the shelf.[23] Reducing choice can actually increase sales in a given category, as experienced by Walmart in the UK (candle sales doubled after being reduced by 65 per cent[24]) as well as in Canada (two of five peanut butter lines were dropped yet overall category sales increased). In 2010, P&G cut its assortment of soap and other skincare products by one-third at one retailer. Similarly, at another retailer, P&G reduced its offering of detergents and other fabric-care items by about 20 per cent. Despite the reduction in choice, sales grew in both categories. In a 2007 study, consultant Bain & Co estimates that SKU rationalization efforts can result in up to a 40 per cent sales increase for a retailer while reducing costs by between 10 and 35 per cent.[25]

As Walmart and other retailers have rationalized the number of SKUs they sell (in order to focus on brand leaders and private label) and heightened their demands for genuine innovation and added value in terms of NPD, major CPG vendors have reacted accordingly. A number of them have reined in NPD, others have pledged to shrink the number of lines they offer, while others have gone further still – disposing of entire divisions (eg Sara Lee, Kraft) in order to focus on their areas of strength, brand leadership, authority and expertise.

Outsmarting the elephant

As we have seen thus far, SKU rationalization is by no means a straightforward task. It requires a deep shopper understanding and ideally on a store-by-store basis. In order to get closer to achieving this, many retailers today are utilizing technology to learn which products are being purchased by which customers and when, why, for whom, how many etc. Data from dunnhumby, the market research company part-owned by Tesco and behind the retailer's Clubcard scheme, shows that 85 per cent of shoppers tend to buy a range of products within one category rather than being devoted to one brand.[26] It's no surprise that retailers are increasingly looking to data to figure out which of those SKUs are interchangeable – therefore removable – and which ones must be kept in.

In fact, Tesco's partnership with dunnhumby allows it to receive hourly grocery sales data for more than 15 million shoppers within days of purchase.[27] Tesco gathers and analyses four billion pieces of data from shopping baskets every week. And for each SKU that goes through the checkout, 45 different pieces of data are analysed.[28] Was it a brand or private label? Was it on sale or full price? Was it being purchased for self-consumption or for someone else in the household? This enables Tesco to segment its shopper base, tailoring both its marketing and its merchandising efforts to reflect the local demographic. In fact, the retailer's direct mail redemption rate is an astonishing 98.4 per cent, compared to the industry average of 1 per cent.[29] Customization means increased relevance of offering and promotions, which translates to opportunities for increased revenues as well as the reassurance that you are unlikely to remove important SKUs. Retail is increasingly becoming a scientific, fact-based business.

In his book, *Any Colour You Like As Long As It's Any Colour You Like*, Martin Hayward comments:

> In 1995, when Tesco Clubcard launched, one of the reasons it was so revolutionary was because the retailer was properly investing in rewarding loyal customers, rather than throwing money at chasing elusive customers it didn't have. And it works. Over the last 10 years the proportion of Tesco's growth from existing

customers spending more, is greater than growth from new customers. This approach represents a sea change in the way marketing investment is spent.[30]

However, there is a cost associated with all this technology and we know by now that Walmart is not a big fan of costs. Every year, Tesco sends out £500 million of rewards to Clubcard holders.[31] Plus there are costs associated with, first and foremost, a subscription to dunnhumby, keeping the technology up to date, printing and delivery costs of the vouchers and labour costs associated with processing customers' vouchers. Many would argue that there is a clear and justifiable return on investment, as seen in the financial improvement by dunnhumby's global clients, including Kroger, Casino, Macy's and Home Depot.

In fact, Walmart's competitors in key markets such as the United States, the UK and Canada are increasingly turning to data mining as a means of battling the giant. They can't always compete on price, so they might as well attempt to outsmart Walmart and drive loyalty by improving the relevance of their product assortment. In Canada, for example, Walmart only got into the food business in 2005 when it opened its first Supercentre. Within five years, Walmart was trading through more than 120 such stores and rapidly expanding into new territories.[32] Considering the opportunity to convert another couple of hundred discount stores to the Supercentre format in Canada, it's fair to say that price competition will remain fierce in future years. Metro, Canada's third-largest grocery retailer, has always been overshadowed by larger domestic chains Loblaw and Sobeys, but it has especially felt the pinch since Walmart began its aggressive march into the Canadian food sector. From 2006 to 2009, sales grew by a mere 0.8 per cent on a compounded basis.[33] It was time to break apart from the competition and differentiate. Metro partnered with dunnhumby in 2009 to re-launch its loyalty card scheme and begin analysing shopper data. They have since experienced an increase in basket size, card enrolment and percentage of sales using its loyalty card. All of this has helped to battle Walmart.

CEO Eric La Fleche commented that the scheme affects 'the assortment we carry, the price we sell for, the promotions we make, the personal offers we can target. That's the kind of stuff we need to compete in this environment with all the discount stores out there. Not to name the big elephant in the room, but Walmart is a big player.'[34]

Going back to the topic of SKU rationalization, data mining in many cases ensures that those important brands do not accidentally get thrown in the bin. In Metro's case, the data led it to change the way it merchandises bottled juices – from beyond displayed by brand to displayed by flavour. 'We were able to grow sales and have a clearer, simpler offer for the customer, with less assortment on the shelf. So we're saving on the cost side... and we're growing sales and margins', La Fleche added.[35]

Meanwhile, in the United States, Kroger, Walmart's largest competitor in the grocery sector, has also used dunnhumby to reduce SKUs effectively in certain categories. In his book, Martin Hayward describes how one of dunnhumby's very first tasks was to streamline the retailer's range of 60,000 SKUs. The company identified 10 categories that could benefit from SKU reduction, and 8–45 per cent of the products from each of the 10 categories were removed. Hayward writes, 'The delisted products were carefully selected according to rules dunnhumby had developed to ensure no essential items were removed. Results spoke for themselves, sales increased in nine out of the 10 categories because shoppers were finding it easier to shop from the edited ranges.'[36]

Donald Becker, former Kroger Executive Vice President, also confirmed that data have been a huge advantage during the process. In 2008, he commented: 'We're not looking at it (SKU rationalization) from, "how much can we eliminate?" But we look at it from our own data on what is the customer buying or not buying?' At the time, Kroger had eliminated nearly 30 per cent of SKUs in the breakfast cereal category. 'The customers were telling us with their wallets what they were buying. And so we eliminated some sizes. We eliminated some different SKUs and even some variety – keeping in mind localization, what was really important to that store or to that area.' The result? A reduction in out-of-stocks and improved category performance, while having to add back only one particular SKU requested by shoppers.[37] The power of data.

As discussed at the beginning of the chapter, both Walmart and Asda failed to perfect the skill of SKU rationalization and, for Walmart's US operation in particular, it has cost them dearly. Meanwhile, Tesco's ability to mine Clubcard data has resulted in a more accurate, localized in-store assortment as well as far more relevant marketing offers, driving coupon redemption and greater spend altogether. Not a bad strategy considering that the cost of retaining loyal customers is far lower than the cost of acquiring new ones.

Walmart asserts that it surveys thousands of customers every month, which allows it to get robust, actionable, statistically significant data all the way down to the store level. And of course it has access to an unimaginable amount of product data through Retail Link, as we will discuss later in the book; however, Walmart has always shunned the idea of running a loyalty card programme, viewing it as an added cost and therefore in conflict with its EDLP pricing strategy. Instead, Walmart asserts that it drives loyalty by offering consistently low prices, a topic that we will now explore in much greater detail.

Notes

1   *The Grocer*, Chloe Smith, 21 February 2009. **http://www.thegrocer.co.uk/articles.aspx?page=articles&ID=197586**

2   **http://www.unilever.co.uk/brands/foodbrands/icantbelieveitsnotbutter.aspx**

3 Campaign, I CAN'T BELIEVE IT'S NOT BUTTER IN UK RELAUNCH. 31 March 1995, CMPN

4 http://www.dairycrest.co.uk/our-brands-products/utterly-butterly.aspx

5 *Marketing Week*, I CAN'T BELIEVE IT'S NOT BUTTER, Thursday, 29 May 1997. http://www.marketingweek.co.uk/home/i-cant-believe-its-not-butter/2023474.article

6 *The Grocer*, Chloe Smith, 21 February 2009. http://www.thegrocer.co.uk/articles.aspx?page=articles&ID=197586

7 UK statistic from *The Grocer* as above. US statistic from Walmart transcript: WalMart Stores, Inc. at Bank of America Merrill Lynch Consumer Conference – Final, 10 March 2011

8 *Media Post*, Food retailers selectively trimming, Jack Loechner, Friday, July 2, 2010. http://www.mediapost.com/publications/?fa=Articles.showArticle&art_aid=130974

9 *The Grocer*, Asda tests brand equity, Adam Leyland, 24 September 2007. http://www.thegrocer.co.uk/articles.aspx?page=articles&ID=122083

10 *The Grocer*, I Can't Believe It's Not Butter is back as Asda bows to shoppers, 20 June 2009. http://www.thegrocer.co.uk/articles.aspx?page=articles&ID=200805

11 Ninth consecutive quarter of comparative decline reported in August 2011

12 *Advertising Age*, Walmart reversal marks victory for brands, Jack Neff, 22 March 2010

13 Wal-Mart Stores, Inc. at Bank of America Merrill Lynch Consumer Conference – Final, 10 March 2010

14 http://walmartstores.com/pressroom/news/10573.aspx

15 http://www.retail-merchandiser.com/dailydose/retail-roundup-archive-/1092-fewer-skus-fewer-customers.html

16 *The Grocer*, 'Cheesegrater' Blackhurst to slice 10 more categories: Asda is removing duplicate brands from 10 more categories. How will suppliers be hit by the range rationalisation? Chloe Smith, 28 February 2009. http://findarticles.com/p/articles/mi_hb5245/is_7894_232/ai_n31465152/

17 http://www.heinz.com/our-company/press-room/press-releases/press-release.aspx?ndmConfigId=1012072&newsId=20100217006929

18 http://blog.nielsen.com/nielsenwire/consumer/too-much-choice-and-variety-assortment-realities/

19 WSJ retailers cut back on variety, once the spice of marketing , Ilan Brat, Ellen Byron and Ann Zimmerman, 26 June 2009. http://www.smartbrief.com/wsj.jsp?id=5499145

20 http://www.sju.edu/resources/libraries/campbell/researchguides/files/Food%20Industry%20Review%202009.pdf

21 http://info.demandtec.com/SKU-Rationalization-with-AMR.html

22   SuperValu transcript: Supervalu Inc. at Goldman Sachs Retailing Conference – Final, 10 September 2009

23   *The Globe and Mail*, In store aisles less is more but customers can still be particular, Marina Strauss, Retailing Reporter, Globe and Mail Update, Tuesday, 18 May. 2010. **http://www.theglobeandmail.com/report-on-business/in-store-aisles-less-is-more-but-customers-can-still-be-particular/article1573518/**

24   *The Grocer*, Less is more at Asda, where cutting lines has increased sales, Chloe Smith, 25 July 2009. **http://www.thegrocer.co.uk/articles.aspx?page=articles&ID=201995**

25   *The Globe and Mail*, In store aisles less is more but customers can still be particular, Marina Straus, Retailing Reporter, Globe and Mail Update, Tuesday, 18 May. 2010. **http://www.theglobeandmail.com/report-on-business/in-store-aisles-less-is-more-but-customers-can-still-be-particular/article1573518/**

26   **http://www.dunnhumby.com/admin/files/relevant-communications-uk.pdf**

27   Martin Hayward, *Any Colour You Like As Long As It's Any Colour You Like*, p 11. **http://www.dunnhumby.com/admin/files/dunnhumby-any-colour-you-like.pdf**

28   *Sunday Times*, Every little bit of data helps Tesco rule retail: The Clubcard keeps an eye on half of the households in Britain, Jenny Davey, 4 October 2009

29   Martin Hayward, p 40

30   Martin Hayward, p 3

31   Thisismoney.co.uk, Tesco sells details of your shopping habits, Sean Poulter, 14 March 2011. **http://www.thisismoney.co.uk/money/news/article-1715030/Tesco-sells-details-of-your-shopping-habits.html#ixzz1UM4FJ7ZM**

32   **http://investors.walmartstores.com/phoenix.zhtml?c=112761&p=irol-unitcount**

33   Company documents

34   *The Gazette*, Loyalty program starts to pay off for grocer Metro, Peter Hadekel, Wednesday, 24 November 2010. **http://www2.canada.com/montrealgazette/columnists/story.html?id=30169a57-7507-48c3-9a3b-b9763d6a3e7b**

35   *The Gazette*, as above

36   Martin Hayward, p 25

37   **http://www.rffretailer.com/Articles/Cover_Story/2009/04/27/Kroger-Powers-Ahead**

It's an EDLP world

05

The consumer advocate and king of deflation

The first RCA consumer colour television set cost a whopping $1,000 when it was introduced in 1954.[1] Prices halved later that year to $495,[2] yet this was still an astonishing 16 per cent of the average American's income. Fast-forward nearly 60 years and today you can buy a TV at Walmart for $130, less than 1 per cent of the average American's income.[3] Deflation has occurred across a number of categories, particularly in electronics. Not only are retailers finding cheaper ways to source and distribute goods, but the mark-up associated with a new product launch is finding its time limited in the face of ongoing technological improvements.

This is to be expected from general merchandise categories such as electronics where higher margins enable a degree of price elasticity. But what about groceries? They are necessities with very little room for mark-ups. So why are American consumers spending less and less on groceries each year?

You can probably guess by now that Walmart is playing a role in this. In fact, it has been estimated that Walmart reduces consumer price inflation by between 0.1 and 0.2 per cent on an annual basis.[4] Walmart, despite its size, only holds a 15 per cent share of the fragmented US food sector, yet its focus on driving low prices has had a ripple effect on the competition, thereby reducing prices throughout the entire industry.

And of course it has been the consumer to benefit. As a percentage of their disposable income, Americans spent just 11.4 per cent on food in 2010. The figure is even more astonishing when we strip out the amount spent on eating at restaurants – a mere 6.4 per cent of disposable income goes towards food-at-home consumption (ie food bought from retailers). This is less than half the amount we spent just 50 years ago – when Walmart was getting started, 14.1 per cent of consumers' disposable income went to the supermarkets.[5]

However, we can't fully blame or thank Walmart for driving down prices because it wasn't until the late 1980s that they even got into the food business. The proportion of income spent on food has generally been in decline since the end of the Second World War when new technologies were introduced to drastically improve efficiencies in agricultural operations. Farming became less cost-intensive thanks to the introduction of machinery, chemical fertilizers and pesticides, and monocultures. This has helped to reduce prices and make food more readily available across different income groups, but today there is much debate about the true price we pay for cheap food. Issues such as factory farming, the use of pesticides and genetically modified ingredients have divided consumers. The tragedy is that many consumers have become accustomed to low prices and now find it hard to justify paying a 'premium' to ensure that issues such as animal welfare are addressed during production.

Despite doubts over the sustainability and longer-term implications of selling cheap food, we cannot deny that Walmart continues to help consumers by offering lower prices on everyday essentials. And increasingly Walmart is working to democratize new areas such as healthcare (through its $4 prescriptions), financial services (which although very popular in Mexico, for example, have been limited in the United States owing to regulation), and healthy foods, the retail giant's latest initiative. Teaming up with First Lady Michelle Obama, Walmart plans by 2015 to reduce sodium by 25 per cent and added sugars by 10 per cent in thousands of food products offered in its US stores. Even Walmart's most severe critics have to applaud its intentions to improve the nation's health. Of course, the commitment, along with a pledge to save consumers $1 billion a year on fresh fruits and vegetables, will also help Walmart to appease city councils as it looks for the green light into America's cities, which we will discuss in more detail later.

In any case, for nearly two decades Walmart's democratization of everyday goods was reflected in its 'Always Low Prices' slogan. Walmart was about offering cheap stuff, but in today's era of product proliferation and fierce retail competition, this is no longer enough. Therefore in 2007 Walmart drastically shifted its messaging away from pure physiological benefits (low prices on necessities) by changing its slogan to the softer, more emotional 'Save Money. Live Better.'[6] If Abraham Maslow were around today, he would applaud Walmart for moving up the hierarchy of consumer needs and reaching the top of the pyramid – self-actualization. By offering an opportunity to 'live better' at Walmart, the retailer is tapping into the emotional psyche of the consumer and demonstrating the ultimate promise on Maslow's ladder – the ability to enrich its customers' lives. It's also a nod to those affluent yet price-sensitive shoppers who were heading to Walmart in droves during the recession.

Walmart therefore must always act on behalf of its consumers. Everything it does is in the name of providing lower prices to shoppers – whether that is driving hard negotiations with suppliers or investing in technology to cut costs. It is both the advocate for, and gatekeeper to, the United States' shoppers. At times, it is difficult for Walmart to reinforce this message owing to the constant nature of EDLP, and this is particularly true in international markets where Walmart may not be the leading retailer. Therefore, initiatives to improve price perception are welcomed with open arms.

In the UK, for example, Asda's Price Guarantee promises British shoppers that its products are at least 10 per cent cheaper than major rivals. If they're not, shoppers get refunded the difference.[7] The marketing investment was made to finally lay to rest the notion that Asda is the cheapest supermarket around. Since then, millions of shoppers have used the service, which is powered by Mysupermarket.co.uk. It's a clever marketing tool for an EDLP retailer, particularly as pricing becomes more transparent with shoppers increasingly utilizing smartphones and price comparison websites. Honest pricing will be a major trend in 2012 and beyond:

> With our stores and low prices, we can really take advantage of mobile technology and this era of price transparency.
>
> (Mike Duke, 2011)[8]

In an exclusive interview with the authors, Asda's CEO Andy Clarke commented: 'There will always be a place for promotions but it's about having the right proportion. EDLP is transparent, simple and it creates trust with our shoppers. The days of promotional gimmicks are gone.'

Equally, price perception can be just as important, if not more so, than the reality of low prices, which makes the Price Guarantee a worthwhile investment. When it was re-launched in early 2011, UK consumers were battling a number of economic hurdles – inflation was well above government targets and unemployment was a major concern, particularly as government spending cuts began to take their toll. To add insult to injury, consumers feared interest rate hikes and VAT had just gone up by 2.5 per cent. Therefore, Asda's price promise was bound to resonate with many penny-pinching customers, despite the fact that it covers only 15,000 SKUs – which is less than half of the total assortment – and that there is a fair amount of administration involved in claiming a refund. It's the perceived value that made it worthwhile for a number of shoppers.

Price perception is a funny thing. In the United States, Walmart doesn't end prices in $.99 as is common practice in supermarkets. Instead, they typically end prices in $.88 or $.89, leading shoppers to believe subconsciously that they are getting a better deal. At the same time, if certain categories are priced too low then that too can have an undesired effect. In Japan, for example, shoppers were suspicious when Seiyu offered a $10 pair of jeans. Surely, quality must have been cut in order to price a product so low, consumers presumed. HBC is another category where low prices can actually have a negative effect on sales. Walmart could easily reduce the prices of its Equate private label line but shoppers would question the quality in a category where they are used to paying a premium. 'In toothpaste, if the national brands are selling for $3.33 a tube and you're at $1.50, well the customer's going to think something's wrong with your product', a Walmart executive told us.

Recession lesson #1: never take your eye off the customer

On a weekly basis, Walmart's low prices attract 140 million shoppers in the United States: 52 per cent, or 73 million, of these shoppers are core Walmart customers with an average household income of over $50,000. Although these core shoppers spend just $61 per month on consumables, they make up more than two-thirds of the retailer's sales.[9] In a weak economy, the need for value is of course heightened, particularly among this lower-income segment. Mr Simon told the authors: 'Our customers in the United States are stretched and stressed. They tell us their primary concerns are job security, the rising cost of groceries and the high cost of gas.' Walmart is learning to adapt to changes in shopper behaviour such as trip consolidation and 'paycheck cycles'.

'One in five Walmart moms tell us that the cost of gas is their top expense after housing and car payments. In an effort to offset high gas prices, customers consolidate shopping trips and they reduce their discretionary spending.' Perhaps more worrying, Mr Simon told the authors that he continues to see a spike in customer visits for necessities at midnight on the first of the month when government assistance funds become available in their accounts. 'These visits taper off significantly, spike again at the middle of the month and then decline drastically through the end of the month. It's called the paycheck cycle. The fact that it has continued over the past few years and is as pronounced as ever speaks volumes about the challenges our customers face.'

With disposable incomes under such pressure, Walmart should have been in a prime position to capitalize on their core customer's quest for value during the most recent recession. So why then did they spend the subsequent two years in decline?

The answer is simple: Walmart saw the recession as an opportunity to engage with an entirely different demographic – the new value-seeking affluents. These higher-income shoppers were spending an average of 40 per cent more per visit than the typical Walmart shopper. They were trading down from traditional supermarkets in a bid for better value. At the same time, the recession sparked a shift in consumer mentality – suddenly frugality became socially accepted. This is a trend we foresee to continue as empowered consumers across a variety of income levels are increasingly utilizing technology such as smartphones and price comparison websites to obtain, share and review product and pricing information. Today, consumers are encouraged to be thrifty, shop smartly and shout about bargains. Asda, for example, told the authors in an exclusive interview that its customers are now sharing online orders so as to split the delivery fee, and promotions such as buy two for £4 were also being shared in-store.[10] Shoppers have never been so savvy, and crucially they expect the retailer to help them save.

Walmart saw the weak economic backdrop and shift in consumer mindset as an opportunity to cash in on more lucrative customers, who perhaps had shunned Walmart prior to the downturn but were now willing to give them a try. Despite a small percentage of sales traditionally allocated towards advertising costs, Walmart ramped up its marketing efforts during the recession in a bid to raise awareness among this new demographic. In 2009, Walmart became the United States' number-one retailer based on measured-media advertising, displacing department store Macy's. That year, *Advertising Age* estimated that Walmart increased its US spending by 14.2 per cent, while global advertising spending increased by an astonishing $300 million to reach $2.4 billion. As a brand, Walmart was the third most advertised in 2009, quite a jump from its ranking at 16th place in 2007 – just before the recession struck.[11]

In addition to ramping up its advertising efforts, Walmart also embarked on a major initiative to revamp its stores, rationalize SKUs as previously discussed, and add more compelling merchandise to the mix. Project Impact, as it was known internally, was aimed at gaining Walmart credibility, reducing clutter, improving shopability and navigation of its stores and creating a more inviting store experience. It was about lowering shelves, widening aisles, improving lighting and removing the bargain-heavy, pallet-led Action Alleys. This was about sophistication, making Walmart about more than just price.

And that is where we had to stop and question whether this was actually the right strategy for Walmart. Walmart is, after all, about price. It's about offering extreme value on a wide assortment of goods. That has always been the attraction among shoppers and the differentiator among competitors – Walmart has been in a unique position to deliver on that promise of both value and assortment. Now you could argue that many of Walmart's stores were in need of a revamp and, of course, improvements in customer service will never be frowned upon in the retail industry. However, unlike most Walmart initiatives, Project Impact wasn't about pure cost investment to provide shoppers with better value. This was about store investment to gain long-term market share. While there would certainly be efficiencies gained on the distribution side, Project Impact was about attracting and retaining a new type of shopper. The strategy carried a great degree of risk. And at a time when value was paramount for Walmart's core customers, its pricing message became muddled.

Looking back on Project Impact, Bill Simon commented in 2011: 'We got enamoured with presentation as an example. We walked people through our [remodelled] stores and they were gorgeous. But they cost more. And if you spend more on your building, your prices can't be as low as you want them to be.'[12] Speaking to the authors, Mr Simon also noted that being in stock is also critically important to shoppers. 'We've found that if we don't get those things right, if we don't take care of the basics, then it doesn't matter how entertaining we make the in-store experience', he told us.

The main merchandising component of Project Impact – 'Win, Play, Show' – was designed to segment its products into three categories. A 'win' category, such as pet care, possessed growth, scale and credibility. Walmart stocked the full range and used the category aggressively to gain market share. Price leadership was vital here. A 'play' category, meanwhile, such as denim jeans, featured a limited assortment because although it may have possessed growth, scale or credibility it certainly did not possess all three (as was the case with a 'win' category).

Finally, a 'show' category such as hardware featured those items that tended to lack credibility at Walmart. These products showed little room for growth but were necessary for Walmart's positioning as a one-stop shop. 'It's important we have hammers, and it's important we have tape measures, but we don't need 28 kinds of tape measures, which we actually had at one time', said former chief merchandising officer John Fleming.

But, as discussed in the previous chapter, before Walmart takes the axe to its sewing machines and office furniture, it must first and foremost take the customer into account. Take the fishing aisle, for example. This was one of those categories deemed cull-able and therefore soon heavily rationalized, leaving customers with an 'anaemic'-looking department as described by Walmart itself. The retailer has since increased the assortment and space of this department and as a result saw comparable sales of items like rods and reels up by 40 per cent. Hunting goods – including the controversial gun category – and fabrics have also been added back into the mix as part of Walmart's 2012 goal of having the broadest assortment available.

Action Alleys have also been added back. So much for clear sophisticated aisles; the absence of pallet-led discounts has hurt Walmart's price perception. By early 2011, Action Alleys were back in two-thirds of US stores, resulting in an increase of 10–20 basis points in comparable store sales.

The path to efficiency

Now, when it comes to Walmart, there's no two ways about it: I'm cheap. (SAM WALTON)

Walmart's business model is very simple – to offer well-known brands at the lowest possible everyday price. Logic would tell us that when a retailer prices a product below what the competition are selling it for, they make less money on the sale. Yet this assumes that two things are equal: (1) the number of units sold and (2) the amount for which the product was purchased. At a very early stage, Sam Walton recognized that, provided the right merchandise was on the shelf, he could undercut the competition on price yet attract enough shoppers so that the high volumes would make up for the price investment:

> ... Say I bought an item for 80 cents. I found that by pricing it at $1.00 I could sell three times more of it than by pricing it at $1.20. I might make only half the profit per item, but because I was selling three times as many, the overall profit was much greater.
>
> (Sam Walton)

As Walmart grew and became more powerful, they were able to achieve better terms with suppliers. Their scale meant that lower purchasing costs could be reinvested in lower prices at the shelf. Of course, it didn't stop at lowering the cost of buying goods. Everyday Low Prices (EDLP) is 100 per cent derived from Everyday Low Cost (EDLC). The entire business is based on this principle. As CEO Mike Duke puts it, 'We must have the most efficient retail organization in the world, and that's the path we're on.' Frugality is truly an understatement here, and this even applies to how the company got its name. Sam Walton had a card with several possible names, all of which had three or four words in the title. Bob Bogle, the first manager of Walton's Five and Dime store in Bentonville, tells the story in Mr Walton's autobiography:

> I scribbled 'W-A-L-M-A-R-T' on the bottom of the card and said, 'To begin with there's not as many letters to buy.' I had bought the letters that said 'Ben Franklin' and I knew how much it cost to put them up and to light them and repair the neon.

Walton embedded a frugal yet diligent business culture within Walmart from day one. It wasn't uncommon to see senior business executives, Mr Walton included, stay at the Day's Inn, often sharing a room with a colleague in order to halve the cost. At Walmart's Bentonville headquarters, furniture is often a 'mismatched hodgepodge of colors and styles, including samples of chairs from suppliers that Walmart, having assessed for purposes of selling them in its stores, has put into everyday service', wrote Charles Fishman in his book *The Walmart Effect*.[13] Trips to visit suppliers were always to cost less than 1 per cent of the purchase and vendors were infamously required to accept collect calls from Walmart's buyers. 'Every time Walmart spends one dollar foolishly, it comes right out of our customers' pockets. Every time we save them a dollar, that puts us one more step ahead of the competition – which is where we always plan to be', Sam Walton wrote in his autobiography. Walmart's ability to offer low prices is the result of its continuous efforts to drive out excess costs in the business, something that has been ingrained in the company since Sam Walton's early days as a merchant:

> What happened was absolutely a necessary and inevitable evolution in retailing.
> (Sam Walton)

Let's not forget that when Walmart was starting out, independent retailing was a hugely inefficient business. A lack of competition meant that small-town retailers could get away with offering a mediocre assortment, closing their stores on Sundays and, critically for Walmart, charging phenomenal mark-ups. And still customers would keep coming back, either because they didn't know any differently or because they just didn't have a choice. Walmart saw this as an opportunity to better serve the customer and in the process they would forever change the way that retailing was done.

How Walmart broke the supermarket pricing model

As the big boy of retail, Walmart takes a lot of heat. For ruthlessly under-cutting its rivals, for tough negotiations with suppliers, for putting smaller companies out of business. It's easy to put blame on the big guy, but we have to remember that Walmart wasn't always so big. Sam Walton was once a small-town merchant. He once felt the wrath of the more established retailers at the time, such as Kmart, and not everything he touched turned to gold. But he did recognize an opportunity to, in his words, 'take things beyond where they've been'. He never marked up a product by more than 30 per cent, thereby offering extreme value to consumers and, most importantly, on a permanent basis:

> When we arrived in these little towns offering low prices every day, satisfaction guaranteed, and hours that were realistic for the way people wanted to shop, we passed right by that old variety store competition, with its 45 percent mark-ups, limited selection, and limited hours.'
>
> (Sam Walton)

While traditional supermarkets primarily focused on high–low pricing strategies, Walmart recognized yet another more efficient way to do busi-ness. The retailer broke from the norm once again by asking suppliers to offer one low price on a permanent basis. Now it's important to understand that trade promotion investment, as it is referred to in the industry, on aver-age accounts for 13–20 per cent of an FMCG supplier's revenue, or more than two-thirds of their marketing budget.[14] It is by far the biggest single expense for a number of FMCG companies. Therefore, you can imagine that a few eyebrows were raised when Walmart told its suppliers to abandon their typical promotional cycles and instead to invest it all into one consist-ently low price.

The cost model of a full-service supermarket is very different from that of a mass discounter, and therefore, prior to Walmart, retailers primarily relied on promotions to drive shopper traffic and incremental sales. In fact, the majority of food retailers today continue to opt for a high–low pricing model, although the two strategies continue to blur.

Doing business with a high–low retailer adds a significant level of disrup-tion and cost into the supply chain. For a given promotion, demand must be precisely forecast in order to ensure that there will be a worthwhile return on investment (ROI) and that there is sufficient supply (if not, suppliers can be faced with leftover stock or empty shelves – neither of which is likely to go down well with their retail customer). In the case of the former, trade sources suggest that as many as 50 per cent of promotions result in negative returns on investment after taking into consideration execution costs and unintended cannibalization. For example, say a can of tomato soup is on a supplier-funded half-price promotion at high–low Retailer X. That same can of tomato soup is offered at regular price at EDLP Retailer Y. In this instance, shoppers are more likely to visit Retailer X, which cannibalizes sales for the tomato soup supplier while disproportionately rewarding the retailer. As Walmart says, high–low retailers simply rent customers and rent market share:

> Don't go in and dump a bunch of coupons in the market and drive artificial volume, hold it steady.
>
> (Bill Simon, 2011)

That said, the increasing use of data is enabling high–low retailers to offer more targeted promotions and thereby improve ROI for both them and their suppliers. As discussed in the last chapter, Tesco's partnership with dunnhumby (the market research company part-owned by Tesco and behind the retailer's Clubcard scheme) is a fantastic example as it enables Tesco to drive long-term customer loyalty by better understanding its shoppers. To Walmart, this is viewed as unnecessary cost. Instead, the retailer's EDLP strategy looks to remove the complexities associated with running a high–low strategy, and in the process it provides both itself and its suppliers with a far greater sense of predictability in the supply chain. Since prices are generally constant, there is no need to worry about forecasting for incremental demand that would occur as part of the binge/purge process of running promotions. This then allows suppliers to achieve greater efficiencies when it comes to planning, manufacturing and distribution.

One private label supplier in the UK that we have spoken to told us that Asda's EDLP approach combined with long-term multi-buys and rollbacks makes for a much more predictable flow of business than it sees with supplying the likes of Tesco and Sainsbury's with their more promotional approach to retailing.

Therefore, EDLP takes the guessing game – and the costs – out of the equation. Take labour and advertising expenses, for example. Labour is one of the largest operating expenses for many food retailers, so any opportunity to reduce this – of course without impacting customer service – is taken. This is why we have seen so much investment in store technology (eg self-checkouts, handheld scanners) over the past decade. Like technology, an EDLP policy can also reduce labour costs as it eliminates the need for employees to physically change price tags each time there is a promotion. Of course, for many retailers this can be as often as once a week, which is a lot of time and money spent changing prices and relocating stock to promotional areas. When Walmart implemented EDLP in Brazil, for example, the number of price changes declined by 60 per cent and checkout lines were reduced by 53 per cent, proof that EDLP can actually help to improve customer service.[15]

Equally, a lack of price changes means that EDLP retailers can save on advertising costs – whether that's mailing weekly circulars or announcing a promotion via TV or radio. While volume-driven food retailers tend to spend a relatively small proportion of their sales on advertising anyway,

Walmart's investment is still remarkably low – a mere 0.5 per cent of sales versus the 2 per cent spent by Target.[16]

Too concerned with trading down over trading out

As you can see, EDLP versus high–low remains one of the most debated topics in the food retail sector. Which actually conveys a stronger value proposition? Walmart would argue that everyday low prices are simple and credible. They eliminate short-term price uncertainty and, in fact, instil trust among consumers once they understand the value proposition. 'It's not easy being an EDLP retailer but nothing builds more loyalty', Mike Duke commented in 2011.[17]

However, high–low retailers would say that EDLP is boring, lacking both stimulation and a sense of urgency among shoppers since the prices are always the same. High–low retailers maintain that shoppers can find better value at their stores by waiting for the promotions, during which time prices are typically lower than at an EDLP retailer. Of course, the catch is that those prices are temporary and an EDLP retailer like Walmart would argue that such short-term discounts erode the credibility of the standard shelf price. 'The two most important words in that equation aren't low prices but every day', said Walmart Canada's former CEO David Cheesewright:

> This promise of the lowest possible prices, day-in and day-out, permits our customers to shop at their convenience without waiting for 'sales'.
>
> (Walmart)

Yet all of this assumes a normal economic backdrop. In a down economy, shoppers become more promiscuous and cherry-pick the best bargains, which puts pressure on retailers to engage in more promotional activity regardless of their pricing principles.

During the recession, Walmart in the United States suffered quarter after quarter of negative comparable store sales growth. In a bid to win quick market share, they made a few pricing blunders. Firstly, there were instances when national brands were priced below the private label equivalent – referred to as 'the cardinal sin in retailing' by a former Walmart executive. In other instances, the cost to Walmart of buying private label was greater than the cost of buying a national brand – another significant faux pas. But perhaps the biggest mistake was Walmart's temporary shift away from its core EDLP policy. They began offering deep discounts on major brands, and in some cases these products were being offered below cost. For example, a 40-ounce bottle of Heinz ketchup was sold for $1. A former Walmart executive told us: 'It was ludicrous. They only sold Heinz and they only sold the 40-ounce bottle so they had restaurants, schools, everyone buying 6 or

7 bottles at a time. You couldn't buy the 24-ounce bottle for that price, let alone the 40-ounce one.'

A similar mistake was made by selling 24-packs of Coke and Pepsi for $5. 'At the end of the day, it didn't bring in any more customers. It just brought the same customer in a lot', the Walmart executive told us. The retailer was arguably more concerned with shoppers trading down than they were with shoppers trading out, in this instance to the dollar stores. At the time, Walmart was losing the pricing battle to these smaller pesky stores, many of which were growing comparable store sales in high single digits while Walmart was in decline. Too preoccupied with SKU rationalization and store remodels, Walmart began to neglect its EDLP principles and in the process alienated its core shopper base. Meanwhile, the dollar stores were busy adding more groceries into their assortment, benefiting from those shoppers defecting from Walmart.

Slashing prices on national brands, and doing so below cost in some cases, was a desperate attempt by Walmart to win back market share. Some point the finger to the host of external executives who have joined Walmart's management team in recent years. The retailer has hired executives from CPG companies and competing retailers, some of whom 'just didn't get Walmart's business philosophy', according to a senior executive. In any case, such pricing was unsustainable and uncharacteristically Walmart: this was high–low behaviour. It's no surprise then that Walmart's number-one goal today is to restore EDLP across its entire corporation. They now aim to have an opening price point – either national brand or private label – in every single category and in 2011 introduced an aggressive ad match policy to restore confidence among shoppers that Walmart offers the lowest prices around.

No need for weapons of mass distraction

Across the Atlantic, Walmart's British operations were also guilty of veering away from EDLP at one point. In the UK, where 40 per cent of all sales were on promotion in 2011,[18] EDLP-driven Asda has struggled at times to compete against promotion-orientated competitors such as Tesco and Morrisons. When you factor in a weak economic backdrop, the temptation to veer away from EDLP becomes even greater. Back in 2009, Asda began to dabble in multi-buy promotions in an attempt to drive shopper traffic and claw back some lost market share. The retailer continued with its efforts to win shoppers over with 'buy one, get one free' (BOGOF) and other limited-timed deals into the following year. In the four weeks to 5 July 2010, the number of promotions at Asda increased by 13.4 per cent on an annual basis to 1,646. This was still below competitors such as Sainsbury's and Morrisons, but in fact greater than Tesco – one of the most promotional supermarkets – which ran a total of 1,615 promotions during the same time.[19]

Despite its intent of improving price perception, the move towards promotional activity simply confused shoppers and in the process made Asda blend in with the rest of the supermarkets. Similarly, as food price inflation eased, Asda found that suppliers would offer more promotions rather than decreasing unit costs.[20] As an EDLP retailer, this is unacceptable, yet, from an CPG supplier's point of view, it's far more favourable to end a promotion early than to push through longer-term base price increases. It turned out that multi-buy offers, or 'weapons of mass distraction'[21] as then CEO Andy Bond famously referred to them, were not in Asda's interests and the retailer is now 'on a journey back to EDLP', Andy Clarke told the authors. Clarke, however, points out that, while low prices are important, having a strong value proposition goes much further. 'We are the best-value retailer in the UK, not the biggest discounter.'

Preço Baixo Todo Dia: is it an EDLP world?

The Asda example leads us to a very important question – does EDLP translate in every market? Generally speaking, Walmart has made significant improvements in flexibility with regard to its international operations, recognizing that not all markets are created equal after failures in Germany and South Korea. For example, in Latin America and Asia, many stores trade under local banner names and merchandising is also very much reflective of the local market. However, when it comes to pricing, there's no two ways about it – a uniform EDLP approach must be adopted by all markets:

> Everyday low prices in every market. No exceptions, no excuses.
>
> (Mike Duke, 2011)[22]

On 6 January 2011, 5,000 miles south of Walmart's cold Bentonville headquarters, its Brazilian division was celebrating something special. And no, it wasn't just a warm summer day in the southern hemisphere, but the day that EDLP was launched in its Brazilian stores. All hypermarkets and supermarkets – including Walmart, Big and Hiper Bompreço – were closed that morning so that employees could permanently reduce prices on 2,000 items by up to 20 per cent. The chain officially reopened at lunchtime as an EDLP retailer.[23]

The conversion had been in the works for nine months, as Walmart worked with suppliers to renegotiate contracts and also with consumers to help educate them about the benefits of EDLP. The new pricing model had been tested in a handful of Brazilian outlets and met with 'fairly good results'. Days before the launch, Walmart ended its Bomclube loyalty programme which had approximately 4 million members in the north-east and south of Brazil. It was time once again to focus on cost reduction and driving everyday low prices.

The move in Brazil is significant for a few reasons. Firstly, Brazil is unique in that it is one of the few retail markets in the world dominated by the large multinational retailers: Companhia Brasileira de Distribuicao (or CBD, which is jointly controlled by France's Casino), Carrefour and Walmart are the country's three most important food retailers. Their efficiency-led approach has helped to drive prices down in what is already an extremely promotional market. As such, there is a tremendous amount of price transparency in the Brazilian food sector. It is not uncommon to see shopping-basket price comparisons at the entrance of Carrefour or Walmart, and Brazilian shoppers are accustomed to finding comparison signage for specific products at the shelf. Walmart's commitment to EDLP therefore puts additional pressure on vendors, who of course sell to both Walmart and its competition.

Now Walmart is certainly an important retail customer for Brazilian FMCG suppliers – but they're not number one. Unlike in the United States where some FMCGs make more than one-third of their sales through Walmart, in Brazil CBD is actually the largest retail account. Therefore, if an FMCG supplier is asked/required by Walmart to adopt an EDLP approach, it is bound to ruffle some feathers when it comes time for negotiations with CBD.

EDLP doesn't exist without EDLC

Our highest priority is to continue being the retailer with the lowest cost structure in the market, so as to be in a position of giving our customers Every Day Low Prices.

(Walmart de Mexico y CentroAmerica 2010 Annual Report)

In order for EDLP to be a success in a new market, it's absolutely vital for two things to take place: (1) EDLC must be well established and (2) prices must be truly cheaper than the competition. 'EDLC is and continues to be a part of our DNA. We invest in low prices which drives volume and enables us to go back and reinvest in price. It's all a cycle and something that is truly unique to Walmart', Asda CEO Andy Clarke told the authors.

But this doesn't always happen overnight – in Mexico it took Walmart eight years from market entry to EDLP implementation. Ownership structure plays a major role in Walmart's ability to offer everyday low prices to shoppers. In Mexico, majority ownership was achieved in 1997[24] and by 1999 EDLP was introduced.[25] Prior to this, Walmart had spent years stripping out excess costs in Mexico in order to fund EDLP, and its vision for EDLC continues to this day. By 2000, the EDLP model had already been established on the back of a lean cost structure whereby general expenses accounted for 15.1 per cent of revenues and operating margin was 5.3 per cent. A decade on, general expenses were reduced even further to 14 per cent of revenues as part of Walmart's relentless drive for efficiency.[26] That year, Walmart de

Mexico invested more than 1 billion pesos in the automation of two of its distribution centres (DCs). How does this affect prices, you might ask? Productivity at those two DCs in Tabasco and Cuautitlán is expected to increase by up to 30 per cent,[27] allowing Walmart to transport merchandise to a larger number of stores more efficiently. The cost savings achieved through DC automation as well as global sourcing and other supply chain initiatives will once again get fed back to the customer in the form of EDLP, enabling Walmart to attract additional shoppers and fund further investment in technology and the supply chain. It is an ongoing cycle, all in the name of lower prices.

While Walmart certainly benefits from the increased traffic and consequent market share gains on the back of price investment, it is by no means a charity and therefore some of those cost savings are used to buffer the bottom line and appease shareholders – over the past decade, Walmart de Mexico has recorded a 280 basis point improvement in operating margin.[28] Today it is the unequivocal market leader in Mexico, with sales reaching $25 billion in 2010.[29]

Kakaku Yasuku – EDLP implementation isn't always seamless

EDLP is a proven recipe in fast-growing, price-conscious markets like Mexico and China; however, the transition hasn't gone quite so seamlessly in the stagnant, more affluent Japanese retail market. Initially, EDLP simply didn't work for Walmart's Japanese shoppers, 90 per cent of whom are women,[30] who were used to finding weekly specials in *chirashis*, newspaper inserts produced by many retailers. We know by now that weekly flyers are a big no-no when it comes to Walmart's EDLP approach; however, when Seiyu attempted to abandon the *chirashi*, sales quickly plunged: EDLP wasn't going to happen overnight.[31]

In Japan, another barrier to EDLP was the fact that many consumers had traditionally been motivated by quality over price, although this has shifted in recent years owing to austerity measures. This is especially true when it comes to fresh food – a vital component of the Japanese consumer's diet. Even for a retailer like Walmart, there is very little room for cost reductions in perishables because most Japanese farms are family-run operations that tend to offer better deals on smaller orders rather than on larger ones.[32]

In fact, many Japanese consumers associated cheap food with inferior quality and let's not forget that, owing to higher population densities, consumers do not have the space in their homes to bulk-buy six months' worth of toilet paper or canned beans. Add to the mix that there is a strong preference for domestic goods and we can begin to see why Walmart struggled for so many years in Japan.

But differences in consumer behaviour were certainly not the only barrier Seiyu faced when attempting to convert to EDLP. Going back to our earlier points about the prerequisites for success with EDLP, Walmart Japan initially failed when it came to both ensuring that it was offering the lowest prices available and achieving EDLC in order to fund EDLP. 'Everyday Low Prices cannot be achieved overnight, but we have to meet the challenge. Otherwise, there will be no rebirth of Seiyu', then Seiyu President Masao Kiuchi said in 2005.[33] Seiyu's stores were dated and prices were not compelling enough – more than a decade of deflation in Japan meant that most retailers were forced to cut prices aggressively:

> When we started talking to the Japanese multinationals about EDLP, and the fact that EDLC was an important part of that, they didn't get it, quite honestly.
> (Scott Price, CEO of Walmart Asia)

Like Mexico, Walmart Japan's ownership structure held them back initially. They entered the market in 2002 by purchasing a 6.1 per cent stake in Seiyu.[34] During the first few years, Walmart had little to do with the day-to-day operations of Seiyu. They were there primarily to learn the ropes of this vastly different but potentially very lucrative new market, so if it all went sour they could easily sell their minority stake. Well, it did go sour for quite a while and many analysts, noting similarities with Germany, questioned Walmart's ability to crack such a difficult, stagnant market. Despite continued losses in Japan, Walmart felt that it needed to hold a more influential role in one of the world's largest economies. Japan may have had its nuances – a finicky consumer, a stagnant economy and an inefficient supply chain – but it was a big market with a fragmented retail sector. This was music to Walmart's ears. It gradually increased its stake over time until Seiyu eventually became a wholly owned subsidiary in 2008.[35] The timing was ideal: the impact of the global financial crisis meant that Japanese consumers who previously shunned lower prices were quickly developing an appetite for cheap goods.

Achieving full ownership gave Walmart more power and flexibility to invest in key areas such as merchandising, store remodels, distribution and logistics, ultimately enabling them to invest in EDLP. Cost reduction on the whole has been a much slower process in Japan compared to other markets, owing to higher wages and underlying complexities in the structure of the grocery distribution system. However, within months of acquiring the final shares of Seiyu, Walmart flexed its muscles by shutting down 20 unprofitable stores and reducing its corporate workforce by 29 per cent[36] – a move that was uncommon in employee-loyal Japan and therefore met with a degree of resentment among both staff and shoppers. Yet it crucially enabled Walmart to invest in price. It began to realize additional economies of scale by processing meat in a central facility (and therefore eliminating the need for in-store butchers and freeing up floor space for higher-margin prepared meals). Walmart began to achieve higher labour productivity in stores from initiatives such as multi-tasking, improved logistics efficiency and lower advertising costs:

> The Japanese customer needs us. Thirty per cent of the Japanese are now classified as working poor.

(Scott Price, 2010)

Kakaku Yasuku (EDLP) was launched in 2008, just months after Seiyu was fully integrated into Walmart's business. Whereas previous half-hearted attempts at EDLP had met with mixed results, the launch of Kakaku Yasuku resonated with today's more price-conscious shopper. There had also been a change in the consumer psyche around quality perception – many now recognize that lower prices do not necessarily equate to lower quality, an area that has been bolstered by Walmart's global sourcing and private label initiatives. Previously, Seiyu lacked a compelling in-store environment and crucially was not always the cheapest, despite its best efforts. Today, renovations have attracted shoppers (traffic was up 2 per cent in 2010) who are also more convinced of their pricing strategy thanks to a series of guarantees which honour competitors' prices if shoppers find a product cheaper in another retailer's *chirashi*. Seiyu reversed seven consecutive loss-making years by turning a profit in 2008 – the year EDLP was implemented.

Global sourcing has played, and continues to play, a major role in Seiyu's ability to offer not only greater value but also more compelling merchandise. Take grapes, for example. Seiyu had been sourcing grapes through an existing supply chain in Japan and selling them to customers for 348 Japanese yen. In 2010, they began importing a different variety of grapes from California, which were offered in a larger package and sold for a whopping 40 per cent discount to the Japanese variety. At 248 Japanese yen, the California grapes not only offer greater value to the customer but it's also a differentiated product with a quality level that is equal to or better than the current option. Now you can argue that this goes completely against the notion of offering locally and sustainably sourced foods, which ironically is a major priority for Walmart at home and in international markets, particularly in India, China and Central America. However, as Mike Duke puts it: 'What's happening is the geographic borders are more blurred and there's more of a global optimization going on as it relates to product.' If Walmart can leverage this and offer greater value to its shopper, you bet it is going to act on it.

Additional examples of Seiyu utilizing Walmart's global sourcing network include US beef, US broccoli, Australian asparagus, US-made household products from Procter & Gamble, Chinese-manufactured home electrical appliances and electronics from Haier, EUPA and Funai, and Walmart private labels such as Extra Special wines from the UK, as well as Mainstays home textile products from India and Pakistan.

In another international market, South Africa, Walmart's entry has been touted as a possible precursor to a bitter price war, with Walmart using its global scale and influence to bring down prices for South African shoppers.

To some extent, this will be true, with Walmart expected – in the longer term – to implement some of its efficiencies and best practices to bring lower costs (and therefore lower prices) to Massmart. Walmart can also be expected to reinforce Massmart's commitment to centralized distribution and will also be keen to expedite the process of centralized procurement.

Owing to the sanctions that were placed on South Africa during the apartheid era, there were very few European or US suppliers that built a significant presence in the South African market, meaning that competition among vendors was largely limited to South African suppliers servicing South African retailers. In an attempt to foster competition, many retailers and suppliers became organized on a regional level, with procurement and logistics often being structured around provinces and then being further segmented around different brands or ranges. The end result is a very frag-mented FMCG market with very many decentralized conversations taking place between retailer and supplier. This will be something that Massmart, guided by Walmart, will seek to remedy. Walmart prefers to have fewer, more senior conversations with its suppliers and will not be content with Massmart's buyers operating on a regional or SKU-specific basis. Suppliers in South Africa will soon be asked to centralize and shift away from the legacy provincial structure.

However, there are also a number of reasons why Walmart's impact on pricing in South Africa might be limited. The first reason is that Massmart is a relatively small retailer – particularly in grocery categories – where it is dwarfed by Shoprite, Pick n Pay and SPAR, meaning that its bargaining power will be limited. Any attempts by Massmart to implement EDLP will be met by resistance from suppliers and from their larger retail customers, who may act punitively towards suppliers if Massmart is seen to be receiv-ing better prices. The second reason why Walmart's impact on pricing might be muted is due to the aforementioned absence or weakness of global FMCG giants in the South African marketplace. The leading suppliers in the market are not Walmart's traditional partners such as Tyson, Procter & Gamble or Clorox, but instead local conglomerates like Tiger Brands and AVI, companies that Walmart will have done little – if any – business with. The retailer will therefore be starting from scratch to some extent in build-ing relationships with local vendors and will be less able to draw on the collaborative relationships that it has historically enjoyed with the likes of P&G.

It is in non-food categories that Walmart might be able to bring about the fastest impact on prices. In areas such as consumer electronics, apparel and toys, where Walmart has made huge progress in global procurement and private label, Walmart should be able to exert a strongly positive impact on Massmart's value proposition: bringing lower prices and higher quality to South African shoppers.

Walmart versus inflation

We're seeing cost increases starting to come through at a pretty rapid rate.
(BILL SIMON, 2011)

What do the following events have in common: political unrest in North Africa, rising affluence in China and floods in Australia? They are all contributing factors to rising food prices. The global food market is far more intertwined than one would imagine. Economic, political, environmental and socio-demographic shifts can all impact the price we pay for everyday foods such as bread, chicken and vegetables.

Inflation is one of the largest concerns for the future of the food sector, and even the mighty Walmart will not be able to fully absorb the cost of inflation. By mid-2008, food prices had reached their highest levels in 30 years. At that time, skyrocketing oil prices were to blame – by July 2008 they had reached an all-time trading record of $147 per barrel. Not only did this make it more expensive to transport food and other products, but it also made it more costly to manufacture and package consumer goods. The silver lining for retailers like Walmart, however, is that shoppers look to consolidate trips when gas prices go up.

> When it goes from $30 to $45 or $50 to fill up your tank, then the one-stop shop becomes more important. We actually see our traffic lift.
>
> (Bill Simon)

In any case, food price inflation eased as oil prices dropped to more normal levels. However, in December 2010, the global food price index rose above its 2008 peak and by February 2011, food prices were up another 2.2 per cent over the previous month, marking yet another record high.

While the 2008 increases were directly linked to soaring oil prices, 2010 rises were primarily climate related. Poor and unusual weather conditions in producer countries pushed up commodity prices, leading to a global increase of 25 per cent for the year. For example, droughts in Russia, the world's third-largest wheat-producing country, and a consequent export ban logically led to skyrocketing wheat prices in summer 2010. It's a simple case of economics: if demand outstrips supply then prices are likely to rise.

Sure, weather and its impact on crops have always led to fluctuations in the price and availability of certain foods. Retailers and manufacturers brace themselves for this by engaging in hedging – locking in prices with producers for an agreed period of time so as to avoid short-term pricing volatility.

Yet, while commodity price fluctuations are to be expected, there are greater forces at play that make inflation a long-term concern for the entire food sector. Agricultural land is being diverted from crop to biofuel production. The United States is diverting close to 40 per cent of corn harvest for fuel while the European Union has a goal of 10 per cent biofuel use by 2020. Hedge funds, meanwhile, have artificially inflated prices through increased speculation in the commodities market. In 2010, the price of cocoa reached a 33-year high after a London hedge fund bought up approximately a quarter of Western Europe's total stocks.

What is most worrying, however, is the projected population growth which will have a major impact on food resources and consequently retailers' ability to sustain low prices for consumers. The world population, at just under 7 billion at the start of 2011, is expected to grow by approximately 30 per cent by 2050. In order to keep up with the projected 2 billion additional mouths to feed – the equivalent of almost seven new United States – the UN estimates that food production will have to double within the next 40 years.

Jason Clay of the World Wildlife Fund believes that 'we will need to produce as much food in the next 40 years as we have in the last 8,000'. To some, this may sound sensationalist but you cannot ignore the rapidly emerging middle classes in Asia, the Middle East and Latin America. By 2050, incomes are expected to triple globally and quintuple in emerging markets. As consumers become more affluent, they spend less of their disposable income on food but they suddenly have the buying power to consume higher-quality, often more expensive foods. For example, newly prosperous consumers in Asia are shifting from vegetarian diets to meat-based ones, which will put further pressure on global meat and grain prices. The UN Food and Agriculture Organization (FAO) suggests that beef could become an extreme luxury by 2050 – 'the caviar of the future' – while a rather more eccentric *Wall Street Journal* article puts together a compelling case for considering insects for dinner – they require fewer resources and produce less waste. Bugs or no bugs, the era of cheap food is well and truly over.

So what does all of this mean for food retailers? The primary implication is that low prices cannot be sustained, a particular worry for those retailers that trade from a value-led, price-driven proposition. Take the single-price point retailers, for example. In 2008, inflation got the best of California-based discounter 99 Cents Only which was forced to raise prices of all items by 0.99 of a cent. Factoring in sales tax, products were soon no longer '99 cents only'. At what point will the dollar stores be replaced by the 'two dollar stores'?

Inflation may be out of the retailers' hands but they should be looking to control that which is controllable. Over the next 5 to 10 years, we can expect to see increased investment in supply chain and technology as food retailers find ways to increase efficiencies. Cost reduction will be vital when it comes to combating inflation, an area, of course, where Walmart is already streets ahead of the competition. In fact, we expect Walmart to benefit disproportionately from rising food prices given its ability to mitigate certain cost increases. It operates one of the most efficient supply chains in the world, and is now beginning to reap the benefits of global sourcing. There is no other retailer in the world that can boast such efficiencies on a global scale. The bigger Walmart becomes, the greater economies of scale it can generate and consequently the lower prices it can offer. Meanwhile, smaller retailers and/or those without a lean cost structure will be exposed and the gap widened:

Furthermore, Walmart's EDLP strategy works well in an inflationary environment since customers are aware that, while there are a lot of overall price fluctuations in the market, Walmart's prices are generally constant and therefore trustworthy. There will, of course, be some exceptions – in 2010, Walmart had to raise the price of jeans, for example. Additionally, in commodities such as rice, it becomes very difficult even for a retailer of Walmart's size to mask inflation.

In such a price-competitive marketplace, the very last thing Walmart, or any retailer, wants to do is pass inflation on to its customers. If the retailer isn't absorbing it and the shopper isn't absorbing it, then that leaves just one party left – the supplier.

> We work with [suppliers] as hard and as long as we can to try and hold down the costs all the way through the supply chain.
>
> (Bill Simon)

This is by no means exclusive to Walmart, or US retailers for that matter. In France, hypermarket chain Leclerc vowed to limit price increases to 2 per cent in 2011, despite requests from suppliers to raise prices by up to 7 per cent to reflect the higher raw material costs. Leclerc promised to reinvest 0.2 to 0.25 points of profit margin in order to maintain its own EDLP status, but the rest would be up to suppliers. A similar message was echoed in Germany by Rewe Group CEO Alain Caparros who in 2011 simply stated: 'We are refusing price increases from food manufacturers.'

Since retailers tend to hold the upper hand, it is often the supplier that is required to find a more economical way of delivering the same product for the same cost. This tends to mean one of two things – suppliers can take the hit on inflation themselves and potentially reduce promotional spend, or, provided they come to an agreement with the retailer, they can reduce the pack size of their product while maintaining the price. The former option isn't sustainable and will quickly eat into profits. The latter option, meanwhile, allows the cost of inflation to be absorbed, but without the shopper necessarily recognizing an increase in unit pricing. During the recession, such downsizing occurred in a number of product categories, including peanut butter, ice cream, orange juice and yogurt. We will inevitably see more of this in the future as retailers and suppliers battle rising commodity costs.

But it's not always so straightforward. Those suppliers that refuse to succumb to retailer demands often meet with an unfortunate fate. Over the past several years, there have been a number of high-profile cases of major brands being delisted from retailers because they couldn't agree on price. In the United States, Costco delisted Coca-Cola for almost an entire month in 2009.[37] In Belgium, Delhaize removed roughly 300 Unilever products for a similar reason.[38] In the UK, following on from soaring wheat costs, Tesco and Premier Foods became embroiled in a public pricing dispute that saw 12 of Premier's 18 SKUs removed from Tesco's shelves.[39] Price negotiations, never a particularly easy process to begin with, are becoming a growing source of contention in the food industry.

The hard fact remains that today the power is very much in the hands of the retailer. It's hard to believe that in Sam Walton's autobiography he refers to initial difficulties getting the large FMCG companies such as Procter & Gamble and Eastman Kodak to sell their products in his stores. 'And when they did they would dictate to us how much they would sell us and at what price.' Today, Walmart is P&G's largest customer, with annual sales of nearly $13 billion generated through the retailer.

Today, an average Walmart store features 96 product categories with 140,000 SKUs. Walmart's US division alone buys from more than 61,000 suppliers in more than 55 countries around the world.[40] Yet, as we will discuss in the next chapter, to one supplier Walmart alone can account for more than half their business. It's easy to see which way the pendulum swings.

Yet amid the fight for power, it's easy to forget that retailers and suppliers are targeting the same end user. There needs to be far greater collaboration in the industry, particularly given the growing expectations of today's savvy shopper. Retailers and suppliers need to think about how they can best serve their shoppers and consumers who will undoubtedly be looking for value at the shelf, but they will also be looking for their favourite brands.[41] As we've seen in the previous chapter, shoppers have the power to vote with their feet if they cannot find what they are after in the store. Leading suppliers with strong brand equity will find a way to remain on shelves simply because there is consumer demand for their products. When Delhaize removed the Unilever products from its stores, nearly one-third of its shoppers defected to the competition because they were loyal to specific Unilever brands. Inflation therefore should be viewed as a long-term trend that will require a more collaborative approach between retailers and suppliers. With that in mind, we will now take a closer look at Walmart's relationship with – and importance to – the world's largest consumer packaged goods companies.

Notes

1   http://www.rca.com/about/the-rca-story/

2   *New York Times*, R.C.A. halves cost of color TV sets, 10 August 1954, p 21

3   Average income in 1954 was $3,156 versus $40,712 in 2009.
    http://www.ssa.gov/oact/cola/AWI.html

4   http://blogs.reuters.com/felix-salmon/2009/11/10/
    wal-mart-does-not-save-families-3100-a-year/

5   http://www.ers.usda.gov/briefing/cpifoodandexpenditures/data/
    Expenditures_tables/table8.htm

6   Bloomberg Businessweek, Walmart is out to change its story with new ads,
    posted by David Kiley, 13 September 2007. http://www.businessweek.com/
    the_thread/brandnewday/archives/2007/09/walmart_is_out.html

7 http://your.asda.com/2011/1/6/your-weekly-shop-will-be-10-cheaper-at-asda-our-guarantee

8 Quote from WMT Shareholders Meeting, June 2011

9 These statistics are from a non-public Walmart document seen by one of the authors

10 Based on an exclusive interview with Judith McKenna

11 *Advertising Age*, Top 100 outlays plunge 10% but defying spend trend can pay off; 26 bold marketers, Bradley Johnson, 21 June 2010. **http://adage.com/article/news/top-100-outlays-plunge-10-defying-spend-trend-pay/144555/**

12 *The Wall Street Journal*, With sales flabby, Wal-Mart turns to its core, Miguel Bustillo, 21 March 2011. **http://online.wsj.com/article/SB10001424052748703328404576207161692001774.html**

13 Charles Fishman, *The Wal-Mart Effect*, 2006, Allen Lane, London, p 30

14 http://members.pricingsociety.com/articles/edlp_and_trade_promotion_roi.pdf

15 Marketwatch, Wal-Mart pitches 'everyday low prices' overseas, Andria Cheng and MarketWatch, 1 June 2011. Read more at **http://www.foxbusiness.com/industries/2011/06/01/wal-mart-pitches-everyday-low-prices-overseas/#ixzz1UMZX5Tlf**

16 *Advertising Age*, Walmart boosted media investment by $300 million, Jack Neff, 16 February 2009. **http://adage.com/article/news/walmart-boosted-media-investment-300-million/134628/**

17 Comments from company Shareholders Meeting in June 2011

18 *The Grocer*, Promotions hit record 40% of all supermarket sales, Charlie Wright, thegrocer.co.uk, 29 March 2011. **http://www.thegrocer.co.uk/articles.aspx?page=articles&ID=217003**

19 *The Grocer*, What about EDLP? Asda ups number of promos by 17%: it has said it will be running fewer deals but Asda has increased its number of promos by more than its rivals over the past month, Ronan Hegarty, 20 July 2010

20 *Guardian*, Battle of the bogofs, Julia Finch, 18 February 2010. **http://www.guardian.co.uk/business/2010/feb/18/viewpoint-asda**

21 *Guardian*, as above

22 Walmart Shareholders Meeting, June 2011

23 Walmart Brazil. **http://www.walmartbrasil.com.br/imprensa/releases_interna.aspx?id=1281**

24 http://walmartstores.com/AboutUs/277.aspx?p=246

25 *DSN Retailing Today*, Resilience and format diversity keep first international entry excelente – Wal-Mart operations in Mexico, June 2001. **http://findarticles.com/p/articles/mi_m0FNP/is_2001_June/ai_75406090/**

26 Walmart de Mexico y Centroamerica 2010 Annual Report, p 13.
**http://www.walmex.mx/assets/files/Informacion%20financiera/
Anual/Eng/Financiero/financiero2010ing.pdf**

27 Walmart de Mexico y Centroamerica 2010 Annual Report, p 13

28 Walmart de Mexico y Centroamerica 2010 Annual Report, p 13

29 Walmart de Mexico y Centroamerica 2010 Annual Report, p 4

30 Comment from Walmart Shareholders Meeting, June 2011

31 Bloomberg Businessweek, Can Wal-Mart woo Japan? 10 May 2004.
**http://www.businessweek.com/magazine/content/04_19/
b3882063.htm**

32 Bloomberg Businessweek, Japan isn't buying the Wal-Mart idea,
25 February 2005. **http://www.businessweek.com/magazine/content/
05_09/b3922073.htm**

33 Bloomberg Businessweek, Japan isn't buying the Wal-Mart idea

34 **http://walmartstores.com/AboutUs/274.aspx**

35 **http://walmartstores.com/AboutUs/274.aspx**

36 Bloomberg Businessweek, Matthew Boyle, 13 October 2009.
**http://www.businessweek.com/managing/content/oct2009/
ca20091013_227022_page_2.htm**

37 MSN Money, Costco brings back Coke, Elizabeth Strott, Thursday, 10
December 2009. **http://money.msn.com/market-news/post.aspx?post=
00000065-0000-0000-35ad-150000000000&_blg=385**

38 Reuters, Delhaize halts Unilever products in pricing row, 10 February 2009.
**http://www.reuters.com/article/2009/02/10/delhaize-unilever-
idUSLA49729320090210**

39 The *Wall Street Journal, Europe Edition*, Bread-price dispute hits British aisles,
Paul Sonne, 29 October 2010

40 **http://walmartinfo.co.za/docs/walmart_economic_benefits_facts.pdf**

41 *Marketing Magazine*, Branding does work – shoppers vote with feet after
Belgian supermarket removes Unilever products, David Benady,
marketingmagazine.co.uk, 17 February 2009. **http://www.brandrepublic.com/
bulletin/brandrepublicnewsbulletin/article/881378/Branding-does-
work---shoppers-vote-feet-Belgian-supermarket-removes-Unilever-
products/?DCMP=EMC-DailyNewsBulletin**

06

Walmart and its suppliers

Having depicted the meteoric rise of Walmart, from a handful of nondescript discount stores in the backwoods Deep South to a globe-straddling commercial colossus that impacts thousands of suppliers, millions of employees and billions of consumers, we can turn our attention to the impact of Walmart on the first group mentioned above: the supplier community.

One of the confusing issues surrounding Walmart is that it gets a very mixed press from a supplier standpoint. Often held up in the media as the bullying giant that squeezes suppliers until their pips squeak, private conversations between the authors and assorted figures in the vendor community often paint a different picture: a retailer that will – after a very difficult first conversation on price – embark on a collaborative relationship with suppliers, offering them the tools they need to grow their businesses (occasionally internationally) and partnering with them to drive efficiencies that benefit both Walmart and supplier and, most importantly, the consumer.

Walmart and its suppliers: the evolution of collaboration

Don Soderquist has portrayed Walmart's traditional, historic relationship with suppliers (and relations between all retailers and suppliers) as a fairly adversarial stand-off: 'The salesperson presents his or her items to a prospective buyer. They discuss a price and negotiate – the salesperson attempts to get the highest price and the buyer attempts to get the lowest price... This was the common practice everyone understood and accepted.'[1] This, indeed, was the situation known and accepted by Walmart until the late 1980s, when two separate events – a much-fabled canoe trip and a dinner with General Electric – led to a total overhaul of how Walmart would interact with its major trading partners.

Canoeing with P&G

In his autobiography, Sam Walton is refreshingly candid in expressing his disdain for middlemen, the jobbers or distributors that acted as go-betweens, getting manufacturers' products on the shelves of retailers (including a nascent Walmart) in exchange for commission. Because these distributors were reluctant to service a remote merchant like Walmart, the company was forced to source directly from vendors – forcing it to develop its own supply chain capabilities, but also ensuring that it was able to procure goods at great prices as no middlemen were involved: 'Because we got used to doing everything on our own, we have always resented paying anyone just for the pleasure of doing business with him.'[2]

As Walmart's first-ever buyer, Claude Harris, noted, even Walmart's very early philosophy chimes with the prevailing wisdom among Walmart's buyers to this day – that of advocacy for the consumer: 'There's a difference between being tough and being obnoxious. But every buyer has to be tough. That's the job. I always told the buyers: "You're not negotiating for Walmart, you're negotiating for your customer."'[3]

This advocacy for the consumer resulted in some very tough negotiations with suppliers, including P&G, which was already a colossus in the world of CPG. As Claude Harris recalls, 'I'd threaten Procter & Gamble with not carrying their merchandise, and they'd say, "Oh you can't get by without carrying our merchandise." And I'd say, "You watch me put it on a side counter, and I'll put Colgate on the endcap at a penny less, and you just watch me."'[4]

Such spats were fairly commonplace and they were often being carried on in a kind of vacuum. In a far cry from today's world of top-to-tops and cross-functional collaboration between Walmart and its suppliers, in the early days it was simply buyers battling salesmen, with little or no dialogue at a higher level.

This changed when Sam Walton's tennis buddy George Billingsley invited Walton on a canoe trip in the late 1980s, also inviting another friend, a P&G vice president named Lou Pritchett. As already noted, the relationship between Walmart (one of P&G's largest customers) and P&G (Walmart's largest supplier, as it remains today) was largely fractious and disconnected. During the canoe trip, Walton and Pritchett concluded that, although both P&G and Walmart were aiming to satisfy the end consumer, they were doing so independently of each other: there was a common purpose, but a disconnect in trying to satisfy the needs of shoppers. As Lou Pritchett recalls, 'We were simply two giant entities going our separate ways, oblivious to the excess costs created by this obsolete system. We were communicating, in effect, by slipping notes under the door.'[5]

This realization heralded the beginning of a new relationship between Walmart and its largest vendor: a senior-level summit followed, which precipitated the formation of a new partnership between the two parties. The partnership saw the creation of a Walmart/P&G team, one of the key outcomes of which was a decision to share Walmart's sales and inventory data with its largest supplier. Through collaboration and data sharing, Walmart was now able to increase efficiency, reduce prices and benefit its consumers. Theoretically, at least, vendors were also able to benefit – seeing improved forecasting, lower costs and (albeit lower) margin on a larger volume of product. Don Soderquist remembers that the problem between P&G and Walmart, however, was slightly more fundamental: 'We didn't trust them, and they didn't trust us.' The resolution of this conflict was the realization that each side could be trusted not to share sensitive data with competitors: 'Ultimately we were not competitors; we were both on the same side, wanting to sell more of our merchandise to our customers.'[6]

Dinner with General Electric

The second pivotal moment in Walmart's relationship with its suppliers happened within a few months of the glasnost with P&G, when Sam Walton of Walmart and Jack Welch of General Electric (GE) had dinner, accompanied by several executives from each business.

Over the dinner, both parties discussed potential ways of making their relationship better and more efficient. David Glass, at that time the Walmart President and CEO, suggested that a combination of exchanging data and exploiting more modern communications technologies would be mutually advantageous. The proposal was for Walmart to capture item-level sales data for GE merchandise and electronically transmit an order based on that sales data on a Monday. GE's computers would process the order overnight, fill the order on the Tuesday and ship the merchandise on the Wednesday. Walmart would get the goods on the Thursday and wire a payment to GE on the Friday. Any anomalies or differences would be reconciled four times a year. Thus was defined the virtuous circle for Walmart and its suppliers: data is shared, technology is exploited and mutual efficiencies are realized.

By rolling out the rapprochement with suppliers (developing trust, sharing state and utilizing state-of-the-art technology) and by convincing vendors that the 'customer' was not the retailer, but the consumer, Walmart was able to generate similar benefits in its relationships with thousands of vendors.

Walmart, clearly, was the main beneficiary in this roll-out of 'mutual advantage' – seeing its costs fall, its prices fall, its attractiveness to value-hungry shoppers improve and its availability reach industry-leading levels. Furthermore, this 'collaboration' required harmonization – of computers, of terminology, of order forms and of supply chain orthodoxies. There are no prizes for guessing that, in the vast majority of cases, it was the vendor that ceded and began to adopt the Walmart way of doing business. It's worth pointing out here that this collaboration saw communication shift from a single buyer/seller interface to more of a cross-functional interaction, with a vendor's technology department talking to Walmart's and a supplier's logistics experts talking to Walmart's supply chain executives and so on. We will take a look in more detail at Walmart's logistics and systems, and how they affect suppliers, in subsequent chapters.

Collaboration takes hold

It was only as recently as 1987 that Walmart devoted a dedicated section of its annual report to the array of suppliers on which it depended to provide the merchandise being devoured by its legions of bargain-hungry shoppers. In it, Walmart noted that it 'requires a reliable supply line of quality merchandise. Our vendors and suppliers are the heart of this supply line. Historically, supplier and retailer relationships have often been short-sighted and adversarial. Contrastingly, we believe that tough but fair negotiations should be the starting point and from there the mutual goal of servicing the customer and increasing sales opportunities should guide this relationship.'

Walmart stated at the time that it collaborated with its suppliers on the following initiatives:

- new product development;
- test marketing;
- package design;
- display techniques.

Walmart concluded in 1987 that the dialogue between itself and suppliers was 'a frequent and open conversation, with Walmart merchants often meeting with senior managers at suppliers. The relationships have been augmented by new technologies such as electronic ordering which improves lead times.'

This was a theme picked up in 2004, with Walmart stating that, through joint business planning, it provides suppliers with the tools and data to better forecast their sales demand and efficiently plan production and delivery schedules. It stated that it shares real-time store and product data with its suppliers, including sales of individual products by store. In return, suppliers were said to aid Walmart in better understanding new markets and staying attuned to customers' needs. Suppliers highlighted in the fiscal 2005 report included PepsiCo, Mattel, Reckitt Benckiser, Kraft, Danone and Kimberly-Clark.

Unilever is an excellent example of a supplier that has enjoyed a great track record in collaboration with Walmart. For example, before Walmart embarked on its joint venture with Bharti in India (providing supply chain best practice and jointly running Best Price Modern Wholesale cash & carries), it consulted with Unilever – which has many years' experience serving Indian retailers and consumers. This, according to Unilever, 'contributed to an even better working relationship and understanding when (Walmart) began opening its stores there'.[7]

Is collaboration on the wane?

One of the negative side-effects of Project Impact (with its SKU reduction programme and more intensive promotional activity) was a souring of relationships with suppliers. The Wal*Mart of old – with its 100,000-plus SKU megastores, EDLP strategy, low private brand penetration, willingness to stick pallets around the store and relative lack of enthusiasm for 'vendor investment' – was pretty well regarded in the supplier community. Sure, the annual discussions over terms and conditions would be fairly robust, but the relationship with Walmart was described by many vendors as one of partnership and predictability. Importantly, some of the less fragrant practices used by supermarkets to make money on the buy rather than on the sell were notable by their absence. Although doing business with Walmart was no walk in the park, there are signs that selling into the Walmart of today has become more of a problematic process, thanks in part to private label penetration increasing, but also due to Walmart attempting to increase pressure on suppliers.

At the time of Project Impact, a number of suppliers told us that category assortment reviews had become somewhat more confrontational as Walmart sought to play suppliers off against one another. Anecdotes suggested that appointments with buyers were organized so that representatives from major vendors within a category all met the buyer back-to-back on the same day, in a move that some vendors told us was engineered to create an environment of heightened competitive pressure.

When we asked a senior Walmart executive whether they thought Walmart was still a truly collaborative retailer to do business with, the candid response was fairly stark: 'No. We've lost our collaborative spirit. Other people are better partners now, like Target and a bunch of other non-food retailers. We're the same as Kroger and all the other guys now.'

This appears to be a sentiment that is shared by the higher echelons of the retailer too. In internal documents seen by the authors, which were presented to the retailers' 2011 Year Beginning Forum held in Florida in March, Bill Simon, President and CEO of Walmart US, stated that a renewed priority for the company would include improving vendor relations: 'Healthy relationships with suppliers, that include trust and collaboration, are critical to success.' Mike Duke, President and CEO of Walmart, added that he saw the 2011 meeting as 'a "family reunion" with valued supplier relationships'. He described the historically collaborative relations that Walmart enjoyed with suppliers as 'growth drivers'. He noted that 'trust with suppliers, transparency, collaboration, customer focus, focus on value and passion for serving our mutual customer' would underpin relationships with vendors going forward. He added at an investor event in 2011 that 'relations with suppliers really have to be on a win–win basis. I think in the long run win–lose doesn't ever work. I had a meeting with a large supplier, the CEO and senior management team. And we talked about how do we work together to create an efficient supply chain from the factory all the way to the store shelf and to the consumer.'

Duncan Mac Naughton, Executive Vice President and Chief Merchandising Officer, told the 2011 Year Beginning Forum that suppliers could look forward to easier accessibility to the retailer, accompanied by robust and open dialogue, and collaborative joint business planning. In return, suppliers should 'have their best team on the Walmart business and empower them to make real-time decisions'.

In a document from the Forum, shared with us by a member of the vendor community, Walmart set down its expectations from the supplier community on a single slide, the content of which is worth reproducing here in its entirety:

Suppliers need to:

Bring consumer insights & competitive insights. Every supplier can participate in Category Management through these insights.

Be positioned well with EDLC

Evaluate and optimize productivity loop

Be aligned well with Walmart business model

Provide collaboration and teamwork

Bring correction of errors (COE) dialogue

Evaluate scorecard, benchmark for success against buyer's objectives

Walmart needs:

Price leadership. Walmart respects our brand, we need to respect theirs by confirming EDLC

Innovation: Pre-planning/collaboration/1st to market

Ownable Innovation – exclusivity with Walmart

Market Share (100 per cent out of the gate/70 per cent within first 6 months/ 40 per cent ongoing)

Excellent operational execution, collaboration

Incremental sales to category

Help to tailor assortment by store: Store of the Community

Unique promotional activity: endcaps/action alley/retailtainment

Growth through Walmart.com

'Tough but fair negotiations'

While all this talk of collaboration, partnership and mutual benefit might present Walmart in a somewhat rosy light, it should not be forgotten that Walmart is a fierce, large and unrelenting negotiator. This aggression is often couched in terms of the retailer being an 'agent of the consumer', with Walmart buyers negotiating not on behalf of Walmart, but on behalf of its shoppers. In 1994, Walmart Chief Operating Officer Don Soderquist noted that 'we think of ourselves as agents for the customers, buying for them rather than selling to them'.

However, it should always be borne in mind that Walmart is a publicly listed business with a fiduciary duty to maximize returns (profits) for its shareholders. In other words, there are very few initiatives enacted by Walmart that do not have at least half an eye on the bottom line. While Walmart is able to achieve a positive spin in terms of PR and advertising from its 'consumer advocacy' – its entire marketing strategy has been based around 'Save Money. Live Better' for a few years now – the savings generated from suppliers also benefit shareholders as well as consumers.

It is a telling phrase that was used by Walmart in its 1987 annual report, with 'tough but fair' discussions over price described as the kicking-off point between Walmart and its vendors. One of many accusations levelled against Walmart over the past 20 years is that its growing scale has enabled it to become slightly over-enthusiastic in its quest for lower prices, driving such a hard bargain that suppliers actually reach the point where they are suffering or losing money just to fulfil their obligations to the retailer.

Former Walmart insider Michael Bergdahl, now a participant on the motivational-speaking circuit, addresses this issue on his website, stating that:

> Sam Walton was a proponent of the Free Enterprise System. The pressure placed upon manufacturers and suppliers today is no different than the pressure Sam Walton himself placed on his early suppliers. Walmart Merchandise Buyers expect suppliers and manufacturers to earn a fair profit on the goods they sell to Walmart and no more. If a supplier can't earn a profit supplying Walmart they should either lower their manufacturing costs to become profitable or make the decision to stop supplying the giant retailer. Supplying Walmart can be a manufacturer's dream come true or their worst nightmare. There are many companies that choose not to supply products to Walmart because they cannot achieve their profit goals. Other companies are too small to supply the insatiable product needs of Walmart. There are companies who choose to supply Walmart whether they make a large profit or not simply to enhance the visibility of their brand. For those who do supply Walmart the expectation is that that supplier needs to partner with Walmart to ALWAYS deliver value to the retail customer. In reality there are three types of companies that supply products to Walmart: those who make a profit, those who break even and those who lose money.[8]

Bergdahl's assertion is a refreshingly candid and honest one. Walmart, as with all retailers, does not expect its suppliers to consistently lose money.

No retailer has anything to gain by driving its suppliers out of business – indeed, the disruption caused can be hugely turbulent and expensive. Bergdahl's statement that Walmart expects its suppliers to earn a fair profit is a very neat and concise summary of Walmart's philosophy regarding its suppliers: they should make a decent return, but not too much; not at the expense of the shopper and certainly not at the expense of Walmart.

When we asked a senior Walmart insider if the Walmart of today is any better or worse to deal with than other retailers in terms of negotiating, their opinion was fairly bleak: 'I think we used to be easier to deal with, but it's much harder now. The buying teams are under-resourced and under much greater pressure than they used to. There have also been a lot of changes, so communication has really suffered. Calls are unreturned, e-mails unanswered.'

A report in *The Independent* published in late 2010 revealed that Walmart's UK division, Asda, had published an 88-page memo for its buying staff that recommended some less than fragrant negotiating skills. The guidance reportedly warned buyers that negotiations would not be easy, and that they should use techniques such as 'good cop/bad cop' in meetings. The report added that one Asda supplier who went through the negotiating process said he felt 'disappointment' with Asda. 'Obviously, you get used to having hard negotiations but this went beyond that and it didn't reflect the partnership approach that you want with retailers. It was all about how much you could screw out of us', he said.

Buyers were also instructed to extract better terms from their suppliers by asking for money to cover areas such as marketing and waste. 'Clearly, suppliers should be challenged to fund marketing costs', it says. It also tells buyers: 'Suppliers should provide compensation for products that are marked down or thrown away because customers aren't buying them.' In addition, suppliers should help fund capital expenditure: 'We invest a huge amount of capital into new space each year and our suppliers can help pay for it.'

The document laid out how to structure a meeting with a supplier. 'Plan your introduction', it said. 'Use this opportunity to take control and set the agenda. Open outrageously (include plenty of fat). The bigger the opening figure, the bigger the settlement figure.' Buyers should have prepared 'three concessions that cost Asda nothing but will assist their trading position. Only concede if you have to. Be tactful, but be firm. A threat is only a threat if it is followed through. Remember always that we are negotiating on behalf of our customers!'[9]

Despite the odd wobble and prevarication – and despite counter-claims from assorted retailers – Walmart's go-to-market strategy in the United States (and in most of its global markets) is everyday low prices. This EDLP strategy is documented in the previous chapter on pricing and marketing, but is worthy of brief consideration here as well. Walmart's ability to single-handedly drive the pricing agenda, to the extent that it is often credited with reducing prices and suppressing inflation across the entire US economy, is a function of many factors. Chief among these is scale: on the one hand, Walmart's size means that it has massive power over US suppliers; while on the other, this very scale means that it is able to offer its suppliers the potential to generate economies of scale and volume efficiencies.

So, what is the extent of this scale and power? And what does it actually mean for vendors that service the world's largest retailer?

The dependence of US suppliers on Walmart

While many suppliers around the would have to be confronted with thumb-screws before they started revealing the names of their biggest retail customers, US Securities and Exchange Commission (SEC) regulations mean that publicly listed businesses in the United States (or those that report for other reasons) are required by the SEC to reveal the identity of those customers that account for a significant proportion of revenues.

With 10 per cent being the threshold at which the loss of a major customer could have a 'material impact' on a supplier in terms of loss of sales and/or profitability, many regulatory filings in the United States unsurprisingly point to Walmart as constituting just such a customer. That said, a variety of other mass merchants (notably Kohl's, Costco and Target), grocery retailers (Kroger, Safeway, SuperValu and Food Lion) and specialist retailers (Walgreens, GameStop, PetSmart, Home Depot, Toys 'R' Us etc) are often cited as key customers for relevant suppliers.

The basis of the research for the following analysis is the 10K annual filings submitted by suppliers with the SEC. Within these filings, suppliers inform investors of the fact of whether or not they have a single customer, or several customers that account for a significant proportion of their revenues, usually 10 per cent. The fact of having one, or several, large customers is something of a double-edged sword in that having these customers suggests certain benefits in terms of volume if nothing else. On the flip side, losing one or more of these customers would mean losing a sizeable chunk of business. In the words of one vendor: 'The loss of sales of any of our products in a major retailer could have a material adverse effect on our business and financial performance.'

By collecting and analysing the percentage of sales reported by each supplier as being accounted for by Walmart (and it is normally a percentage – only one or two vendors report dollar sales volumes), this percentage is applied to the vendor's total sales to deliver a dollar value for sales to Walmart, enabling us to compare different vendors in terms of share of sales to Walmart, dollar sales to Walmart and growth in sales to Walmart over time. It is worth noting that many of the percentages supplied by vendors are issued with no decimal places, so there is an evitable margin of error, but one that we feel comfortable in analysing and publishing.

Before we reveal some of the finding of this research, it is worth highlighting some background issues and technical points to put the findings in context.

Pharmaceuticals and alcohol have a convoluted route to the shopper

Planet Retail estimates show that Walmart is the third-largest retailer of pharmaceuticals in the world,[10] so one would expect to see it figure as a major customer for the likes of Pfizer, Wyeth and Bristol-Myers Squibb. Owing to the structure of the US pharmacy market, which still relies to a huge extent on wholesale giants such as McKesson, Cardinal Health and AmerisourceBergen, however, it is these groups, not Walmart, that figure as the major customers for pharmaceutical manufacturers.

An even more complex distribution system confronts US brewers, distillers and vintners. As any frequent visitor to the United States will attest, the country is a patchwork quilt of different regulations and laws concerning both the on-trade and off-trade sale of alcoholic beverages. Regulations vary state by state and even county by county, and also vary by category, with different laws covering beers, wines and liquor. As a result of this fairly archaic legislative framework, a fair proportion of alcohol consumed in the market reaches consumers via a complex network that can include wholesalers, state-run distributors and liquor boards, retailers and restaurants. For this reason, while we would assert that Walmart is a significant eventual global customer for major alcoholic beverage suppliers, this is not apparent in regulatory filings owing to the indirect distribution model in the US market.

Tobacco & confectionery – the McLane clause

A similar factor is in evidence in other categories in which wholesalers have traditionally played a major role, such as tobacco and confectionery in the fragmented c-store sector. One such wholesaler is McLane, the former Walmart-owned business that is still responsible for supplying the retailer with confectionery and cigarettes. Walmart, presumably, has continued with this arrangement as it makes economic sense compared to the alternative – bringing it in-house – and it means that for suppliers like Hershey and Altria, McLane is the principal way that they get their products onto Walmart's shelves. McLane has revealed that 30 per cent of its sales go to Walmart, so we assume that for major candy and tobacco concerns, Walmart is again a significant eventual customer, but there is no precise way of confirming this assertion.

Lack of disclosure from private and international businesses

Clearly, there are some limitations to the following analysis, the most notable of which is the fact that huge parts of the vendor community do not provide these data, as they are private companies or based outside the United States. No doubt, if we were able to secure similar levels of data from private companies or those listed outside the United States, then names such as SC Johnson, Reckitt Benckiser and Nestlé might be figuring highly in this analysis. It is noteworthy that European-based suppliers tend to be less overwhelmingly reliant on a single retailer, as European grocery markets are dominated by strong local players such as Tesco, Carrefour, Migros, Delhaize and Ahold, meaning that sales tend to be spread more thinly across more customers. Unilever, for example, states that only 20 per cent of its global sales are channelled through 10 major retail chains. The bulk of its sales are distributed through wholesale to millions of smaller retail enterprises: Unilever has commented that its products can be found in over 10 million small stores in Africa and Asia alone. Nonetheless, the availability of the data that we present below means that we are able to glean interesting insights into what it means to participate in the Walmart vendor community.

Reliance on Walmart as high as 55 per cent

Our research shows that around 120 vendors or service providers name Walmart as a major customer. On average, Walmart accounts for 21 per cent of total sales for the 120 suppliers, with the proportion reaching as high as 55 per cent. Garan, the manufacturer of the Garanimals range of children's apparel, generated over 90 per cent of its sales through Walmart in 2010. As this range is virtually exclusive to Walmart, Garan does not qualify as a multi-retailer supplier for consideration here.

It is noteworthy that, of the 10 vendors with the highest dependency on Walmart, nine are sellers of fairly niche non-food categories such as DVDs, firearms accessories, kitchen gadgets or apparel or are the providers of services such as the operation of photo studios within Walmart stores. Only Del Monte, the seller of canned vegetables, fruit and tomato products and pet care, can be classed as a grocery vendor and it is indeed the largest vendor on the list shown in Table 6.1 (its involvement in private label – a growing component of Walmart's grocery business – should see Del Monte's reliance on Walmart increase in the future). Some of the suppliers in the table are relatively small operators, where even a tiny piece of business in absolute terms can account for a substantial proportion of their turnover.

DAC Technologies Group is a leading manufacturer of gun-cleaning kits, gun safety devices and other outdoor products. In fiscal 2009, it generated

TABLE 6.1 The 10 vendors with the highest dependency on Walmart

Vendor	Product category	% of sales to Walmart
DAC Technologies Group	Gun accessories	55.0
Emerson Radio	Electricals	53.0
CPI	Photographic studios	52.0
Tandy Brands	Belts & accessories	47.0
CCA Industries	HBC	45.0
Crown Crafts	Baby products	43.0
HBB (Nacco Industries)	Kitchenware & small appliances	36.0
R. G. Barry	Footwear & accessories	38.0
Del Monte Foods	Food & pet care	35.0
Lions Gate Entertainment	Films & DVD	35.0

SOURCE: SEC filings; 2010 & 2011

a whopping 55 per cent of sales to Walmart, with its other customers including sporting goods retailers, distributors and catalogue companies. It should be noted that sales to Walmart were an eye-watering 71 per cent of total sales in 2008. DAC's administrative offices and primary warehouse facilities are handily located in Little Rock, Arkansas, and the company also operates a warehouse facility in Los Angeles which is used primarily to ship products to Walmart distribution centres. DAC notes that its products are primarily sourced from manufacturers and suppliers located in China. In 2009, DAC entered into a trademark licensing agreement with Olin Corporation to market certain of its gun-cleaning items under the Winchester brand name to Walmart.

Emerson Radio is a supplier of televisions, DVD players and video cassette recorders (VCRs), audio accessories, microwave ovens, home theatre, high-end audio products, office products, mobile stereo and wireless products. Walmart accounted for 53 per cent of 2009 net revenues, progressing steadily from the 46 per cent seen in 2008. Target is Emerson's other major customer, accounting for 25 per cent of sales in 2009. Emerson notes that 100 per cent of its products were sourced overseas, primarily from China.

CPI is owner and operator of Sears Portrait Studios and PictureMe Portrait Studios in Walmart and is the leading portrait studio operator in North America, offering photographic services in over 3,000 locations. Its reliance on Walmart owes much to the acquisition of its rival PCA in 2007, a transaction that saw it become the sole operator of portrait studios in Walmart stores in the United States, Canada, Mexico and Puerto Rico. The company operates under the trade names PictureMe Portrait Studio in the United States, Walmart Portrait Studios in Canada and Estudios Fotografia in Mexico. As of 2010, PMPS operated 1,923 studios worldwide, including 1,549 in the United States and Puerto Rico, 260 in Canada and 114 in Mexico.

Crown Crafts is a vendor of infant and toddler products, consisting of bedding, bibs, infant soft goods and accessories. The company's products are manufactured primarily in China. Walmart accounts for 43 per cent of sales (down from 47 per cent in 2008) and Toys 'R' Us accounts for another 21 per cent. Target ceased accounting for more than 10 per cent of sales in 2009.

Tandy Brands is a leading designer and marketer of branded men's, women's and children's accessories, including belts, gifts, small leather goods, eyewear, neckwear and sporting goods. Its merchandise is marketed under a broad portfolio of licensed and proprietary brand names, including Totes, Wrangler, Dockers, Dr. Martens, Amity, Rolfs, Canterbury, Prince Gardner, Princess Gardner and Surplus, as well as private brands for major retail customers. Tandy sells its products through all major retail distribution channels throughout North America, including mass merchants, national chain stores, department stores, men's and women's speciality stores, catalogue retailers, grocery stores, drug stores, golf pro shops, sporting goods stores and the retail exchange operations of the US military.

In 2010, private brand products sold to a variety of retailers accounted for 59.6 per cent of net sales. One of the company's principal private brand activities is the supply of Faded Glory SKUs for Walmart, which accounted for 47 per cent of total sales in 2010. Unsurprisingly, the principal source country for Tandy's procurement is China, with other imports coming from the Dominican Republic, India, Italy, Mexico and Taiwan.

CCA Industries is a creator and vendor of a fairly broad selection of health and beauty products, designed to cater for a variety of requirements such as teeth whitening, scar reduction, nail polishing, weight loss and the eradication of bikini bumps. Given the focus of its product portfolio – which includes 'cosmeceutical categories' – drugstore customers are also a significant sales channel. In fiscal 2010, Walmart accounted for approximately 41 per cent of net sales, with Sam's Club accounting for a further 4 per cent. Other key customers include Walgreens (13 per cent), CVS (5 per cent), Target (4 per cent), Dollar General (3 per cent) and Rite Aid (3 per cent).

Nacco Industries is, to say the least, one of the more esoteric conglomerates you could wish to discover, with subsidiaries active in forklift trucks, kitchenware stores, small domestic appliances and coal mining.

Its Hamilton Beach (HBB) small appliances division supplies brands such as Hamilton Beach, Proctor Silex, Eclectrics, Traditions, TrueAir and Hamilton Beach Commercial to leading retailers and to restaurants, hotels and bars. Hamilton Beach states that it has approximately 1,300 active accounts and enjoys category-management responsibilities at Walmart (United States and Mexico), Target, Kmart, Sears and a number of other food, drug, and mass merchandise retailers throughout the United States and Mexico. Its highlights of dealing with Walmart include receiving accolades such as Vendor of the Year and vendor innovation and quality awards.

In addition to its own consumer brands, HBB supplies Walmart with GE-brand kitchen electric and garment-care appliances under Walmart's licence agreement with General Electric Company. HBB also supplies Target with Michael Graves-branded kitchen appliances under Target's store-wide Michael Graves line. In addition, HBB supplies Kohl's with Food Network-branded kitchen appliances and supplies Canadian Tire with small kitchen appliances under the Lancaster brand. Walmart accounted for approximately 36 per cent of HBB's revenues in 2010. The majority (98 per cent) of HBB's products are supplied to its specifications by third-party suppliers located in China.

R. G. Barry is an industry leader in the dynamic world of slippers, but also supplies other categories such as hybrid and active fashion footwear, sandals, slipper socks and hosiery. The company enjoys a strong reputation in its area: in 2008, Walmart US selected R. G. Barry as category manager and sole supplier for its sizable replenishment slipper business; the Utopiaä brand team was named Target's 2008 Vendor of the Year in the men's essentials area; and Sam's Club named the company their Accessories Supplier of the Quarter in the first quarter of 2009.

In 2009, the company followed in the footsteps of FMCG businesses by realigning its structure to better serve key retail customers. It reorganized its internal sales resources so that key customers would be served by specialized cross-functional account teams. The business already operated a sales administration office in Bentonville to support its business with Walmart, its largest customer which accounted for 38 per cent of revenues in 2010. On the manufacturing front, R. G. Barry sources its slipper-type products from 14 different third-party manufacturers, all of which are located in China.

Del Monte Foods (not to be confused with global produce giant Fresh Del Monte) is a major player in the canned food and pet food markets. It generates 35 per cent of its sales to Walmart, with Walmart representing the largest customer in all of Del Monte's product segments.

Interestingly, Del Monte is one of very few suppliers to happily confess to participating in the private label arena, noting: 'The company also produces, distributes and markets private label food and pet products.' Del Monte provides some Great Value vegetables and tomatoes as well as some of

Walmart's Ol' Roy dog food – partly explaining some of the vendor's deep reliance on Walmart.

Lionsgate is a leading studio with a major presence in the production and distribution of motion pictures, television programming, home entertainment, family entertainment, video-on-demand and digitally delivered content. Lionsgate directly distributes to the rental market through Blockbuster, Netflix and Rentrak. In August 2009, it also entered into a multi-year distribution agreement with Redbox which made its titles available through 22,000 Redbox DVD rental locations. Lionsgate also distributes or sells directly to mass merchandisers such as Walmart, Kmart, Best Buy, Target and Costco. Sales to Walmart accounted for approximately 35 per cent of net home entertainment revenue in fiscal 2010.

Before we go on to take a look at the largest identified vendors to Walmart, it is worth assessing those vendors that have generated the most impressive growth to Walmart over the past three fiscal years, both in terms of pace of growth and also volume of incremental sales.

Table 6.2 represents those vendors that have seen the fastest growth. The most stellar performer in this regard has been Iconix Brand Group, which has seen sales from its three licences with Walmart rising from 3 to 21 per cent of the company's sales over the past three years. The company – which is responsible for annual eventual retail sales of $12 billion – kicked off its business with Walmart in March 2007 through Iconix's acquisition of Danskin, through which Iconix acquired a licence with Walmart for the exclusive sale of Danskin Now product in the United States, Canada, Central America and Argentina. In August 2007, a deal was signed for Walmart to be the exclusive retailer of Ocean Pacific (OP) in the United States. The agreement also granted Walmart rights to use the brands in Brazil, China and India, as well as the right of first negotiation with respect to other international territories. In December 2007, Iconix entered into an agreement with Walmart to use the Starter trademark in the United States, Canada and Mexico.

These moves were followed by the 2008 launch of OP in the United States, with the OP brand expanding to Canada, Mexico and Argentina in the following year. As a result of these moves, Iconix has seen direct-to-retail sales increase from 25 per cent to 50 per cent over the past three years and its sales to Walmart grow exponentially. Tellingly, Iconix describes Walmart International as a key global partner. Iconix also owns Bright Star, a business that provides design direction and arranges for the manufacturing and distribution of men's private label footwear products primarily for Walmart under its private labels.

Other vendors that have seen their sales to Walmart grow rapidly include Smucker (which saw sales to Walmart accelerate rapidly thanks largely to its acquisition of the Folgers coffee business); video game supplier Activision; and private label grocery specialist Ralcorp.

Ralcorp (which has recently acquired American Italian Pasta – also included in the rapid growth list) has presumably benefited from Walmart's push for higher private label penetration. The company's private label lines include

TABLE 6.2 Vendors that have seen the fastest growth

Vendor	Product category	Rate of growth of sales to Walmart 2008/10 (%)
Iconix	Apparel	1,012
Smucker	Grocery	146
Activision	Entertainment software	122
Ralcorp	Grocery	121
Moneygram (US)	Financial services	114
Smart Balance	Grocery	106
American Italian Pasta Company	Grocery	72
Coinstar	Kiosks	67
Maidenform Brands	Apparel	60
DemandTec	Consumer demand software	58

SOURCE: SEC filings

cereal, pasta, frozen bakery items, cookies, snack nuts, savoury snacks, preserves and jellies, peanut butter, table syrups and dressings. As previously discussed, Ralcorp is also active through its own consumer brands, such as Post cereal.

While Ralcorp will have benefited to an extent from the strategic push by Walmart to boost private label sales, it will have been hurt by Walmart 'encouraging' its branded vendor partners to participate in enhanced Rollback activities. With Ralcorp active in both branded manufacturing and private label supplies, it is very difficult to identify whether the positive impulses from its largest customer outweighed the negative, but the fact remains that Ralcorp has seen the share of sales to Walmart increase from 15 to 19 per cent over the past three years.

Having rapid growth is all well and good, but to assess the sheer scale and some of the business added with Walmart, Table 6.3 represents the incremental sales volumes generated through Walmart over the most recent three fiscal years.

TABLE 6.3 Incremental sales volumes generated through Walmart

Vendor	Product category	Added sales volume 2008/10 ($m)
McLane	Convenience wholesaling	1,032
PepsiCo	Grocery	883
Kraft Foods	Grocery	876
Smucker	Grocery	738
General Mills	Grocery	597
ConAgra	Grocery	487
Hershey	Grocery	477
Ralcorp	Grocery	404
Kellogg	Grocery	404
P&G	Grocery	383

SOURCE: SEC filings

It is no great surprise to see major players in grocery supplies being the largest recipients of extra sales volume through Walmart. The 10 largest gainers between them garnered an extra $6.3 billion in sales to Walmart over the past four years (Table 6.3); a period during which Walmart increased its global sales by $44 billion to $419 billion and Walmart US saw sales increase by $19 billion to around $260 billion.

At the same time as this monumental growth, Walmart's sales mix has been shifting towards grocery, which has gained in share each year, climbing from 47 per cent of sales in 2007 to reach 54 per cent of sales in 2010 (please note that in the intervening years, the Puerto Rican division was folded into the US division, accelerating the growing share of grocery as the Puerto Rican unit is dominated by supermarket chain Amigo). While this shift does not sound particularly seismic in itself, it is worth remembering that the modest-looking increase in grocery share translates into grocery sales increasing from $112.6 billion in 2007 to $140.6 billion in 2010 (an increase of $28 billion). For the sake of context, market-leading grocer Kroger's total sales are $82 billion.

TABLE 6.4 The 10 largest vendors, 2006–10

Vendor	Sales	% of sales to Walmart	Sales to Walmart ($m)
P&G	78,938	16	12,630
McLane	32,687	30	9,806
PepsiCo	57,838	12	6,941
Kraft	49,207	14	6,889
Tyson Foods	28,430	13	3,810
General Mills	14,797	23	3,403
Kellogg	12,397	21	2,603
Kimberly-Clark	19,746	13	2,567
ConAgra	12,079	18	2,174
Dean Foods	11,158	19	2,131

SOURCE: SEC filings

While this is nominally good news for grocery vendors, it should be pointed out that apparel vendors will have had to face up to shrinking sales within Walmart, with apparel sales declining from $28.7 billion to $25.8 billion in the United States over the past three years (this figure still leaves Walmart as the overwhelming leader in the US apparel market, however).

P&G leading the way

As we've seen earlier in this chapter, P&G, one of the world's largest FMCG businesses, is one of Walmart's most long-standing and important vendor partners. It has a veritable arsenal of global power brands in household, HBC and pet care such as Pampers, Tide, Ariel, Always, Pantene, Bounty, Pringles, Charmin, Downy, Iams, Crest, Actonel and Olay. Walmart and P&G blazed a trail with their adoption of a top-to-top collaborative approach on information sharing and supply chain, shifting away from the tradition-ally adversarial approach that typified relationships between retailers and vendors. Their collaboration – which was a key step in the creation of Retail Link over the longer term – has enabled lower costs, minimized inventory and allowed a greater focus on the customer.

McLane's reliance on Walmart is due mainly to the fact that it used to be owned by the retailer. McLane is a supply chain services company, providing grocery and foodservice supply chain solutions for thousands of convenience stores, mass merchants, drug stores and military locations, as well as thousands of chain restaurants throughout the United States. It counts among its customers 7-Eleven, Yum! Brands, Target, The Pantry, Conoco-Phillips and Exxon Mobil, in addition to relying on Walmart for over a third of its annual revenues. Following its sale by Walmart, McLane is now owned by renowned investment group Berkshire Hathaway. McLane supplies Walmart with much of its merchandise in areas such as confectionery and tobacco.

PepsiCo tells its investors that 'retail consolidation and the current economic environment continue to increase the importance of major customers'. In 2010, sales to Walmart, including Sam's Club, represented approximately 12 per cent of total net revenue. The company's top five retail customers represented approximately 31 per cent of 2010 North American net revenue, with Walmart and Sam's Club representing approximately 18 per cent. These percentages include concentrate sales to PepsiCo's bottlers which are used in finished goods sold by them to Walmart and Sam's Club.

PepsiCo has recently been lauded for its work with Walmart, with PepsiCo China beverage group named Supplier of the Year by Walmart China and Walmart Mexico naming PepsiCo Beverages Mexico as its Supplier of the Year.

Generating nearly $7 billion in annual sales to Walmart, Kraft's leading categories are confectionery (thanks to the Cadbury deal), snacks (bolstered by the acquisition of Danone's biscuits unit), beverages, cheese, convenience foods and general groceries. With iconic brands such as Kraft, Kool Aid, Ritz Philadelphia and Oscar Mayer, Kraft generates 49 per cent of its sales in North America, meaning that its relationship with Walmart is very close.

Kraft's contentious acquisition of Cadbury has significantly increased its exposure to emerging markets and bolstered its activities in categories such as gum and candy. Kraft is an active partner with both Walmart US and Sam's Club in terms of operating co-branded promotions and states that it is 'taking full advantage of our size and broad reach. We're working closely with our global customers like Carrefour, Tesco and Walmart.'

PepsiCo is a leading global food, snack and beverage company. Its global brands, which include Quaker Oats, Tropicana, Gatorade, Frito-Lay and Pepsi, are accompanied by strong regional brands such as Walkers, Gamesa and Sabritas. The company's largest operations are in North America (United States and Canada), Mexico and the UK, which, coincidentally or not, are Walmart's largest markets too.

Tyson Foods, with headquarters in Arkansas, is the world's largest processor and marketer of chicken, beef and pork. The company produces a wide variety of protein-based and prepared food products that it sells to both retail and foodservice customers. Often tagged the 'Walmart of meat', thanks to its Arkansas roots and dominant scale in its industry, its sales to Walmart are generated in its chicken, beef, pork and prepared foods segments.

General Mills, the world's sixth-largest food company, is dominated by its US retail division, a fact reflected by the importance of Walmart to the company. Its other divisions – International, Bakeries & Foodservice and Joint Ventures – account for much less than half of sales. In the United States, General Mills' major product categories are ready-to-eat cereals, refrigerated yogurt, ready-to-serve soup, dry dinners, shelf stable and frozen vegetables, refrigerated and frozen dough products, dessert and baking mixes, frozen pizza and pizza snacks, grain, fruit and savoury snacks, and a wide variety of organic products including soup, granola bars and cereal.

During 2010, Walmart accounted for 23 per cent of consolidated net sales and 30 per cent of net sales in the US Retail segment. Walmart also represented 5 per cent of net sales in the International segment and 7 per cent of net sales in the Bakeries and Foodservice segment.

Kellogg is the world's leading producer of cereal and a leading producer of convenience foods, including cookies, crackers, toaster pastries, cereal bars, fruit-flavoured snacks, frozen waffles and vegetarian foods. The company's brands include Kellogg's, Keebler, Pop-Tarts, Eggo, Cheez-It, All-Bran, Mini-Wheats, Nutri-Grain, Rice Krispies, Special K, Chips Deluxe, Famous Amos, Sandies, Austin, Club, Murray, Kashi, Bear Naked, Morningstar Farm, Gardenburger and Stretch Island. Walmart accounted for approximately 21 per cent of consolidated net sales during 2010, comprised principally of sales within the United States.

Kimberly-Clark's global brands are sold in more than 150 countries, with the business estimating that 1.3 billion people use Kimberly-Clark products every day. With well-known family care and personal care brands such as Kleenex, Scott, Andrex, Huggies, Pull-Ups, Kotex, Poise and Depend, the company states that it holds the number-one or number-two share position globally in more than 80 countries. Kimberly-Clark, with two offices in Arkansas, is closely aligned with Walmart, through which it generated 13 per cent of sales in 2010.

ConAgra Foods is one of North America's leading food companies, noting that its brands are to be found in 97 per cent of America's households. ConAgra's Consumer Foods segment manufactures and markets leading branded products to retail and foodservice customers in the United States and internationally. Its flagship brands include Egg Beaters, Healthy Choice, Hunt's, Orville Redenbacher's and PAM, just to name a few. Stating that one of its key strategies is 'aligning with customers to leverage consumer insights', ConAgra has seen its sales to Walmart rocket over the past four years from 13 to 18 per cent of sales, adding nearly $500 million in sales over the past three years alone. This growth will have been attributable to both branded and private label foods sold through Walmart.

Market leader in the US dairy industry, Dean Foods sells milk and a full range of related products under more than 50 well-known local and regional brands, and a wide array of private labels. It operates through two divisions: Fresh Dairy Direct-Morningstar, the largest processor and distributor of milk and other dairy products in the country; and WhiteWave-Alpro, the maker of an extensive line of nationally branded products such as Horizon Organic dairy products, Silk soymilk and International Delight coffee creamers.

Fresh Dairy Direct-Morningstar's largest customer is Walmart, which accounted for approximately 19 per cent of Fresh Dairy Direct-Morningstar's net sales in 2010. WhiteWave-Alpro's largest customer is also Walmart, accounting for around 16 per cent of WhiteWave-Alpro's net sales in 2010.

The power is now with Walmart

It will take people with long memories in some markets to cast their minds back to a time when suppliers ruled the roost. This was a time when suppliers were so big compared to fragmented national retail sectors dominated by independents and small regional chains that they called all the shots in terms of which retailers could sell their products, the minimum (or 'recommended') retail price at which products could be sold and how the products should be merchandised.

The 1970s and 80s were a period in which the evolution of the FMCG industry stepped up a gear, with the consolidation of national speciality brands into national FMCG powerhouses that grew through acquisition to include different brands and products across food and drink, health and beauty, pet care, household products and beyond. At the same time, M&A was becoming increasingly international in scope, leading to the development of the FMCG giants that we see today – multi-billion-dollar leviathans often active in 100+ countries with a broad arsenal of $1 billion+ brands that are present in billions of households across the globe.

As this consolidation and internationalization process in the supplier community gathered pace, a similar process was at play in the world of retailing. The mid- to late 1990s saw retailers in mature markets build on their dominant domestic market positions by venturing overseas in a concerted attempt at building scale. While the likes of Ahold, Delhaize, Walmart, Tesco and Carrefour were busy constructing global empires, some commentators were asserting that this cross-border push was an attempt to establish global buying power – an observation that we will subsequently argue is something of a fallacy in an FMCG industry that is still typified by negotiations and deals that are conducted on a national level.

Nonetheless, the emergence of global retail superpowers like Walmart has expedited the consolidation process in the FMCG manufacturing sector. Deals such as P&G's acquisition of Gillette are widely understood to be an attempt to wrest back some control from the retailers by building multinational FMCG operations that should theoretically be able to better stand up for themselves against the might of the retailers. Despite the FMCG sector bulking up in an effort to build self-defence capabilities against major retailers on a national or international level, it remains the case that it is the retailers like Walmart that are in charge of the distribution of products to consumers and it is those retailers that are the ultimate gatekeepers for suppliers to reach shoppers.

With approximately 70 per cent of purchasing decisions thought to be made at the shelf in-store, it is clear that the influence of brand marketers is to a certain extent limited. The concept of 'must-have' brands is becoming diluted, although still relevant, and retailers including Walmart have pursued strategies such as range rationalization and increased private label sales, while at the same time increasing their demands for vendor investment and the delivery of category and shopper insights.

At the risk of stating the blindingly obvious, it is worth reiterating the fact that retailers have become colossal businesses in their own right, with Walmart, Tesco and Carrefour growing to such a scale that they dwarf many of their suppliers by a monumental margin – a far cry from the 1960s and 70s when big food, drink or HBC businesses bossed relatively tiny retailers around.

It is worth remembering that Walmart's sales in 1980 were 'only' US $1 billion and that many vendors would refuse to visit Bentonville – suppliers had bigger accounts to manage and saw little benefit in collaborating with a backwater southern retailer with less than 300 fairly modest stores.

Fast-forward to 2012 and Northwest Arkansas continues to be one of the fastest-growing communities in the United States in terms of population growth. US and international vendors are falling over themselves to establish a physical presence in Bentonville, Springdale and Fayetteville to service Walmart. Why? Because the backwater southern retailer now trades through around 9,000 stores in around 30 countries, generating net sales in excess of $400 billion and serving more than 176 million customers a year.

If one compares the total net sales of the world's leading FMCG producers with the world's leading retailers, it becomes clear that the scale and power have very much shifted to Walmart and other global retail giants. What becomes obvious is that there are very few vendors that can compete with the global retailers in terms of scale: to provide some context, Walmart International alone is now bigger than Nestlé and, indeed, Walmart's annual expenditure on private label – at over $100 billion – tops Nestlé's annual revenues.

We will point out in the next chapter why this global scale has yet to translate into genuine global buying power for Walmart, but it is worth reminding ourselves here that retailer scale has already exerted a profound impact on a national level. Walmart's sheer size in the United States has confronted suppliers with a huge customer that can insist on change. These demands can impact prices, promotional programmes, marketing support, supply chain, sustainability initiatives, packaging, sales volumes and profitability. Walmart's other initiatives – including a drive for higher private label penetration, SKU rationalization and inventory reduction – have been wreaking a seismic impact on the vendor.

Walmart's shopper-centricity driving customer-centricity from suppliers

Having seen already in this chapter that US suppliers are becoming increasingly dependent on Walmart, with around a fifth of the business going through the retailer, we turn now to one of the more successful responses to the trend – that of customer-centricity. It is noteworthy how frequently many of the multinational suppliers that we have spoken to identify four key strategic customers on a global basis. Usually, these would be Walmart, Carrefour, Tesco and Metro, although these can often be augmented with a 7-Eleven, McDonald's, PetSmart, Home Depot, Best Buy, Aldi, Kroger, Walgreens, etc depending on geography or the product specialization of the supplier in question.

Regardless of what retailers are on the list, the simple fact remains: individual retailers, led by Walmart, have now become so important to suppliers that many of them have dedicated headcount, offices and strategies to better serve their most important customers. By the same token, it should be noted that the ball is in Walmart's court when it comes to influencing or even deciding which products shoppers should buy. Through strategies such as range rationalization, private brand development and increasingly sophisticated promotions, merchandising and marketing, and despite the billions of dollars thrown at NPD and advertising by suppliers each year, it is Walmart that controls what its shoppers buy. Even if a vendor creates the greatest product ever, if that vendor is not aligned with the needs and strategies of Walmart, then that product is unlikely to be a success.

At the time of its merger with Gillette, a P&G executive remarked that the move was a reaction to the fact that 'the power has shifted to the consumer'. While the comment is true, a more realistic observation would have been that the deal was a reaction to the fact that the power has shifted to Walmart: it has become the ultimate gatekeeper to American shoppers.

It is fairly old hat to observe here that Walmart has been endeavouring to put its shoppers at the heart of what it does for many years now, that is, pursuing a shopper-centric strategy. Shopper-centricity is a long-term strategy requiring retailers to place the shopper at the core, even at the expense of short-term profit. In its most basic form, shopper-centricity is simply the ability to offer the right assortment to the right shopper at the right time.

While price is clearly one of the key drivers of shopper loyalty, especially in these economically uncertain times, it is worth remembering that price is one of myriad loyalty drivers, the other main categories of which comprise quality, experience, product and location. Price leadership has always been a key strategic focus for Walmart, seizing on initiatives such as private labels (economy lines in particular), EDLP messaging and enhanced promotional activity in an attempt to convince shoppers of its value credentials.

Price has proven to be an effective weapon for Walmart, but it is a fairly blunt instrument with which to deal with increasingly sophisticated shoppers. In order to maintain many of its key metrics (sales, margins, market share etc), Walmart has been moving beyond price alone in order to better compete in what is a fiercely competitive market awash with different options for demanding consumers who are often short of both time and money. Some examples of shopper-centric initiatives being pursued by Walmart include: offering tiered private label assortments; utilizing shopper and category data to tailor in-store assortment, merchandising and marketing; rationalizing SKUs to increase the relevance of assortments; engaging directly with shoppers via social media; investing in the in-store experience through store remodels; and diversifying its range of formats (Supermercado de Walmart and Walmart Express are two good examples) based on shifting consumer patterns.

Successful Walmart suppliers have already realized that, in order to better reach the end consumers that are the subject of Walmart's shopper-centric strategies, they should take on the challenge of becoming more Walmart-centric in order to better serve their biggest customer. Which leads us to reiterate a point made earlier – the role of Walmart as gatekeeper to the shopper.

Is Walmart lacking insight?

The ability to offer a targeted, localized and customized product mix is a fundamental component of Walmart's shopper-centric strategies. One of the key tactics in ensuring that Walmart is meeting the requirements of its shoppers is through the effective use of shopper data. We would argue that the most effective way of delivering these data and insight has been through the use of loyalty card data, as demonstrated by the likes of Kroger, Casino and Tesco utilizing insights from dunnhumby. Walmart would argue that its use of shopper surveys married up to Retail Link data delivers similar levels of actionable insight, an assertion that would be more than open to debate. Indeed, Walmart insiders have told us that many of the mistakes made during Project Impact were a direct result of Walmart's inability to generate and benefit from granular insight into the preferences and behaviour of its shoppers.

Walmart already tailors stores and assortments by location to a certain extent. Being able to tailor merchandising mix by time of day, week etc requires a very deep level of customization – in terms of inventory maintenance and employee costs when it comes to restocking – and is therefore one of the least-used tactics by retailers. However, Walmart (in Mexico and the UK) has begun offering more premium, higher-margin products around pay day and more promotions from mid-month onwards when shoppers are feeling strapped for cash. Walmart is also tweaking its assortment in the United States as well, offering smaller pack sizes with lower prices towards the end of the month.

As Walmart evolves, suppliers must follow suit

As Walmart continues to evolve its strategy in order to better serve shoppers, this process is directly impacting suppliers. Walmart's emphasis on a shopper-centric approach, helping its shoppers 'save money so that they can live better lives', has created both threats and opportunities for vendors. It has therefore become more vital than ever for vendors to gain genuine understanding and alignment with Walmart's shopper-centric way of going to market and the strategies that result.

In terms of tangible steps, those we have seen successful suppliers adopt include:

- Engaging with Walmart's strategy setters to better understand its strategy and priorities.
- Collaborating with Walmart to understand its shoppers and how to better connect with them.
- Shifting from a transactional relationship with Walmart to a more collaborative partnership.
- Vendors need a seat at the strategic table. This can be delivered by supporting and enabling routine top-to-tops and cross-functional meetings with Walmart.
- Driving Joint Business Planning with Walmart for win–win growth and mutual margin enhancement.
- Providing shopper and/or category data and insight to support Walmart's objectives.
- Focusing on suitable categories and brands to align with Walmart's objectives.
- Establishing the correct structural alignment. Walmart wants a Customer Business Unit organized around it, not a supplier that is organized around countries or categories.
- Resourcing accordingly: having the correct personnel and infrastructure (eg an office in Bentonville).
- Partnering on logistics, supply chain etc to deliver efficiencies and unlock mutual value.

- Supporting and adhering to Walmart's environmental sustainability objectives.

Structural alignment is key

As mentioned above, getting the right structural alignment in place is vital for a vendor wanting to thrive in its relationship with Walmart. As we note above, the ideal structure for dealing with Walmart includes establishing a Customer Business Unit (CBU) that is organized around Walmart. We have heard of several instances of frustration being directed at those vendors who retain their historical structure of being organized purely by country or by product/category. A typical CBU operated by a major supplier to Walmart might include some or all of the following features:

- global/regional/national engagement at Walmart HQ (be that Bentonville, Miami or Leeds);
- central management of account with P&L accountability;
- cross-functional support;
- joint marketing and innovation;
- insights and category advisory;
- functional customer teams;
- support teams covering insights, marketing, finance, supply chain etc.

As the archetypal success story in terms of dealing with Walmart, P&G is often held up as a good example of how to structure to win with Walmart. P&G's Walmart CBU can be summarized with the following points:

- global customer team leaders with P&L responsibility;
- direct reporting from Walmart team leaders to P&G HQ;
- cross-functional teams (marketing, logistics, merchandising etc);
- global Walmart council led by P&G HQ;
- internship scheme at Walmart;
- regular top-to-top meetings and cross-functional meetings.

When we asked a senior executive at Walmart if P&G was a good example to emulate, and if they had any other views on structural alignment, they said:

> P&G has historically done well. They've always been pretty good. A team in Bentonville is pretty much essential. A team in each Walmart market is also good. The key issue is communication. We have vendors with a team in Bentonville, and a team in, say, Brazil. What can happen is the Walmart team in Brazil reports to the head of Brazil or the head of Latin America. What's the point of that if the Walmart Brazil team don't report into the Walmart team in Bentonville? Local teams need to roll up to the central team in Bentonville.

Assortment editing and the impact on suppliers

Alongside Walmart's acceleration in private label development and penetration, perhaps the greatest threat to brands from Walmart has been the SKU rationalization process, also known as range rationalization or assortment editing, that occurred as part of Project Impact. In fact, the two phenomena were inextricably linked: Walmart trimmed brands from its assortment and replaced delisted secondary brands with expanded private label ranges.

At the risk of being unfair to the global CPG business, there are simply too many products available to consumers, and there have only recently been signs that manufacturers are thinking of decreasing the rate at which new products and their new variants are being churned out to an increasingly indifferent world of consumers.

Following decades of NPD by CPG manufacturers, private label innovation by retailers and the emergence of huge out-of-town retail concepts, the array of products greeting a typical supermarket or Supercenter shopper has grown exponentially. According to the Food Marketing Institute, by 2008 nearly 47,000 distinct products filled a typical US supermarket's shelves, up more than 50 per cent from 1996. At any one time in the United States, there is a pool of over one million items available to consumers, according to AMR Research. Of that 1,000,000+ assortment, shoppers typically only use approximately 340 unique items per year (down from 390 in 2009).

One of the main impacts of product proliferation was that Walmart shoppers were increasingly faced with a bewildering array of choices when attempting to navigate a store, a department and a category. Prior to Project Impact, a Walmart Supercenter carrying 100,000 SKUs would be shopped for 22 minutes by an average consumer, implying that a thorough evaluation of each product carried would require an investigation of 75 items per second! This is clearly a preposterous piece of statistical analysis on our behalf, but still fairly telling in that it reveals that consumers had become over-served in terms of the array of products on offer.

A good example of the benefits of SKU rationalization from a consumer's perspective can be found in the case of Walmart Canada and peanut butter. Walmart dropped two of its five lines of peanut butter to free up shelf space for cinnamon spreads. The retailer didn't see a decline in peanut butter sales: with fewer selections to browse, customers ended up purchasing more than before. 'Folks can get overwhelmed with too much variety', Duncan Mac Naughton, Chief Merchandising Officer at Walmart Canada at the time, told the *Globe and Mail*. 'With too many choices, they actually don't buy.'[11]

As previously discussed in the book, the SKU rationalization process enabled Walmart not only to reduce inventory and labour costs but also to give private label items greater prominence on the shelf. As Walmart remarked, the process resulted in 'improved planning, reduced inventory, higher customer satisfaction scores and better merchandise sell through over the course of 2009'.

One other positive spin-off for Walmart from its SKU rationalization programme was that the process enabled another opportunity for the retailer to enjoy enhanced leverage over its vendor partners. We have encountered several vendors that have told us that the SKU rationalization resulted in a quasi-auction process where those suppliers more willing to contribute the largest amount of marketing contribution or promotional support have retained their place on the shelf, despite not necessarily being the stronger or most popular brand.

While most of the SKU reduction programme was undertaken in consumables as well as in non-food categories like sports, the process was broadened to include a wider array of non-food categories. The assortment editing process was not without certain issues. Walmart found itself in 2009 losing shopping trips to drugstores, grocers and category specialists like Home Depot because it had axed certain SKUs that were trip-drivers in their own right. Walmart admits that it made mistakes, and arguably these mistakes were made due to the lack of credible customer data that other retailers – notably those with loyalty cards – have available to them.

As discussed earlier, in order to rectify its mistakes, Walmart has been adding thousands of SKUs back into the mix. The retailer has engaged with suppliers to review its assortment to make sure that it has the breadth of inventory that Walmart customers have come to expect. Walmart is restoring thousands of products to its assortment and adding new items. Bill Simon stated at the time: 'We plan to win in every category and let customers decide through their purchase decisions what to include in our assortment.'

As Walmart and other retailers have rationalized the number of SKUs they sell (in order to focus on brand leaders and private label) and heightened their demands for genuine innovation and added value in terms of NPD, major FMCG vendors have reacted accordingly. A number of them have reined in NPD, others have pledged to shrink the number of lines they offer, while others have gone further still – disposing of entire divisions in order to focus on their areas of strength, brand leadership, authority and expertise. P&G, for example, pledged to reduce its product assortment by 14 per cent over a two-year period. In an interesting experiment of sorts, the company reduced the number of skincare products it sold through one Canadian retailer by a third and reduced its household SKUs by 20 per cent at another retail customer. In both instances it reported sales increases.

Vendors and sustainability

Beyond the usual spheres of promotions, terms and conditions etc, retailers are exerting their powers in other areas, with two notable examples including the inextricably linked issues of packaging and sustainability.

Retailers have not enjoyed the best of reputations in the media and in the general public consciousness in recent years, with constant allegations of bully-boy tactics, unethical sourcing and worker exploitation surrounding the retail industry around the world. Clearly, Walmart has proven to be a large and easy target for criticism in this regard. Walmart has acknowledged that the PR issue was part of the reason for its enthusiasm for all things green. Matt Kistler, Walmart's Senior Vice President for Sustainability, told the *Guardian* in 2010: 'At first it was a little bit of a reaction to the negative pressures as a company we'd been receiving. But very early on, from day two, there was a tremendous appetite not only from an environmental point of view but from a business point of view to do what we're doing.'[12]

Faced with this bad press – and also the need to reduce costs and increase efficiency – Walmart has been busily pursuing an environmental agenda in recent years, seeking to minimize both inputs and outputs in order to reduce the overall environmental impact of its operations. It has become increasingly apparent that Walmart has been looking to maximize the PR impact of its environmental initiatives and the company has been eager to involve its suppliers as much as possible in its efforts to reduce its ecological impact.

We are happy to acknowledge that Walmart is pursuing the environmental agenda because it is the 'right thing' or a 'good thing' to do, but it would be churlish not to acknowledge that its eco-friendly strategies are also being followed thanks to the significant positive spin-off that many of them have for cost reduction. Indeed, it is worth remembering that many initiatives being launched by Walmart and other retailers (minimizing plastic bag usage, backhauling, packaging reduction etc) were first pioneered or championed by hard discounters – not because they help save the planet, but because they help save money.

As in many other issues, Walmart has been in the vanguard of pushing a sustainable vision of retailing. We don't doubt for a second that this has been at least partly motivated by a desire to improve its image (the retailer has traditionally been something of a corporate enemy number 1 in the United States), but Walmart has always been more than transparent that its motivations for greener retailing are – as with all it does – a combination of lower prices for shoppers and higher profits for itself.

Walmart has been proactive in the realm of environmentally responsible retailing in markets such as the UK, the United States and Mexico (indeed, the retailer has initiated some impressive projects in all of its operating markets). Walmart has little time for the expensive showboating and grandstanding exhibited by some other retailers around the world. For an environmental initiative to be worthwhile for Walmart, it must have a positive impact on profitability. As noted by a Walmart executive in Canada, the retailer is anxious to demonstrate that 'environmental sustainability can go hand-in-hand with business sustainability'.

It is worth remembering that Walmart faces something of an uphill battle when it comes to burnishing its eco-credentials, involved as it is in importing tonnes of Chinese imports produced with grotesque environmental side-effects.

That said, there is no doubt that Walmart is genuinely attempting to offset its impact on the environment. Through programmes of change, Walmart is making tangible progress in areas such as refrigeration, heating, ventilation and cooling; store design; lighting; water use; packaging use and recycling; general recycling initiatives; eco-friendly/ethical sourcing and supply chain logistics.

Alongside these in-house initiatives, vendors around the world are being exhorted to support Walmart's environmental improvement programmes. Through mechanisms such as packaging scorecards, carbon foot printing and basic minimum standards, suppliers are facing up to the fact that – in order to continue to do business with their major retail customers such as Walmart – they must adhere to a set of criteria and uphold a series of values that they might not otherwise participate in. Obviously, many major vendors have already embarked on sustainability programmes of their own, but are now facing the burden of matching the requirements of Walmart.

As John Compton of PepsiCo told investors in 2010, 'I'm in the consumer products business, so if I'm going to have a company in the next five or ten years, I better change my practices because Walmart is not going to sell my products if they're not sustainable'.

Walmart's broad environmental goals are simple: to be supplied 100 per cent by renewable energy; to create zero waste; and to sell products that sustain people and the environment. To this end, one of the key developments kicked off by Walmart is a planned worldwide Sustainable Product Index, which is expected to lead to higher quality, lower costs and measure the sustainability of products. According to Walmart, 'one of the biggest challenges we all face is measuring the sustainability of a product. Walmart believes a research-driven approach involving universities, retailers, suppliers and non-government organizations can accelerate and broaden this effort.'

The first step has been the implementation of a Supplier Assessment in which Walmart will provide each of its 100,000 global suppliers with a survey of 15 simple questions to evaluate their own company's sustainability. The questions include some familiar queries on greenhouse gas emissions and location of factories, but the list also includes some new areas, such as water use and solid waste produced. Walmart asked its top-tier US suppliers to complete the survey by the end of 2009. Outside the United States, the company has developed timelines on a country-by-country basis for suppliers to complete the survey.

The 15 questions for suppliers comprise:

- Energy and Climate: Reducing Energy Costs and Greenhouse Gas Emissions
    1 Have you measured your corporate greenhouse gas emissions?
    2 Have you opted to report your greenhouse gas emissions to the Carbon Disclosure Project (CDP)?
    3 What is your total annual greenhouse gas emissions reported in the most recent year measured?
    4 Have you set publicly available greenhouse gas reduction targets? If yes, what are those targets?

- Material Efficiency: Reducing Waste and Enhancing Quality
    5 If measured, please report the total amount of solid waste generated from the facilities that produce your product(s) for Walmart for the most recent year measured.
    6 Have you set publicly available solid waste reduction targets? If yes, what are those targets?
    7 If measured, please report total water use from facilities that produce your product(s) for Walmart for the most recent year measured.
    8 Have you set publicly available water use reduction targets? If yes, what are those targets?

- Natural Resources: Producing High Quality, Responsibly Sourced Raw Materials
    9 Have you established publicly available sustainability purchasing guidelines for your direct suppliers that address issues such as environmental compliance, employment practices and product/ingredient safety?
    10 Have you obtained third-party certifications for any of the products that you sell to Walmart?

- People and Community: Ensuring Responsible and Ethical Production
    11 Do you know the location of 100 per cent of the facilities that produce your product(s)?
    12 Before beginning a business relationship with a manufacturing facility, do you evaluate the quality of, and capacity for, production?
    13 Do you have a process for managing social compliance at the manufacturing level?

14 Do you work with your supply base to resolve issues found during social compliance evaluations and also document specific corrections and improvements?

15 Do you invest in community development activities in the markets you source from and/or operate within?

The general sustainability index followed the 2007 launch of a packaging scorecard system across its supplier base. The aim of the programme was to measure Walmart's 60,000 worldwide suppliers on their ability to improve packaging and conserve resources. This initiative was projected to reduce overall packaging across the Walmart global supply chain by 5 per cent by 2013. In February 2007, Walmart shared the packaging scorecard with its global supply base of more than 60,000 suppliers, allowing them to input information and track their performance relative to other suppliers. From February 2008, Walmart began to measure and recognize its entire world-wide supply chain based upon the packaging scorecard.

Walmart's environmental initiatives, particularly the scorecarding, could be viewed on the one hand as another onerous example of Walmart burdening its suppliers with more work and expense. On the other hand, it also provides more opportunity for mutual benefit through collaboration. Once again, Unilever provides some good examples. The European supplier has been providing expert support to Walmart's sustainable value networks (SVN) for several years. Unilever participates in 4 of these 13 SVNs, which aim to bring Walmart's suppliers together to share best practice. In the Food & Agriculture SVN, Unilever has taken the lead in water by developing a reliable way to measure how efficiently suppliers are using water to grow crops. Unilever ran an irrigation study among Californian tomato growers, the results of which contributed to a sustainability scorecard for Walmart suppliers. Also, working in close cooperation with Walmart, in the summer of 2008 Unilever set up 'sustainability kitchens' at Asda superstores around the UK. The objective was to encourage shoppers to make environmentally friendly changes, for example washing laundry at 30°C, which could also save them money. As part of this activity, Asda ran a promotion on selected Unilever brands with strong sustainability credentials such as Hellmann's, Persil and PG Tips, resulting in a significant sales increase during the period.

Having looked at Walmart's interaction with major global suppliers, we now turn to evaluate the retailer's attempts to increase the clout it holds over suppliers in general: its strategic push to more direct global sourcing.

Notes

1 Soderquist, D (2005) *The Wal-Mart Way: The inside story of the success of the world's largest company*, Thomas Nelson, Nashville, TN, p 166

2 Walton, S with Huey, J (1992) *Sam Walton: Made in America*, Doubleday, New York, p 235

3 Walton, p 235

4 Walton, p 236

5 Walton, p 238

6 Soderquist, p 167

7 Unilever annual report 2010

8 http://www.michaelbergdahl.net/q5.htm

9 http://www.independent.co.uk/news/business/news/leaked-memo-reveals-how-asda-sought-to-beat-down-suppliers-2102448.html

10 Category sales estimates from the **www.planetretail.net** database

11 http://www.theglobeandmail.com/report-on-business/in-store-aisles-less-is-more-but-customers-can-still-be-particular/article1573518/

12 http://www.guardian.co.uk/business/2010/jan/12/walmart-companies-to-shape-the-decade

Removing the margin-takers:
Walmart and global procurement

07

The globalization of the economy is a hefty topic and one that is better left to economists to discuss. What we can discuss here, though, is Walmart's role in this globalization process and how just one retailer's procurement has reshaped – for better or worse – the pattern of global trade and the economic well-being of countries as diverse as the United States and China.

The Chinese imports issue is one of the most frequently used sticks with which to beat Walmart. The *Guardian*, for example, in 2010 reported that Walmart gets many of its products from low-cost Chinese suppliers (and, as we shall see elsewhere in this book, many of Walmart's leading suppliers themselves get their products manufactured in China and other low-cost economies). The pressure group China Labour Watch estimates that if it were a country, Walmart would rank as China's seventh-largest trading partner, just ahead of the UK, spending more than $18 billion annually on Chinese goods.[1]

That Walmart sources a great deal of merchandise from China and other low-wage economies is in no doubt, and there have been frequent allegations that Walmart suppliers flout a wide variety of basic regulations on working conditions, pay and welfare.

In 2010, the *Guardian* quoted Michael Bride, deputy overseas organizing director at the United Food & Commercial Workers Union in Washington DC, as stating that: 'With the scale the company has, the economies of scale it can command, it basically extracts every last nickel out of its suppliers. If you're a Chinese supplier and Walmart is pressing you down, you probably can't go and negotiate your electricity rates or your rent down. But you can cut costs when it comes to labour.' An investigation by China Labour Watch of five factories supplying Walmart found 'illegal and degrading conditions', according to a report released in November 2009 by the New York-based human rights group. At one plant in Dongguan, which supplies candles and Christmas tree lights, it found that workers were required to work 24-hour overtime shifts during busy periods and painted a bleak picture of pay as low as 44 cents per hour, bathrooms without running water and unsanitary canteens. Although Walmart uses independent auditors to check on ethics at its suppliers, the *Guardian* added, the group found evidence of workers being obliged to sign false pay receipts. Walmart responded to the report by saying it had begun an immediate probe into the factories: 'We take reports like this very seriously and we will take prompt remedial action if our investigations confirm any of the findings.'[2]

Walmart/Asda was also targeted in a 2009 War on Want 'Let's Clean Up Fashion Campaign' which included some not altogether unexpected conclusions, such as: textile workers in Asia are not paid a great deal of money; retailers pressure suppliers to reduce their prices; and retailers make a great deal of margin on each garment.

Among the retailers highlighted in the report was Asda, which received a two out of five rating (meaning, according to the report's authors, that Asda acknowledges that minimum and industry benchmark wages are not sufficient, but has made no real efforts to apply a living wage).

The report stated that:

> It is extremely disappointing that a company as large as Asda/Walmart is still failing to seriously address an issue as important as wages and judging by its submission is falling well behind its closest competitors in regard to the quality of its work in this area. Although it's good to see that Asda's audit programme picks up on shortfalls, the case study they supplied makes clear that Asda is applying minimum wage standards to its work in this area. In Bangladesh this equates to just under 1,700 Bangladesh taka. This is well below a living wage. The Asia Floor Wage campaign sets this as over 10,000 Bangladesh taka in Bangladesh. Their work on productivity also offers no guarantee of improving wages for workers. Although some workers may gain greater potential for increasing their earning through becoming more skilled it is unclear how the project intends to raise wages across the board. The benefits of productivity projects can fall straight into the pockets of suppliers and result in additional stress on workers. Without worker involvement and input into the process, a key element of any credible project on wages which is not mentioned anywhere by Asda, it is unclear that workers themselves will see any benefit.[3]

Asda, for its part, stated in its submission to the campaign: 'Suppliers need to take ownership of compliance in their factories. They need to demonstrate that they are regularly and rigorously auditing their own factories... Our code addresses both wage and freedom of association considerations.' And, following the publication of the report, an Asda spokesperson told the *Guardian*: 'As the report itself states, the methodology isn't perfect, which in our view makes comparisons between retailers meaningless. At Asda, we're committed to doing the right thing for our customers, colleagues and suppliers. We believe the most sustainable solution to this complex issue is to align worker pay with productivity improvements. That's why we're working directly with factory owners to improve conditions and improve production techniques.'[4]

The issue of working conditions in Asian factories is a complex and thorny one, but it does seem puzzling that, in the never-ending discussion over retailers and their sourcing in low-wage economies, it is nearly always positioned as the retailers' fault that employees in Asian factories get a raw deal in terms of wages and working conditions. Somehow, it never seems to be the fault of suppliers or, indeed, the governments of the countries in question. And it is never the responsibility of shoppers who seem to have an insatiable desire to pay as little as humanly possible for anything. Walmart could (and probably should) do more to make sure that its vendors are not mistreating their labour forces, but surely the onus should be on governments to enact monitoring systems and living wage requirements for their own citizens.

It is worth pointing out here that, ever since the unfortunate Kathie Lee Gifford incident in the 1990s, Walmart has been more vigilant than most in making sure that its reputation in terms of sourcing is not plunged into controversy. (The Kathie Lee Gifford incident, in 1996, saw the TV celebrity and Walmart become mired in controversy after some items sold under her name at the retailer were revealed to have been sourced from a Honduran sweatshop.) In 2008, it conducted 11,502 factory audits, and over the past two years it has conducted training sessions attended by more than 14,000 supplier and factory employees, covering topics such as best practices sharing or on-site practical training. The company has stated that 'Walmart's Ethical Standards team works collaboratively with government and non-government agencies as well as other global retailers to develop, implement, and monitor programmes that make a difference.'

The other anti-Walmart sentiment derived from global sourcing is due to the perception that, by sourcing from China and other Asian markets, Walmart is somehow destroying US manufacturing jobs. We would argue, however, that the US manufacturing industry was already in decline before Walmart initiated any sort of serious global sourcing capabilities and that Walmart is merely the biggest example of a general trend in US retailers sourcing most of their products from overseas, benefiting from the lower costs to be found in Asia and elsewhere.

Some examples would be useful here: Abercrombie and Fitch states that it sources from 209 vendors located primarily in Asia and Central and South America. Rival fashion chain Gap notes that only 1 per cent of all items that it sells (representing approximately 2 per cent of total cost) are produced in the United States. Approximately 27 per cent of merchandise units were produced in China. Electronics market leader Best Buy states that its private label range is manufactured under contract by vendors based in South-east Asia. Leading discounter Dollar General, meanwhile, states that 'In 2009, we imported approximately $629 million of goods, or 8 per cent of total purchases at cost. We believe we have the potential to directly source a larger portion of our products at significant savings to current costs. We are currently increasing our direct foreign sourcing efforts, which we believe offer significant opportunity for gross profit enhancement in the future.'

Another issue with any sort of reliance on China as a source of imported product is that Walmart can be seriously affected by rising costs in that market. When asked at a 2011 investor conference whether increasing prices from Chinese suppliers were impacting Walmart, Walmart US CEO Bill Simon stated that:

> prices are coming up from Wisconsin, so dairy prices, cheese prices, I mean, we're starting to see inflation in lots of different places, not just from Asia. Our job as Walmart and as merchants at Walmart is to find ways to pull cost out of the system, work with the suppliers where we can, engineer the costs and the price to the place where we get the lowest possible we can. And then if we can't, we have to pass them through because that's EDLP. We can't just absorb it. I do believe if you look back historically what you'll find out is that in inflationary periods, we do really well because of our size and our scale. We have the ability to hold prices down longer with the size of the buys that we will make and the influence it will have on our supply chain and our ability to move it pretty quickly through the system much more efficiently than others. And if we can get – hold prices down longer, go up last, what we will have is a very big opportunity in the marketplace.

The evolution of global sourcing at Walmart

Walmart, like virtually all retailers that started out in the middle of the 20th century, sourced virtually all of its products from distributers, wholesalers or direct suppliers located in their domestic market, in Walmart's case, the United States. Not that all of the products it sold were manufactured in the United States, by any means, but it was certainly the case that they were sourced from US agencies. As we discuss elsewhere, it took Walmart a while to gain the scale and clout to cut out the middlemen and start sourcing directly from manufacturers, and it took longer still for Walmart to start sourcing directly from overseas.

In its fiscal 1977/78 annual report, Walmart stated that it had developed a direct import programme from what it quaintly referred to as 'the Orient' that saw its buyers visit the region six times a year. The company noted that less than 8 per cent of its merchandise was sourced directly from Asia, with those products mainly comprising those that involve 'intricate labour'.

In 1981, the retailer established a buying office in Hong Kong to provide greater opportunities in the retailer's direct import programme, a move that was augmented later that year by the addition of a buying office in Taipei to supplement the Hong Kong base.

At the same time as Walmart was establishing its procurement infrastructure in Asia, concerns over sourcing from Asia and the impact it was having on US manufacturing and US jobs became a big news story. In response to these concerns, Walmart initiated its 'Buy America' programme in 1984, with the aim of supporting US manufacturing and preventing the flow of jobs abroad. The retailer stated that it was encouraging US manufacturers and retailers to mutually consider the programme, whereby they support the purchasing of products manufactured in the United States in order to help address the issues of the trade deficit and prevent the erosion of US manufacturing jobs. In 1985, in an update on the Buy America programme, Walmart reported that $200 million in merchandise purchases had been returned to the United States, creating or retaining 4,500 jobs. By the following year, Buy America was described as no longer a mere programme but part of Walmart's philosophy. The retailer reported that it had converted or retained $693 million in purchases (at retail) – equivalent to 10,554 jobs – in the United States.

The Buy America programme continued apace in the late 1980s, with Walmart noting in 1988 that it was trying to offer the same terms and conditions to US suppliers that it offered to overseas vendors. The retailer stated that it was trying to offer US suppliers longer lead times and more predictable orders in terms of quantity. The programme was said to have created or retained more than 41,000 jobs since its inception in 1984. Tellingly, 1988 was the last time that Buy America was referenced by the retailer in its annual reports, although 1992/93 saw the initiation of short-lived 'Buy Mexican' and 'Buy Canadian' programmes in each market. Several high-profile PR disasters in the 1990s (Bangladeshi-made textiles merchandised under Buy America banners and some infamous TV appearances by David Glass and Kathie Lee Gifford) rendered the Buy America programme something of a poisoned chalice, with Walmart beginning to pick up its (largely unjustified) reputation as the poster child for importing from low-wage economies.

The following decade saw a change in tone from Walmart, with the Buy America programme safely swept under the carpet and the retailer seemingly happier to acknowledge the benefits of international procurement. In 2001, Walmart told its investors that, in the preceding few years, it had improved the quality of its goods – as well as its supply logistics and retail prices – by acquiring certain products for all of its stores around the world from a single source, a process Walmart referred to as 'global sourcing'. Walmart added that the concept works with items that are global in scope and need, whether they're items for sale or for use by employees. Items like copy paper, light bulbs, hangers, fabric or clothing zippers were cited by Walmart as typical candidates for global sourcing.

In 2002, Walmart assumed responsibility for global procurement from a third party that had been acting as Walmart's agent. This allowed the retailer to better coordinate the entire global supply chain from product development to delivery. In addition, the global procurement programme was said to allow Walmart to share its buying power and merchandise network with all of its operations throughout the world.

Three years later, with regard to global procurement, Walmart reiterated the old maxim that 'knowledge is power', and that its in-depth knowledge was critical when it came to choosing merchandise suppliers from around the world to deliver the right mix of quality and value to Walmart shoppers:

> That's why Global Procurement is establishing groups of technical experts – specialists that focus on the many important dynamics of a particular category purchase. For example, in apparel, Global Procurement has brought together individuals who have a specialized understanding of various apparel manufacturing techniques, screen printing, finishing, etc – as well as individuals who have an extended understanding of different fabrics such as cotton, synthetics, knits and wovens. These specialty groups work closely together with our team members responsible for ethical sourcing and logistics. It's all to make certain that every day we bring our customers quality products at unbeatable prices.

New global sourcing strategy unveiled in 2010

In January 2010, Walmart unveiled a new global sourcing strategy that involved the creation of Global Merchandising Centers, a change in leadership and structure, and a strategic alliance with Li & Fung, a global sourcing organ- ization. Walmart Vice Chairman Eduardo Castro-Wright said at the time that the moves were 'important elements in the company's strategy to deliver even greater value to its customers and shareholders'.

Walmart first announced its consolidated global sourcing structure centred around new Global Merchandising Centers (GMCs) in October 2009. The new structure was designed to leverage the company's global scale in both general merchandise categories and global food sourcing. 'The newly- established Global Merchandising Centers represent the largest and most important element of our new sourcing strategy', Castro-Wright noted. 'These centres will create alignment between sourcing and merchandising and drive efficiencies across various merchandise categories.'

The core of the company's overall global sourcing strategy will be to continue increasing direct sourcing for the company's private brands, which represented more than $100 billion in purchasing annually at the time. 'Our new strategy and structure should drive significant savings across the supply chain', Castro-Wright said.

Walmart was hoping to cut billions of dollars of costs from its sourcing operations by aggregating some components of its purchasing across its operating markets. The overall objective of this process is to increase the share of total buying that it purchases directly from manufacturers instead of through third-party wholesalers or procurement agencies – the recurrent theme of eradicating the middlemen. Less than $20 billion of the $100 billion that Walmart spent each year on procuring private label merchandise, for example, was bought directly from manufacturers.

As part of this new strategy, Walmart also finalized a series of agreements with Li & Fung. The agreements were non-exclusive and did not include volume or shipment commitments. The strategic alliance between the two companies has allowed Walmart to 'realize the benefits of consolidating a portion of its sourcing portfolio'.

Does global buying really exist?

Global buying power and the notion of global procurement are oft-touted concepts and they have been used as a justification of sorts for much of the internationalization of retailing that has taken place over the past couple of decades. By becoming bigger and more international, the argument goes, retailers will gain greater leverage over international suppliers and will secure better deals across different markets. A fine theory, but slightly flawed when it comes to tangible results.

Where global buying power has actually gained traction is in non-resaleable products (shopping trolleys, point-of-sale (POS) equipment etc) and also in services such as IT systems for labour scheduling, warehouse management, merchandising and such like. These types of products and services can be bought centrally for global usage by Walmart employees and genuine global buying power can be exploited.

To a lesser extent, the same is true for certain non-food categories such as toys, apparel and household products, particularly those that are sourced as private labels. Indeed, Asda has often commented that it is able to sell its George brand of clothing so cheaply because it buys fabrics by the mile rather than by the yard – a benefit of being part of the Walmart global family.

That said, it's worth remembering that idiosyncratic features of Walmart's different operating markets mean that the 'one size fits all' approach to buying apparel – both literally and metaphorically – would not work for supplying shoppers in the US and Japanese markets, for example.

Theoretically, the same level of scale could be achieved by Walmart in categories such as entertainment and electricals, but again there are obstacles to making this a reality. From the huge variances in national tastes in music and cinema to the different voltages and plugs used in each country, there are a number of reasons why Walmart will find it difficult to achieve genuine scalability in its purchasing.

There has been some progress in this regard, however. As early as in 2001, Walmart's Global Sourcing Team discovered that stores in Argentina were selling an entry-level microwave oven at twice the price of those sold by the company elsewhere in the world. The situation was quickly rectified when the Argentine Walmart stores contacted the company's global microwave supplier. Global sourcing also helped the company negotiate prices for fans and air conditioners, allowing its Asda stores in the UK to cut prices on the items by 50 per cent, tripling sales of the products. According to Walmart at the time, global sourcing was not just about US suppliers helping out stores in other countries; Walmart stated that it also procured items from Europe and other regions of the world for sale in the United States and elsewhere.

Grocery is still a national business

On a number of occasions, various Walmart personnel in several international markets have told us that being part of by far and away the world's largest retailer is all well and good, but really cuts no ice when it comes to sourcing groceries in each market.

Senior individuals at Asda have remarked over the past few years, for example, that they are consistently charged more than Tesco by suppliers. That Asda is able to claim to offer equal or lower prices than its arch-rival in the UK is testament to the welcome fact that Asda is the UK's lowest cost to operate (ie most efficient and cost-effective) supermarket but also testament to the less welcome fact that its margins are typically much lower than Tesco's, a product, at least partially, of less favourable general terms and conditions from suppliers in the UK.

Despite theoretically being able to say to suppliers in the UK 'we are Walmart, please give us your best prices', the reaction will be 'you might be Walmart, but in the UK you are a third the size of Tesco and we negotiate on a national basis'.

Walmart will have experienced a similar situation in its ill-fated sojourn in Germany (where many local retailers 'encouraged' suppliers to be less than collaborative with Walmart) and perhaps encounters similar issues in grocery categories in Canada.

Retailers including Walmart have hitherto been unable to engineer global, or even regional, deals because of the fact that it is national retail hierarchies that determine suppliers' attitudes towards doing business with major retail customers. Despite the fact that Walmart accounts for 14 per cent (or $6.6 billion) of Kraft's sales, this will have little impact on Kraft subsidiary Cadbury's dealings with Tesco and Asda.

There are other, more mundane reasons why negotiations or buying are likely to remain national in scope, such as: linguistic issues; different regulations on formulations, genetically modified ingredients and food safety; and the simple fact that – despite the best efforts of businesses such as P&G and Unilever – the world of branded FMCG is still extremely fragmented and country-specific.

Global buying for FMCG is therefore something of a phantom menace, in that consumer goods procurement is still very much a national procedure for a number of reasons:

- It is national retail leaders that command the best terms and conditions.

- The world of branded FMCG is still extremely fragmented and country-specific. Some of the big brands that Walmart sells in the United States are simply unheard of in Brazil or the UK.
- Many global brands are manufactured, processed or bottled locally. Different cost bases and tax regimes make the possibility of common pricing across markets extremely problematic, if not impossible.

When we asked a Walmart director about his thoughts over the likelihood of making much progress on global promotions, for brands in general, he told us: 'There has been no real progress on promotions at all; certainly no success stories that I've heard of. There have been a few attempts, but the thought of global promotions is more of a fantasy than a vision at the moment. We simply do not have the resources to execute.'

In terms of establishing global agreements for brands, the director in question expressed a slightly more optimistic outlook: 'It really depends on the category. Depends on the supplier, too. It won't happen in food. Ninety per cent of food is produced locally and negotiated locally: branded groceries will remain a national game. Non-food is a different matter to grocery. We've some big global agreements coming on stream in 2011/12 – some centrally negotiated deals that will be rolling out in all markets.'

Walmart's quest for leverage

However, what Walmart is hoping is that, over time, its global scale and importance to large multinational FMCG vendors will actually begin to translate into tangible progress in establishing genuine regional and/or global buying. Walmart terms this 'leverage'.

The list below shows how Walmart is hoping to positively impact its bottom line around the world by leveraging a number of key attributes such as size, processes and, perhaps most importantly, relationships with brands and manufacturers:

- leveraging scale and expertise;
- process consistency;
- global brand relationships;
- global supplier relationships;
- price communications;
- merchandising;
- sustainable thinking;
- integration.

Walmart's Vice President for International Purchase Leverage Hernan Muntaner featured in a 2011 *Business Week* report, which set out Walmart's aspirations to piggyback on their suppliers' own sourcing activities. The report noted that Walmart had approached PepsiCo with the suggestion of buying potatoes jointly for a lower price than either company could get on its own. *Business Week* reported: 'So far, Pepsi isn't playing along. But with sales slowing in the United States and the price of sugar, meat, and wheat on the rise, the world's largest retailer is jointly purchasing a growing share of raw ingredients with manufacturers of food and household products sold in its stores. Products already being purchased with suppliers include sugar, which goes into the company's store-brand soda and paper, used in Walmart's back-office printers.'

'Around the world, we found we were buying the same raw materials that Walmart suppliers buy,' Muntaner told *Business Week*. 'When you put the volume together of what we bought and what [suppliers] bought, and buy from just one supplier, you can reduce the cost.' As of early 2011, *Business Week* reported that only makers of private label goods sold under Walmart's house brands have joined in its so-called collaborative sourcing programme. Manufacturers of branded products have taken a pass because they're loath to share pricing data and product formulas, say executives at three companies approached by Walmart.

Business Week went on to state that Muntaner's primary job is to travel the globe helping Walmart's international divisions, from China to Japan to Brazil, find ways to use the company's massive buying muscle to lower what it spends on everything from copier paper to store-branded bottled water. Increasingly, that means selling the benefits of sourcing collaboratively. Muntaner says a soda maker, which he declines to name, has teamed up with Asda in Britain to buy sugar. The soda company paid 14 per cent less, he says. Asda's sugar costs also fell, savings it used to lower the price of bags of its own house brand of sugar.[5]

While Walmart might find it difficult to engineer global deals with suppliers, it is seeing some success in using its scale (in particular its scale in the United States) to positively impact its global operations. When we asked a senior Walmart associate active in procurement if Walmart's global buying abilities were limited, his answer was fairly frank: 'For the time being yes. It's very hard to get Walmart US to care much about it, as they don't get anything out of it. They already have all the scale and buying power they need. Adding in the UK or Brazil would make no difference to them. For private label it's happening, but for brands it feels like a bit of a non-starter.'

But, that's not to say that, in more general terms, 'global leverage' is not being achieved. The Walmart procurement director told us that: 'The way that global leverage has been working has been through the US guys helping International out. These are not global deals as such, but different Walmart countries leveraging our strong US presence.' A good example told to the authors was related to Item X and the allocations that Supplier X was giving countries. Asda requested a certain number of units, but were allocated only a third of that amount. Brazil wanted another amount but was allocated only 15 per cent of the total requested. A source told us how the buyer of

Item X in the United States came down hard on Supplier X: pretty soon after, both Asda and Walmart Brazil got their full allocation. The procurement director added: 'The system is basically Walmart International leveraging American contacts to get more muscle.' (The identity of the item and the supplier has been excised by the authors.)

Another way that Walmart is achieving greater leverage is through technology. One technique is through e-auctions, using its own internal resources. A Walmart spokesperson described the process as follows:

> an e-auction is where you go ahead and you write a very specific specification. You find out who are the people who would like to sell you that specification. You organize it on a computer and then there's a certain time period. Let's just say it's a couple of hours. All those manufacturers or suppliers of that product get to see the bids of themselves and the other competitors at the same time. And what winds up happening is it gives an opportunity for them to say, hmm maybe I'd like to change my bid. Now one of the interesting things is we've done over 60 of these in the last six months. The majority of the time the incumbent actually wins but there is a very meaningful saving. So this isn't like a way to make the supplier relationship a very short-term way. This is a way of getting price transparency so that we're able to see are we paying the right amount for what it is we're looking for.

Walmart has also established an internal online product catalogue that enables merchants from all over Walmart's global operations to see over 1,000 items that are being bought by their counterparts in other Walmart countries. According to the retailer: 'They can click on it. They can get their specifications and eventually they could actually order it, a great facilitator.'

Global Brands Imports gaining traction

Global leverage is a fine notion, but there are signs that Walmart is taking physical steps to make it reality. In an internal e-mail from May 2010 seen by the authors, we learnt of Walmart International's appointment of Fernando Serpa to its Purchase Leverage team. He was appointed as the Vice President for Global Brands Imports and took on responsibility for progressing Walmart International's efforts to facilitate access, supply chain efficiencies and cost advantages on branded products for its markets around the world.

Scott Price, EVP, President and CEO of Walmart Asia, described in 2011 how one example worked, with Walmart selling Canadian Nestlé water in its stores in Japan. Answering his own question of 'how can you ship water from somewhere else in the world and sell it cheaper?' he answered: 'Two things: one, the Japanese beverage industry is terribly inefficient and the second is that there are a lot of empty containerships that are coming back from the United States or North America empty on their way back to Asia. We're able to get really great prices.' Price described how Walmart loads up those ships in Canada with Nestlé water and gets them to stop in Japan on their way back to wherever they're headed in Asia. The bottles are augmented with a Japanese language sticker and then sold for 50 per cent cheaper than any other bottled water in Japan. Price added that 'the margin is significantly higher for us than any other of our beverages, again, the idea being that our Japanese customers like the idea of these value products. They trust the Nestlé brand. They're quite surprised at the value we can get. Our sales in terms of the particular category are great. Nestlé loves it, of course, because they're now breaking into the water industry in Japan, in which they hadn't had a position.'

GMCs yielding results

Walmart's aspirations towards global leverage and global sourcing form part of Walmart's virtuous circle general business model (below) with which the retailer is seeking to use its undoubted scale and global presence in order to generate efficiencies, reduce prices for consumers, improve product quality and drive profitability. Walmart's revamped global sourcing strategy was formally unveiled in January 2010, although it is worth remembering that a number of its global sourcing strategies and mechanics were already under way several years before the announcement was made.

The Walmart business model: → Operate for less → Buy for less → Sell for less → Grow sales → Operate for less → etc.

A key feature of the enhanced global sourcing structure was the formation of GMCs. The motivation behind the formation of the GMC structure was to eradicate billions of dollars of costs for Walmart by cutting out the agents, brokers, wholesalers, importers and exporters that have historically dominated the often complex processes that have enabled products to make the journey from producer to end consumer. As the model below shows, Walmart neatly (and accurately) describes these middlemen as 'margin-takers' – entities that add cost and complexity throughout the value chain. Through centralizing procurement through its GMCs, Walmart is endeavouring to increase the share of total buying that it purchases directly from manufacturers instead of through third-party wholesalers or procurement agencies. As Asda's Andy Bond noted in 2010: 'Thanks to Walmart, we have a unique opportunity to remove middlemen from the global supply chain to lower costs. We believe that the creation of global merchandising centres, be that in food, non-food or apparel, will enable us to save our customers money.'

Walmart's global procurement model: → Leverage scale → Remove margin-takers → Consolidate volumes & activities → Leverage scale

While there is a long, long way to go before Walmart can dream of leveraging its global scale in areas such as branded groceries in any meaningful sense, the retailer, through its UK arm Asda, has already made genuine strides in this direction through one of its UK GMCs, International Produce Limited (IPL). IPL is set for a period of rapid growth as Walmart seeks to exploit its expertise and scale, with the intention of enabling Walmart to reduce prices for imported produce such as melons, stone fruit, apples, pears and grapes. IPL is now buying in greater volume on behalf of Walmart stores (and shoppers) in markets as diverse as the United States, Canada and Japan.[6]

Formed in 2004, IPL was acquired by Walmart/Asda at the end of 2009 and is now a wholly owned subsidiary whose sole purpose is to 'cut out the middleman'. As the two models below reveal (the first flow depicts the traditional produce supply chain, the second flow represents the IPL scheme), the IPL business model removes at least three 'margin-taking' layers from the traditional value chain that links grower to shopper, delivering on IPL's objectives of controlling the supply chain, improving product freshness and quality, developing grower/manufacturer relationships and developing shopper advantage through points of difference.

Traditional produce supply chain: Grower → Pre-packer → Agent exporter → Agent importer → Supplier/packer → Regional distribution centre → Walmart store

Walmart produce supply chain: Grower → Pre-packer → Regional distribution centre → Walmart store

In a little over six years since its inception, IPL has become the UK's largest produce importer, sourcing fruit from South Africa, Latin America, Europe, Morocco and New Zealand and employing 1,000 people globally. Following its success in fruit, IPL has successfully expanded its remit to include corned beef from Brazil, cooked meats from Italy, cheese from Italy and Greece, fresh pasta from Italy, olive oil and wine. Nick Scrase, the MD of IPL, told us that, while it tends to have 'very hard negotiations' and 'tough discussions' with its suppliers, the opportunities for both IPL and its suppliers to leverage volumes are substantial, also offering both parties the opportunity to increase the quality of the products under discussion and enhance margins following the removal of the middlemen in the process.

Feta cheese is a good example. Asda had been using the same feta cheese supplier for some 15 years, sourcing the product through a third-party agent and a third-party transportation provider. Following the intervention of IPL and the removal of these third parties, Asda was able to secure a 13 per cent cost saving, immediately benefiting consumers in the UK through lower prices and also providing Asda with enhanced margins. Other benefits cited by IPL of this more direct procurement method include greater visibility into the provenance of food and drink and fairer prices for suppliers as well as enhanced levels of food safety and food security.

Over the next five years, Walmart is planning to grow IPL fivefold, making it one of the 10 largest food companies in the UK. While one growth generator will be an acceleration of direct procurement for Asda itself, another avenue of growth will be through the ongoing expansion of IPL's reach to service other Walmart markets around the world, with plans already afoot for it to become the sourcing arm for Walmart globally in certain categories (it already supplies South African fruit to Walmart in Japan, the United States and Canada).

IPL claims that, thanks to its evolution into a large-scale specialist organization, it has developed the most efficient logistics and transport function of any UK retailer, due in part to its strong relationship with shipping line Maersk and logistics provider Damco, enabling it to get produce off the tree and into stores in a relatively short space of time.

Once picked on a broad variety of South African farms and orchards, produce is pre-cooled to zero degrees centigrade before being loaded onto temperature-controlled 40-foot containers. These are trucked (for anywhere between two hours or one day) to Cape Town, Durban, Port Elizabeth or Maputo Port (in Mozambique) where they are plugged in at the port and may be stored at the port for between one and three days. The containers are then loaded on a boat for their 14-day journey to the UK, during which they are still chilled (although the chillers might be turned off early for stone fruit to 'stimulate ripening'). Once the containers arrive in the UK (Tilbury, Felixstowe or Sheerness), it takes two days to unload and clear the containers from the port. They are then taken by truck or train to IPL's storage and packing facility in Yorkshire. The combined processes involved mean that it takes less than seven days for fruit to hit the stores after arriving in the UK, and up to a total of 28 days to travel from 'field to fork'.

In 2011, we visited one of IPL's key South African produce suppliers, DuToit, a Ceres-based company that produces around 130,000 tons of fruit (apples, pears, nectarines, peaches and cherries) and more than 50,000 tons of onions, potatoes and salads each year. It has a major position in the apple market in South Africa – accounting for around 12 per cent of the market – and also accounts for nearly 7 per cent of pear production. IPL is DuToit's largest single customer, supplying Asda with 750,000 cartons of apples and pears (10,000 tonnes), although DuToit also supplies local South African retailers Woolworths, Pick n Pay, Shoprite/Checkers, Fruit & Veg City and SPAR (noting that only 60 per cent of produce is sold through organized trade in South Africa). DuToit spoke very highly of IPL's systems and cited the positive impact of IPL on driving range, value and availability.

DuToit had supplied Asda since 1997 through importers, moving to a direct relationship when IPL was formed in 2004. While all of DuToit's sales to IPL have traditionally been exported by IPL, DuToit told us that it was 'very excited' about the possibility of supplying Massmart's food retail and wholesale activities when Walmart took control of the South African retailer. Pieter du Toit, the managing director of marketing for DuToit, said that, since becoming a supplier to Asda, the firm had to integrate its planning with Asda's planning to cut packaging costs in the UK. It also had to adhere to audits on food and people safety and ethical standards. DuToit director Gysbert du Toit told us, 'The relationship with Asda creates stability in our business.'

IPL has been aggressively broadening its remit into wine. In South Africa, Asda already sources between eight and nine million litres of wine each year and IPL sees great potential in taking control of the bottling process, enabling it to negotiate directly with wine producers rather than importers/exporters. Furthermore, by transporting wine in vast 24,000-litre 'wine boxes' for bottling in the UK, Asda is able to benefit from cheaper bottling and also generate substantial environmental benefits and cost savings, as transporting wine in bulk 'wine boxes' uses 50 per cent fewer containers than transporting actual bottles of wine.

While in South Africa, we visited Fairhills, a Fairtrade wine producer and bottler based in Stellenbosch, which is a joint venture between Origin Wine, Du Toitskloof Winery and its worker community. Origin Wine is a provider of logistical services to the South African wine-making industry. Founded in 2002, Origin processes more than 40 million litres of wine per annum. The Fairhills project collaborates with local vineyards to bottle Fairtrade Wines that are mainly sold into the UK, including private label ranges for retailers such as the Co-operative and Asda. In fact, the premium private label range wines supplied to Asda under the Extra Special brand also sell well in Japan, where the Extra Special range has become a best-selling line through Walmart's Seiyu network of stores. The relationship is now handled by IPL.

Asda's early involvement with direct sourcing through IPL, it is worth remembering, was met with a degree of derision from competing super-markets and also from within the fresh produce industry at the time. Just six years later, IPL is the largest produce importer in the UK, with turnover thought to be in the region of £1 billion. Not only has it grown rapidly, but IPL has realized that its produce-sourcing model is a very portable concept that can be replicated across many other product categories. Indeed, a similar company has already been set up for pork and pork products and, as we have seen, the model also suits dairy, wine, oils and cooked meats. IPL has told us that its long-term ambition is not to become a food processer or manufacturer in its own right, but instead to broaden its presence across different commodities, different geographies and different aspects of the value chain.

With Walmart's geographic presence expanding (it seems to be completing one major international acquisition each year), the long-term potential for IPL – and therefore its suppliers – is substantial. With consumers across the world enthusiastically embracing the concept of permanent global summer-time (ie the almost constant availability of products once only available on a seasonal basis), the ability to source a broad variety of produce at low cost and in high volumes is a key cornerstone of success for grocery retailers. Thanks to the innovation and scale of IPL, Walmart is – as in so many aspects of retailing – a step or two ahead of many competitors.

Having the scale and reach to exert such an impact in the world of procurement is one thing: having the means to distribute the products to stores with incredible efficiency is another. So, we now turn to look at Walmart's leadership in distribution – one of the very foundations of its global retail supremacy.

Notes

1 http://www.guardian.co.uk/business/2010/jan/12/walmart-companies-to-shape-the-decade

2 As above

3 http://www.waronwant.org/campaigns/supermarkets-and-sweat shops/extra/inform/16683-lets-clean-up-fashion-2009

4 http://www.guardian.co.uk/money/2009/oct/07/retailers-factory-workers-asia

5 http://www.businessweek.com/magazine/content/10_42/b4199023758279.htm

6 The rest of this chapter is based on Bryan Roberts' trip with Asda to visit South African produce and wine suppliers. Originally published as an article on **www.kantarretailiq.com**

Still leading in logistics

08

Having seen how Walmart's scale enables it to buy products with an un-paralleled advantage, it is time to look at another area that has enabled Walmart to establish and maintain its position as by far and away the leading retailer in the United States and the world: getting those products where they need to be quickly and cheaply.

As in other areas such as IT systems, the development of Walmart's much-lauded leadership in supply chain and logistics was dictated by a typical mixture of necessity, improvisation and savvy strategy. Walmart's distribution system has evolved into a state-of-the-art technology-driven model of efficiency, but began in the early days with Walmart's characteristic make-do-and-mend approach (its first warehouse was a disused garage in Bentonville), coupled with Sam Walton's tireless enthusiasm for learning from, and recruiting from, retail competitors around the country.

A testament to the importance of logistics for Walmart is that two of its CEOs spent much of their Walmart careers working in the logistics department and today the logistics division is one of Walmart's key business units and one of its undoubted competitive advantages, enabling the retailer to maintain industry-leading metrics in areas such as inventory, efficiency and stock-turn. As Don Soderquist remarks, Walmart's strategy on logistics 'hand-in-hand with Walmart's use of technology, allowed the company to blow past competitors in areas of cost, real-time management of merchandise, and customer satisfaction'.[1]

Perhaps the best summary of Walmart's competitive advantage derived from its abilities in supply chain is what we were told by a senior Walmart director: 'Our biggest single advantage globally is our supply chain. We still kick ass in logistics.'

The scale of Walmart's logistics system

As of 2011, Walmart's US logistics division comprises more than 40 Regional Distribution Centres (RDCs), each of which is over 1 million square feet in size. They operate 24 hours per day, 7 days per week, using between 5 and 12 miles of conveyor belts in each RDC to move over 9,000 different lines of merchandise. Each RDC supports between 75 and 100 stores within a 250-mile radius – the same 'hub and spoke' model used by Sam Walton in the early stages of the retailer's growth. Back in the 1970s, Walmart opened its stores in a 350- to 450-mile radius around a DC, a distance that was described as a day's drive for Walmart's trucks.

In addition to the general merchandise RDCs, Walmart also operates speciality DCs for categories such as grocery, jewellery, pharmacy, clothing and footwear and a network of DCs dedicated to supporting the Sam's Club chain. Speciality DCs also support Walmart's e-commerce activities and Site to Store delivery service.

The scale of Walmart's distribution infrastructure is breathtaking. As of 2010, its logistics division employed 85,000 people, working in 147 DCs and over 50 transportation offices. Its trucking unit oversaw around 7,200 tractors and 53,000 trailers operated by nearly 8,000 drivers.

During fiscal 2011, 79 per cent of the Walmart US segment's purchases of merchandise were shipped to Walmart's stores through its distribution centres. The balance of merchandise purchased was shipped directly to stores by suppliers. General merchandise is transported to stores primarily through Walmart's private truck fleet, while the retailer has contracts with common carriers to transport the majority of perishable and dry grocery merchandise.

Walmart US is supported by 123 distribution facilities (as of January 2011), located strategically throughout the United States and Puerto Rico. Of these 123 distribution facilities, Walmart owns and operates 105. Third parties own and operate the remaining distribution facilities. In addition to servicing the Walmart US segment, some Walmart DCs also service the Sam's Club chain for certain product categories.

Sam's Club, in fiscal 2011, received 63 per cent of its purchases from dedicated Sam's Club distribution facilities and several Walmart US DCs. Sam's Club is supported by 25 distribution facilities. Of these, Walmart owns and operates eight. Third parties own and operate the others. The principal focus of Sam's Club's distribution operations is on cross-docking merchandise, while stored inventory is minimized. Cross-docking is a distribution process under which shipments are directly transferred from inbound to outbound trailers. Shipments typically spend less than 24 hours in a cross-dock facility, sometimes less than an hour. Sam's Club uses a combination of its private truck fleet and common carriers to transport non-perishable merchandise from DCs to clubs. As with Walmart US, Sam's Club contracts with common carriers to transport perishable grocery merchandise from DCs to clubs.

In-house supply chain development

Unlike many other retailers which grew to rely on third-party wholesalers and distributors, the development of Walmart's logistics system was largely achieved in-house. This was largely due to the fact that Walmart's early pattern of growth saw it set up outlets in often isolated rural communities – meaning that distributors found it uneconomical to deliver to Walmart's stores. The retailer was therefore pretty much left to its own devices when it came to distributing products to its stores: if Walmart didn't distribute its products, then no-one else was going to do it for them.

This self-reliance saw Walmart build and run its own DCs and also own and run its own fleet of trucks. Similarly, the implementation of the automation and mechanization of DCs and the introduction of inventory management and merchandise-tracking technologies were all developed and implemented internally by Walmart. Finally, the inclusion of suppliers within a vertically integrated, data-driven supply chain was initiated by Walmart and developed using Walmart technologies like Retail Link.

Don Soderquist recalls how Walmart began by using warehouse automation technologies bought off the shelf from vendors but soon began demanding that suppliers provide the retailer with custom-designed technologies better aligned to Walmart's own business and objectives. He notes that 'before long, the warehouses were transformed into state-of-the-art, full-line distribution centres, including conveyor systems equipped with barcode scanners to read and sort cartons of merchandise and move those cartons from one place in the warehouse all the way to a specific point on the shipping dock and into a waiting trailer'.[2]

Establishing a supply chain in the 1960s

In Walmart's early stages of development, distribution to its stores was a problematic affair. Sam Walton recounts how his stores were too small to receive full pallets of merchandise from suppliers or distributors, so suppliers would deliver pallets to Walmart's warehouse (the rented old garage in Bentonville) where the pallets would be broken down and redistributed by the retailer to its stores. According to Walton, 'it was expensive and inefficient'.

The evolution of Walmart's embryonic supply chain strategy was shaped by Bob Thornton, a warehouse manager hired by Sam Walton from variety store chain J.J. Newberry. Thornton soon set about preparing a design for a warehouse, a 60,000 sq. ft unit that was part of the retailer's new head office development in Bentonville – still the home of Walmart to this day.

Walmart's approach to expansion was based around a kind of hub and spoke approach – all stores had to be within a day's drive of a distribution centre. Sam Walton noted that when a new DC had been opened, the retailer would open a store as far away as possible from the DC while still observing the day's drive rule and then backfill the region until Walmart had 'saturated' the market.

Distribution in the 1970s

Walmart began the early 1970s servicing its 38 stores through one major hardlines distribution centre in Bentonville, AR, which had been doubled in size to 124,800 sq. ft in 1971. The following year saw the completion of additional 88,000 sq. ft extension to the hardlines DC as well as the completion of 22,000 sq. ft facility dedicated to the marking and distribution of clothing, enabling Walmart to reduce its freight costs and complete the turnaround of its apparel ranges more quickly.

The late 1960s and early 1970s also saw Walmart build on its practice of 'backhauling' – the use of its trucks to bring merchandise from manufacturers back to the DC instead of making the return journey back from stores with an empty trailer. In 1971, Walmart's trucks backhauled 954 loads over the year, making a 'substantial contribution to our profit structure'. Walmart's finessing of the backhauling system means that, nowadays, over half the merchandise received at its DCs is delivered to them by the retailer's own trucks.

Walmart's growth in the 1970s was orchestrated by Sam Walton and Ron Mayer, whom Walton had lured away from regional discounter Duckwall Stores. Mayer was responsible for steering Walmart away from the dropshipment system, with stores placing their own orders and receiving their supplies direct from suppliers or distributors, and towards the merchandise assembly technique of receiving supplies centrally and assembling store-specific deliveries at the DC. The same era saw Walmart take the decision to purchase its own tractors and trailers rather than relying purely on contract carriers.

By 1973, when Walmart was trading through around 80 stores, its DC processed 55 per cent of the products sold by the retailer. A new 150,000 sq. ft DC commenced operations in January 1975, designed to consolidate case-pack merchandise previously shipped directly to stores by suppliers. Even at this stage of its development, Walmart was at pains to point out that its DCs were not warehouses intended to stock products. Instead, Walmart always keenly emphasized that its DCs were redistribution points for bulk merchandise received in substantial volumes. The new DC included eight railway car doors and 37 truck doors and was designed in such a way that loads could be transferred directly from truck or train into waiting Walmart trucks without being stored in the DC: while not using the term itself, Walmart was leading the way in what is now known as cross-docking. At the time, the benefits of the new DC and its operations were said to include lower costs, more flexible ordering and faster delivery. The space created in the old DC by the transfer of activity to the new DC was used for additional warehousing. By January 1975, 60 per cent of merchandise was being distributed by the retailer itself; a ratio that improved to 80 per cent a year after the new DC began operating.

As its supply chain developed, Walmart's proficiency in distribution was benefiting from the technological advances that we will look at in more detail in a later chapter. For example, 1975 saw the implementation of a new clothing unit control system that used computer-prepared magnetic tickets to track the sales rate of fashion merchandise. The system provided Walmart's apparel buyer with distribution information to better manage inventories and replenishment.

Another new 150,000 sq. ft DC was unveiled in Bentonville in November 1976, creating a total DC of 300,000 sq. ft. All stock moved through the enlarged DC on a 2½-day cycle. The year 1976 was also notable for the appointment of future CEO David Glass to run the distribution division. Glass, recruited from a discount drugstore retailer, was credited by Sam Walton as responsible for building the 'sophisticated and efficient' logistics system that underpinned Walmart's rise to supremacy.

By 1977, Walmart's two DCs in Bentonville covered some 540,000 sq. ft, providing its stores with basic and promotional items. These facilities, it said at the time, enabled Walmart to buy in bulk and pass on the resultant savings to shoppers. Plans were unveiled in 1977 for a new 390,000 sq. ft combination warehouse and DC in Searcy, AR, that was designed to service half the retailer's stores. The Searcy DC featured a 'revolutionary' conveyor system capable of moving freight at 200 feet per minute. Distribution, Walmart noted, 'plays such a vital role in the company's overall operation and success'.

The year 1978 saw the establishment of a separate division for the distribution of hobby and crafts merchandise in order to improve the in-stock position of stores in these categories, an initiative accompanied in the following year by the opening of a new 390,000 sq. ft DC in Bentonville to 'further enhance our expansion capabilities'.

Rapid growth in distribution capacity in the 1980s

In 1980, Walmart announced extensions to the relatively new DCs in Bentonville and Searcy of 202,000 and 142,000 sq. ft, respectively, and the retailer also completed a new 510,000 sq. ft DC in Palestine, TX, to service the Texas and Gulf Coast markets. A new DC opened in 1982 in Cullman, AL, which operated as a full-line DC as well as housing a secondary processing centre for apparel and a centre for the warehousing and processing of sporting, hobbies and crafts products.

Walmart's rapid growth in the mid-1980s was accompanied by a flurry of development in the distribution side of the business. In 1983, construction started on a new 650,000 sq. ft DC in Mount Pleasant, IA, and in 1985 Walmart announced the construction of new DCs in Douglas, GA (opening January 1986); Brookhaven, MS (August 1986); Plainview, TX (September 1986) and Bentonville, AR (December 1985), adding 2,598,000 sq. ft to distribution space in 1986, an increase of 66 per cent during the year.

By 1986, Walmart's distribution system was providing 77 per cent of the goods sold by Walmart. It comprised 10 DCs, over 7 million sq. ft of space, 750 trucks and serviced each store around five times per week. Each DC – by now averaging around 650,000 sq. ft – received and shipped around 30 million cases per year (equivalent to 96 trailer loads each day). Each DC serviced around 150 Walmart stores. In 1987, Walmart added 1.477 million sq. ft to its distribution network. The increase included the expansion of three DCs plus the opening of the company's 11th DC, a 583,000 sq. ft facility in Laurens, SC.

Walmart's 16 DCs (10 RDCs, three speciality facilities, and three support facilities) in 1988 were said to distribute over 75 per cent of the merchandise sold in the retailer's stores. Another DC was completed in New Braunfels, TX, and the year saw Walmart's 10,000 distribution employees processing over 300 million cases of product. Walmart's on-time delivery rate stood at 99 per cent and filling accuracy exceeded 99 per cent.

Food for thought

In the late 1980s, Walmart began entering the grocery market in a concerted way. The ultimately unsuccessful opening of Hypermart*USA stores began in 1987, with the Walmart Supercenter concept making its debut the following year. As Walmart began to ramp up the amount of food offered through its stores, the retailer began to contemplate how best to integrate grocery products into its logistics infrastructure.

Walmart had some experience in grocery supply chain, thanks to the bulk food assortment carried in its Sam's Club chain which had been trading since 1983. Nonetheless, it lacked the necessary expertise in grocery supply chain for its retail operations, so initially began servicing its Hypermart and Walmart Supercenter chains by using specialist wholesalers. Hypermart was a joint venture with Cullum Companies, the Texan food retail concern that operated a number of supermarket brands including Tom Thumb, now operated by leading US supermarket chain Safeway, so it was able to draw on Cullum Companies' expertise in food supply.

Walmart soon began developing the capability to handle a wide variety of grocery categories, retrofitting coolers and freezers to existing DCs and adding specialized chilled and freezer trailers to its trucking fleet. Eventually, when the volume of groceries Walmart was selling reached viable levels, it began adding specialist grocery DCs to its network, as well as acquiring grocery distributor McLane (see below).

Walmart's square footage of distribution facilities increased from 11.8 million to 14.6 million sq. ft in 1990. The extra space included the new DCs in Seymour, IN, Searcy, AR, and Loveland, CO, as well as a specialist shoe distribution facility in Ft Smith, AR. The year 1991 saw the addition of three new DCs – each in excess of 1 million sq. ft – in Porterville, CA, Sutherland, VA, and Greencastle, IN. In 1992, Walmart's convenience wholesale division McLane opened its first full-line grocery DC in Clarksville, AR. The 705,000 sq. ft DC was designed to serve the nascent Walmart Supercenter chain with food products.

By the early 1990s, Walmart's distribution system comprised 22 DCs averaging nearly 1 million sq. ft and had 'made just-in-time inventory management a reality for us and our vendors'. New DCs were being built in Menomonie, WI, and Clearfield, PA, as well as a speciality facility in Hurricane, UT, and a long-term storage facility in Buckeye, AZ.

The development of Walmart's general distribution infrastructure was accompanied by the growth of speciality distribution functions that Walmart acquired. By the 1990s, McLane was serving selected Walmart, Sam's Club and Supercenter units, while speciality distribution subsidiary Western Merchandisers provided videos, cassettes, CDs and books to around 850 Walmart stores. Western Merchandisers became a Walmart subsidiary in 1990 before being sold to Anderson News Corporation in 1994.

Acquired in late 1990, McLane was a leading wholesaler and distributor of grocery products for around 26,000 retail customers (mainly convenience stores as well as supermarkets, restaurants and general merchandise chains) and operated 14 DCs in 11 states, providing over 12,500 SKUs of perishable and non-perishable groceries and general merchandise.

Although McLane was sold in 2003 to Warren Buffett's investment vehicle Berkshire Hathaway, it is still a vital component of Walmart's distribution capabilities. As previously discussed, McLane is still responsible for supplying the retailer with confectionery and cigarettes. Walmart, presumably, has continued with this arrangement as it makes economic sense compared to the alternative – bringing it in-house – and it means that for suppliers like Hershey and Altria, McLane is the principal route to getting their products onto Walmart's shelves.

Project Remix

Possibly the biggest recent step change in the evolution of Walmart's distribution network was the 2006 'Remix' project. This initiative saw the merging of Walmart's Grocery DC network and its Regional General Merchandise DC network. Each network was once a specialist operation – the Grocery Network handling dry grocery goods, such as cereals and snacks, and the Regional Network moving primarily general merchandise, such as household cleaners, paper towels, toys and electronics. In 2006, that changed when approximately 4,000 items switched networks, meaning that high-velocity items – both grocery and general merchandise – were combined and sent to the stores from the 'High Velocity Distribution Centres'.

Walmart described the process as an innovative 'Remix' which meant that items needed most by customers arrived at stores on one truck, so they could be unloaded and moved faster to the shelves. Pallets were assembled in DCs with the store layout in mind, enabling them to be rolled directly onto the shop floor for rapid replenishment. Previously, FMCGs were delivered on the same trucks as slower-moving lines such as clothing and household goods, often meaning that store staff had to hunt through a mixed delivery to seek out the items most in need of replenishment. The move also meant that Walmart could reduce the number of additional RDCs it needed in its network going forward. Stores benefited from improved merchandise flow and in-stock positions, while Walmart reduced its capital spending needs. Furthermore, Remix meant that Walmart was pushing complexity and costs further up the supply chain and away from itself: a typical move from the retailer.

In addition to reducing costs, the main objective of the Remix programme for Walmart was to improve its in-stock position. Walmart's availability rates were already high, typically ranging between 97 and 98 per cent, Vice President of Supply Chain Systems Randy Salley told industry journal *Chain Store Age* at the time. But the out-of-stocks tended to be in the retailer's fastest-selling lines, such as paper towels and toothpaste and other consumables. After Remix, Salley noted that 'the primary difference is that everything that comes out of a grocery or high-velocity DC is loaded on a pallet that goes directly onto the trailer. Then, the pallet rolls out onto the sales floor for quick shelf restocking.'[3]

A third-party solutions provider involved in the Remix programme was DSC, a company that assisted suppliers through offering consolidation programmes. Walmart's Remix initiative acted to increase the number of orders received by vendors and at the same time reduced the size of those orders, causing a shift to less-than-truckload (LTL) deliveries. LTL deliveries are less efficient for suppliers, meaning that vendors needed to convert LTL to truckload (TL) deliveries to gain efficiencies and improve their service to Walmart. DSC offered this consolidation service for suppliers at five Multi-Vendor Optimization Strategy (MOST) centres across the country.

The MOST consolidation centres (in Dallas, TX, Atlanta, GA, Chicago, IL, Los Angeles, NV, and Allentown, PA) combined orders for multiple Walmart vendors and delivered full truckloads weekly to each of Walmart's 40 regional Remix DCs. DSC managed Walmart's appointment process, ensuring that loads arrived on time and were compliant with Walmart's delivery expectations. With DSC, Walmart suppliers were able to prevent out-of-stocks, make deliveries more consistent and achieve shorter transit times. Tests conducted by Walmart revealed that vendors who participated in a consolidation programme enjoyed a 37 per cent better on-time performance, with the retailer noting that consolidation reduces costs, improves service and increases sales.[4]

Supplier collaboration

Walmart was a fairly pioneering retailer in that it sought to collaborate with its suppliers in order to improve logistics in a way intended to benefit Walmart, the supplier and the shopper. The development of Retail Link and similar systems and technologies enabled Walmart and its suppliers to achieve previously unheard of visibility and predictability within the supply chain, allowing Walmart to create huge efficiencies (and therefore lower prices) and to present consumers with industry-leading availability.

Don Soderquist states that, while Walmart was busily improving its supply chain capabilities, there was still something of a disconnect in the system: 'to put it simply, we were doing our thing, and the suppliers were doing theirs... we were not working together for the benefit of our customers.'[5] We will return to the issue of supplier collaboration, including technologies such as Retail Link, in more detail in the following chapter.

Globalizing supply chain excellence

In its global operations (as of March 2011), Walmart utilized a total of 134 distribution facilities in Argentina, Brazil, Canada, Chile, China, Costa Rica, El Salvador, Guatemala, Honduras, Japan, Mexico, Nicaragua, Puerto Rico and the UK, including two export consolidation facilities in the United States. Through these facilities, Walmart processed and distributed both imported and US products to the operating units of the Walmart International division. During 2010, approximately 77 per cent of the International segment's purchases flowed through these distribution facilities. Suppliers shipped the balance of the International segment's purchases directly to stores in the various countries in which Walmart traded. Of the 134 distribution facilities, Walmart owned and operated 34 and leased and operated 38. Third parties owned and operated the remaining distribution facilities.

As Walmart expanded from its humble Arkansas roots to become the global giant with a foot in every continent, it faced – and arguably met – the challenge of exporting its undoubted supremacy in supply chain and logistics to all of its operating markets. Indeed, it is noteworthy that supply chain (along with systems and procurement) has been cited as a key benefit of Walmart entering a new market and/or acquiring an international business to bring into the global Walmart family. This observation has been more pronounced when Walmart has entered a so-called 'emerging' market such as Africa or India.

Walmart's 2010/11 move into sub-Saharan Africa through the acquisition of a 51 per cent stake in South African retailer Massmart is a case in point. The two retailers noted during the progression of the deal that:

> As the largest retailer in the world, Walmart is renowned for its operating, retailing, marketing and merchandising skills and its leading-edge procurement and supply chain capabilities developed over many years of investing and trading across developed and developing countries. By gaining access to Walmart's experience and capabilities relating to procurement and supply chain, particularly in relation to fresh food retailing, Massmart will be able to deliver a wider selection of quality products which are more consistently available to customers.

A similar logic was at play in Walmart's entry to India, this time effected through a joint venture with local conglomerate Bharti. The joint venture, which has seen the opening of easyday stores run by Bharti and cash & carry stores operated by the joint venture itself (a reflection of the government's protectionist restrictions rather than any strategic preference from Walmart), has been widely flagged as potentially one of the best things to have happened to the sometimes chaotic and often wasteful Indian supply chain. Walmart's expertise in supply chain – particularly in relation to perishable and agricultural categories – has been identified since the first days of the joint venture to be a key attribute that it brings to the project. As the companies have remarked, Walmart is 'renowned for its efficiency and expertise in logistics, supply chain management and sourcing. The joint venture is establishing wholesale cash & carry and back-end supply chain management operations.'

It is these back-end supply chain operations that both Bharti and Walmart hope will have a transformative impact on the Indian fresh chain:

> The joint venture works with the existing supply chain infrastructure to help make it more efficient, thereby maximizing value for farmers and manufacturers on the one end and retailers, and in turn, consumers on the other. The supply chain operation supports farmers and small manufacturers who have limited infrastructure and distribution strength and help minimize wastage, particularly of fresh foods and vegetables. An efficient supply chain can play an important role in transforming farmers and small manufacturers into successful entrepreneurs.

While such a statement should always be viewed through the lens of stripping away corporate flimflam, we find it hard to disagree that Walmart's influence, know-how and ruthless efficiency will have anything but a hugely positive impact on the evolution of Indian farmers' efficiency and speed to market. The same could be said of Walmart's global competitors in India – most notably Carrefour and Metro – but Walmart's pre-eminence in supply chain suggests that its legacy might be more impactful and enduring.

Globalizing one country at a time

Unlike with the export of its IT and systems capabilities, where global standardization is very much the norm for Walmart (90 per cent of its systems around the world are virtually identical), Walmart's supply chain operations on a global level are developed on a market-by-market basis.

Walmart has dubbed this supply chain strategy 'best in market', preferring to adapt its logistics capabilities on a country-by-country basis rather than adopting a completely standardized global model to serve its stores in markets outside North America. This strategy was influenced by experiences such as the markedly different logistical challenges that Walmart encountered in markets as diverse as Mexico, China and Germany. Indeed, Walmart's failure to fully grasp the idiosyncratic realities of the German supply chain (and, to be fair, a remarkably uncooperative bunch of suppliers) was one of the straws that broke the camel's back in that particular market.

As Bjorn Weber, the supply chain expert at Planet Retail, notes, Walmart's abject failure in the German market was at least partially attributable to the retailer's cack-handed attempts to export US supply chain orthodoxies to an entirely unsuitable market: in Germany, Walmart tried to replicate its domestic system of suppliers of certain categories delivering directly to stores. The net result was very long queues of trucks at the front of stores with one or two receiving gates, causing huge frustration among both the vendor community and Walmart's in-store personnel.[6]

Experiences such as this resulted in Walmart adopting a more localized approach to subsequent international adventures. In 2009, Walmart's Senior Vice President of International Supply Chain Gary Maxwell reported at a conference that the 'best in market' strategy has worked well for the company. When Walmart acquires a foreign company or moves into a new market, the retailer now examines the situation in each locale, analysing factors such as land and labour costs, local regulations, asset utilization, and risk. 'In some places, you can't afford automation [in a warehouse]', Maxwell said. 'In other markets, if regulations tell how many pounds a worker can lift, you're going to put in automation.' Maxwell noted that when Walmart sets up a supply chain for a particular country, it takes into account what consumers in that country can afford.

Referring to Bharti-Walmart's first DC in India – an 80,000 sq. ft dry grocery warehouse located in Chandigarh, Punjab, Maxwell noted that 'Our first warehouse in India was small and had no automation. We had racks and forklifts because that was what the customer could afford.' In Japan, on the other hand, consumers have a different set of expectations, and Walmart's warehouses employ technology such as sortation systems, radio-frequency picking, automated cranes and mini-load systems. 'Each piece of technology [in Japan] is targeted at keeping product at a certain quality', he said. As the retail market in a particular country matures (and presumably as labour costs rise), Walmart responds by introducing more sophistication (ie automation) into its supply chains. 'We need to build a best-in-class supply chain for today,' Maxwell said, 'and then we'll evolve the supply chain'.[7]

In 2011, Walmart provided some interesting insight into the benefits it can bring to an acquired business – in this case its Japanese division Seiyu.

Japanese retailing and wholesaling has traditionally been characterized by a fairly labyrinthine (ie inefficient) network of wholesalers, distributors and agencies (or as Walmart would refer to them: margin-takers). Scott Price, Walmart EVP and President and CEO of Walmart Asia, stated that the entire supply chain and the distribution process were 'an opportunity to take waste out of the system'. He stated that Seiyu, when Walmart acquired it, had a very inefficient operating structure: 'They had 48 distribution centres, which we felt was actually ineffective. We were able very quickly to go from 48 down to 25. After we went into those 25 in parallel, we were also introducing a number of initiatives to be able to ensure that those 25 were actually pretty efficient in terms of costs.'

Price reported that Walmart introduced a lean operation:

> We increased the cube, the volumetric utilization of all the trucks that were going in and out of those distribution centres, and then we optimized the truck and the delivery routing to be able to reduce the number of trucks required but also to improve the fuel efficiency. The final phase of that initiative was to take back control. So, we were outsourcing those 25 following the old model. We did a test, which was to take over self-operation of two distribution centres. And what we found is, even after all that lean operation effort, there was still room in terms of being able to take cost out of the system.

Having seen the benefits of the first two DCs being brought back in-house, Walmart then sought to bring all them into self-operation. The results were pretty impressive: a 52 per cent increase in terms of the DC cases per labour hour but as well a 36 per cent decrease in the overall cost per distribution centre per case.

Greening the supply chain

As in virtually every other part of its business, the issue of environmental sustainability is pervading Walmart's logistical operations. Sustainability is one of those areas – including e-commerce, private label and some aspects of marketing – where Walmart International leads the agenda as much as, if not more than, its parent company in the United States.

Throughout the following examples, it is always worth remembering that virtually all of them illustrate the fact that saving money (or pursuing its EDLC strategy) is at the heart of most Walmart strategies. To its credit, Walmart makes no bones about this fact: the retailer has little time for the expensive showboating and grandstanding exhibited by some other retailers around the world. For an environmental initiative to be worthwhile for Walmart, it must have a positive impact on profitability. As noted by a Walmart Canada executive recently, the retailer is anxious to demonstrate that 'environmental sustainability can go hand-in-hand with business sustainability'.

In early 2010, Walmart Canada was a key protagonist in a major Green Business Summit, an event that brought together Walmart suppliers, competitors and high-level executives from the technology, telecommunications, retail, finance, education, architectural and environmental sectors to share business initiatives that are 'good for the planet and good for the bottom line'. Speaking alongside the event, David Cheesewright, President and CEO of Walmart Canada, stated: 'We have a great opportunity to usher in a new era of collaboration and sharing when it comes to green business practices. While much work still needs to be done, there is already some strong sustainability work happening across Canadian organizations.' Also at the event were senior executives from Maple Leaf Foods, Coca-Cola Bottling Company, Alcan Packaging, McDonald's, The Home Depot Canada, 3M Canada, Bissell, Canadian Tire, Hewlett-Packard Canada, Kraft Canada, PepsiCo Foods Canada and SC Johnson.

Walmart Canada used the stage of the Green Business Summit to unveil a raft of new sustainability initiatives, some of which are already making a clear impact on the Canadian vendor community. Walmart has been proactive in the realm of environmentally responsible retailing in markets such as the UK, the United States and Mexico (indeed, the retailer has initiated some impressive initiatives in all of its operating markets) and Canada has seen some interesting new schemes that the retailer hopes will be benefiting not just the planet, but also its profitability.

Alongside the revelation of plans for an environmentally friendly distribution centre in Balzac, Alberta (see below), Walmart also unveiled its Sustainable Product Index, a scheme that had already been implemented by Walmart US and was designed to help customers across Canada evaluate the sustainability of the products they purchase, all the way through from raw materials to disposal. Announced by Walmart in the United States in 2009, Walmart Canada was the first Walmart operation outside the United States to initiate the process for the product index. 'Customers want value and quality when buying products', said David Cheesewright. 'They also want to know that products are being made in a responsible way. Once launched, the Sustainable Product Index will give customers transparency into the entire lifecycle of the products they buy, so they know they're safe, made-well and produced responsibly.' The scheme involves suppliers answering 15 key questions regarding the sustainability credentials of its sourcing, manufacturing and packaging processes before being evaluated against an as yet undetermined set of criteria to create an overall index measure that can guide consumers on making more informed environmental choices.

This is but one example of initiatives being undertaken by Walmart divisions around the world to lessen the environmental impact of the supply chain and logistics functions upon which we all depend as consumers. A few more examples from around the world of Walmart are presented below.

Sustainable distribution centres – Canada, Mexico and Brazil

In late 2010, Walmart Canada opened its sustainable fresh food distribution centre, a state-of-the-art facility that is an estimated 60 per cent more energy-efficient than the company's traditional refrigerated centres. One of North America's most energy-efficient distribution centres, the Balzac facility was described by the retailer as a 'living lab of sustainability' and included Walmart Canada's first pilots of hydrogen fuel cells, solar thermal and wind power, as well as many other sustainability features and products.

Andy Ellis, Walmart Canada's SVP of Supply Chain and Logistics, stated: 'Our sustainable distribution centre showcases the immediate business returns of investing in green innovations and the positive impact of a sustainability mind-set through all phases of a project.' Walmart Canada has also been working with its suppliers to increase its logistics efficiency and to incorporate sustainable practices and initiatives into the processes, operations and mind-set of its third-party suppliers. The company has instituted no-idling policies in all its stores and distribution centres, improved fill rates on trucks and increased use of long-combination vehicles.

It is not just in Canada that DCs are being targeted for environmental improvements. A recently opened DC in Culiacán, Mexico, was built to stringent environmental guidelines and includes sustainable features such as a wastewater plant, two artificial lagoons for rainwater harvesting, extensive recycling facilities, energy-saving lighting and ventilation with intelligent controls. A similar project was undertaken in Betim, Brazil, with the DC there featuring a sewage treatment system, permeable paving, solar water heating, skylights and dimmable lights.

Walmart – notoriously a tough competitor to cross swords with – is to be lauded for launching an inclusive forum to which its competitors were welcomed. It is only through collaborative strategies such as this that any meaningful environmental progress will be made.

Shifting to rail rather than road

As early as 2006, Walmart US worked with shipping supplier SCM to change the mode of shipping from road to rail on 10 of its existing routes. For those routes that could not be replicated by rail, Walmart US converted the vehicles to electricity. The combined effort reportedly reduced CO_2 emissions by 2,600 tonnes and fuel consumption by 40,000 litres and paid back $2 million per annum in savings.

Walmart's UK business, Asda, has also been a key advocate of using more rail transport within its transport repertoire. Since 2001, Asda has worked on moving the transport of goods from road to rail. By 2008, Asda's rail service operated six days a week, moving 40 containers per day, from Daventry to Grangemouth and from Grangemouth to Aberdeen. This saved approximately 7.2 million miles of road travel, an increase of 3.3 million miles since 2007. The Asda produce train also runs throughout the summer season from Tilbury to Wakefield with produce from South Africa. The train makes 800 journeys per year and delivers containers to within two miles of their destination, saving 200,000 miles a year.

Using more efficient trucks

Walmart US aims to increase the fuel efficiency of its fleet by 100 per cent by 2015 (using 2005 as a baseline). By 2008, Walmart US Transportation had achieved more than a 25 per cent increase in fuel efficiency, exceeding one of its early sustainability goals. Of the 25 per cent efficiency gain, 15 per cent resulted from a change in the fuel additive mix, coupled with the use of more efficient tyre compounds and the installation of small diesel generators. The remaining 10 per cent reduction came from aerodynamic improvements and the use of lighter components. Again, cost reductions were not far away: savings were estimated at between $35 million and $50 million.

Packaging Scorecard

Walmart aims to achieve a 5 per cent reduction in overall packaging by 2013, an achievement that Walmart believes could create savings in its supply chain of $3.4 billion, and in the global supply chain of nearly $11 billion. A key component of this effort was the introduction of Walmart's Packaging Scorecard in 2008. The scorecard measures: the average distance that each product is transported; its size; the energy used and greenhouse gas emissions created during the production of the packaging; the sustainability of the packaging material; the use of recycled content and its ability to be recycled after use. By August 2008, 199 unique vendors had accessed the scorecard website and more than 170,000 products had been entered onto the system, and Walmart has also developed versions of the scorecard for Canada, Latin America and Europe. The packaging reduction programme also applies to Walmart's private label products in addition to manufacturers' brands: Walmart's Kid Connection line of toys saw a reduction in packaging that led to the retailer needing nearly 500 fewer containers to ship the same number of items. This has led to an approximate saving of (according to the retailer) $2.4 million in shipping costs, 3,000 trees and 1,000 barrels of oil per year.

Implications for suppliers

For vendors, it is worth remembering that partnering with Walmart in environmental matters is an effective way of bolstering the relationship with

Walmart and also improving sales. A number of suppliers have told us that participating in Walmart initiatives on issues such as packaging reduction, improving a product's green credentials or boosting logistical efficiencies have led to a better relationship with the retailer and a more mutually beneficial way of doing business.

The same goes for vendors and service providers in the spheres of supply chain and technology. Any innovation that reduces environmental impact and increases efficiency (and therefore profits) will be smiled on by Walmart, so there are clear opportunities for suppliers to participate in Walmart's greening of the supply chain. It seems increasingly likely that Walmart's 'best practice' supply chain initiatives (in terms of environmental responsibility and efficiency gains) will be taken global by the retailer, so vendors that deal with Walmart across the world might be well advised to consult with their colleagues in the United States, Canada, Mexico or the UK on the best way to engage with this process.

Walmart's leadership in distribution was developed hand-in-hand with its pioneering approach to the adoption of technology. In the following chapter we will assess Walmart's leadership in technology and the impact that the retailer's early adoption of such technologies had on the growth of its business.

Notes

1   Soderquist, D (2005) *The Wal-Mart Way: The inside story of the success of the world's largest company*, Thomas Nelson, Nashville, TN, p 151

2   Soderquist, p 157

3   http://goliath.ecnext.com/coms2/gi_0198-285227/
Wal-Smart-the-world-s.html

4   http://www.dsclogistics.com/solutions_spec_wmr.php

5   Soderquist, p 165

6   www.planetretail.net

7   http://www.supplychainquarterly.com/conferences/post/?doc_
id=1&utm_medium=email&utm_source=Email%20marketing%20
software&utm_content=610891743&utm_campaign=Post-ConferenceCS
CMP20092009Oct8+_+kuhlm&utm_term=Wal-Martbuildsbest-in-
marketsupplychainforoverseasstores

The surest way to predict the future is to invent it

09

Alongside its sheer scale, the areas of supply chain and systems have been justifiably lauded as two of Walmart's key competitive advantages. In the words of Don Soderquist:

> Technology has been an enabler and facilitator of change throughout Walmart. It has made it possible for us to dramatically change not only the way we do business, but also the way that business is conducted in the entire industry. As a result of the support of senior leadership, Walmart has consistently been on the leading edge of practical technological breakthroughs in equipment, software, and communications technology, a proactive approach that has kept us far ahead of all competitors in taking advantage of the opportunities that technology affords.[1]

This is a sentiment echoed by Bob Ortega, who notes that 'Men such as Jack Shewmaker and David Glass, who were quick to grasp the implications of these technologies, put Walmart at the forefront of this revolution; and it would be hard to overstate how crucial Walmart's head start would be to its success'.[2]

James Hoopes remarked in his excellent analysis of the role of 'growth through knowledge' in Walmart's rise to leadership: 'Information technology has made Walmart superbly efficient not in spite of but because of its gargantuan size and highly centralized organization. Fleeter of foot than the smaller forms with flattened hierarchies that are supposedly the nimblest competitors in the knowledge economy, Walmart shows that high technology is fostering its own form of the huge, highly centralized corporation run with ruthless, hierarchical efficiency.'[3]

When we asked a senior insider at Walmart if the retailer was still occupying its place at the bleeding edge of technology, they answered, 'Not really anymore. We obviously used to be the leader, but everyone else has caught up. Our biggest single advantage globally is our supply chain. We still kick ass in logistics.' So, while some, if not all, of Walmart's advantage in IT and systems has been eroded by competitors in a wide variety of retail sectors, it remains the case that Walmart's use of technology was one of the key underpinnings of its emergence into true global retail supremacy. In the words of one-time Senior Vice President and Chief Information Officer Randy Mott, 'The surest way to predict the future is to invent it.'

The retailer (which can translate as Sam Walton in the early years), as in many areas, grudgingly and almost resentfully embraced the need for investment in technology. That is not to say that Sam Walton did not appreciate the exciting potential afforded to the retailer – he most certainly did – but it is equally certain that he resented the large initial capital outlay on what was then relatively unproven technology. As with supply chain development, Walmart's adoption and implementation of technology, despite being a fairly ad hoc and relatively thrifty transformation, was one of the genuine enablers that propelled Walmart from being a backwoods discounter to become an epoch-making commercial powerhouse.

Many of those who worked for and with Walton in the 1960s, 70s and 80s recall – with a discernible level of fondness – how Walton would have to be badgered into making technology investments, or how some projects would be developed behind his back until such time as he could be presented with a compelling business case or a virtual fait accompli. As Walton himself acknowledged, 'Jack (Shewmaker) is absolutely right about me and systems, though. I rarely get excited about them.'[4]

Walton went on to admit that 'as Chairman of Walmart, I, of course, was the one who ultimately authorized all of those expenditures for technology, which proved absolutely crucial to our success. But truthfully, I never viewed computers as anything more than necessary overhead. A computer is not – and never will be – a substitute for getting out in your stores and learning what's going on. In other words, a computer can tell you down to the dime what you've sold. But it can never tell you what you could have sold.'[5] This statement was undoubtedly true at the time that Walton wrote it, but it should be noted that technology has moved on since. Modern predictive analytics is being used within retail to fill in the gaps in the demand curves that retailers build for forecasting, taking into account variables such as availability, assortment and shopper trends.

As with so many key developments in retailers' evolution, the advent of the computer-powered Walmart was fuelled by Sam Walton's thirst for knowledge and improvement and his proactive stance on meeting, and learning from, other key figures in the US retail industry. In this case, it was a late 1960s meeting with Abe Marks, the head of department store chain Hartfield Zody's and first president of the National Mass Retailers' Institute. With a desire to learn about IBM computers, Walton travelled to an IBM school for retailers in Poughkeepsie, NY, and it was there that he met Marks, one of the speakers at the event.

The two struck up a friendship and Walton subsequently visited Marks to try to learn as much as possible about retail technology. As Marks recalls:

> He (Walton) has just been a master of taking the best out of everything and adapting it to his own needs... By being at that conference, he was absolutely in the right place at the right time. There were no such things in those days as minicomputers and microcomputers. He was really ten years away from the computer world coming. But he was preparing himself. And this is a very important point: without the computer, Sam Walton could not have done what he's done. He could not have built a retailing empire the size of what he's built, the way he built it. He's done a lot of other things right too, but he could not have done it without the computer. It would have been impossible.[6]

Technology takes hold in the 1970s

By the early 1970s, Walmart was able to boast a Data Processing Department, and it was this department that installed a Singer System 10 network to communicate with stores. By the end of the year, the system was 'polling' (ie extracting data from) 22 outlets. The department also put the retailer's softlines DC 'on line', enabling it to review styles and create a shipping manifest. Other highlights at this time included the creation of a vendor system for DC rebuyers and the replacement of an IBM 360/20 mainframe with an IBM 370/125. It should be pointed out that both these models were mainframes rather than more modern servers, which had yet to be invented. Indeed, readers are likely to have more computing power in their iPhone than either of these mainframes had, but they were state of the art at the time and proved remarkably durable: even Tesco was still running some systems on very stable, very old mainframe infrastructure as recently as a few years ago.

By 1975, Walmart was leasing an IBM 370/135 computer to track inventory on an item level for merchandise in the retailer's DC and on a category level in stores. The computer also held data on payroll, accounts payable and sales by department for each store, and provided income data for each store. Walmart noted in 1975 that it ran Singer electronic cash registers in 64 stores and NCR mechanical and electronic registers in 71 stores.

The late 1970s saw an acceleration of investment in technology, with Sam Walton being pushed by some of his hires to implement key innovations. As Walton recalls:

> David Glass and Jack Shewmaker were pushing hard for heavy investment in more and more, better and better computer systems, so we could track sales and merchandise and inventories across the company – especially instore transactions. When Jack became our President in 1978, he worked really hard at getting me to invest in bar coding and SKU item control, which is a computerized stock keeping unit inventory control system. Jack was also heavily involved in the creation of our satellite system, which turned out to be one of our tremendous competitive advantages.[7]

In 1977, Walmart completed the installation of a company-wide computer terminal network and stated that it was one of very few US retailers to possess an 'intelligent' in-store computer terminal. The terminals enabled messages to be sent to and from stores. Stores were therefore able to place merchandise orders directly, as the terminals 'talked' to Walmart's computer (note the absence of a plural there), enabling orders to be processed more quickly. Corporate payroll was also installed on the system, enabling store managers to keep abreast of each store's payroll costs and transmit those to head office. Tellingly, Walmart stated that these developments enabled it to 'communicate with its 195 stores within hours – not days'.

The following year signalled a step change in Walmart's approach to information technology: the construction of a 16,000 sq. ft facility designed to house the 'latest in technological advancements in data-processing equipment'. Walmart noted that each new store was equipped with an IBM 3774 terminal and that it enjoyed better communications with its 229 stores than it did when its store-count was only 40.

Noting that each store was in constant communication with each warehouse, Walmart added that its General Office handles over 500,000 'item reactions' each week, with communications being transmitted over telephone lines. The retailer said that the information carried on each computer was 'mammoth', including data on payroll, bank deposits, daily sales from each store's 36 departments, estimated sales figures, warehouse inventory and hot-selling items. The year 1978 also saw an effective doubling of Walmart's IT capacity: the retailer stated that it was the proud owner of two central computers: IBM 370s, Model 148. With signs that the retailer was realizing the potential of this nascent technology, it revealed the existence of a 'computer development group' tasked with keeping up to speed with technological advances in order to accelerate communications and refine the usability of data.

In a fit of honesty – perhaps even humour – Walmart concluded that: 'The financial savings and the number of personnel hours saved daily by using the computer centre is incalculable – even by the computer.'

The 1980s: technology acceleration in-store

At the start of the new decade, Walmart lauded the benefits of the progress it had seen in its store computer terminal network, as it enabled the tracking of inventory, provided a mechanism for replenishment and kept management informed of sales trends.

In a progressive development, Walmart revealed that it was trialling scanning technology in order to improve accuracy and the front-end experience for shoppers. In a prescient comment (some 30 years before the same suspicions were levelled at the introduction of self-checkout by many retailers, including Walmart), the retailer insisted that new technologies were designed to be people-supportive, not implemented to replace people.

The next few years saw a number of key developments, including the 1981 deployment of a purchase order management system and successful completion of the trial of point-of-sale scanning systems. The next year witnessed the upgrade of in-store back-office computers to offer greater capacity and lower running costs. Further tests were completed of point-of-scale electronic scanning systems and the company's merchandising function was adapted to enable electronic purchase order management.

The year 1983 saw the completion of the back-office computer upgrade and a reaffirmation of Walmart's commitment to a test of electronic scanning of the UPC (Uniform Product Code) at point-of-sale by expanding the test to 25 stores. An additional 70 stores were pledged, with the trial being expanded to 200 stores in the following year. Don Soderquist recalls of the embryonic barcoding system: 'the retailing industry did not generally accept UPC in its early days. Many thought it would be impossible to get everyone to agree on standardization and that the method would ultimately cost too much for everyone to adopt. Our perseverance prevailed, though, and we made it happen.'[8]

Other initiatives in 1983 included the installation of bespoke computers in a number of pharmacies and the start of work on a regional merchandising system to account for the idiosyncrasies of certain regions and individual stores.

The year 1984, ironically the title of George Orwell's 1949 dystopian vision of the future which predicted a world of technology-enabled surveillance, was the year that Walmart announced the signing of a contract for the purchase of a satellite communications system intended eventually to link all stores and DCs with its head office. The system was intended to allow information to be simultaneously sent and received from office to stores as well as the transmission of television communications to announce company news and conduct training. Initial testing began with the installation of earth stations at head office and two distant distribution facilities.

In another sign of Walton's reluctance concerning hefty technology investments, Jack Shewmaker recalled how 'Glenn (Habern, data processing manager) and I came up with the idea of using the satellite and I said "Let's pursue it without asking anybody." So we got it to the point where we were ready to make a proposal and we told Sam. He just listened, he didn't necessarily discourage me. But he didn't encourage me either. Sam never gets excited about systems.'[9]

With regard to the satellite network, Sam Walton described the fundamental part it played in the retailer's success:

The satellite turned out to be absolutely necessary because, once we had those scanners in the stores, we had all this data pouring into Bentonville over the phone lines. Those lines have a limited capacity, so as we added more and more stores, we had a real logjam of stuff coming in from the field. As you know, I like my numbers as quickly as I can get them. The quicker we get information, the quicker we can act on it. The system has been a great tool for us, and our technical people have done a terrific job of figuring out how to use it to our best advantage.

The same year saw Walmart provide an update on its purchase order management system. The company stated that the system allowed its merchandising division to store information on vendors and merchandise and access order information through computer terminals. Walmart added that Telxon handheld terminals enabled in-store personnel to reorder merchandise. In-store associates were also able to use the handset to scan shelf labels in order to access information on quantities ordered and the cost and retail price of the item. Walmart concluded that the system saved time and improved the efficiency of the reordering process.

In an update on its regional merchandising programme, Walmart reported that the programme relied on CAD (computer-aided design) to tailor each store's offer based on 128 traits such as climate, ethnic orientation, recreational preferences and the characteristics of local catchment areas (which were classed as rural/urban, military/college town etc.). The findings were used to determine store layout and departmental adjacencies. The retailer also revealed that it had installed a Human Resources System in 1984, enabling it to maintain a profile of each employee that included details such as salary information, training details and education etc.

Scanning at checkout was also gathering pace. While the retailer noted that it had historically limited data collection at checkout to the barest minimum in order to expedite the checkout process, Walmart described how the testing of electronic scanning of the UPC at checkout had enabled it to rapidly process price and merchandise information, assisting in replenishment efforts, as well as creating a much speedier checkout process for customers. As a consequence, Walmart pledged that all 115 new stores opened in 1985 would feature UPC scanning and that the system would eventually be rolled out across the chain.

In 1985, the company confirmed that UPC scanning had been expanded to 235 stores and that the satellite system had been installed and was functioning in a number of locations. The Walmart Satellite Network (WSN) was to be rolled out to 600 stores and seven DCs over the course of the year, with complete deployment scheduled for the middle of calendar 1987. The benefits were said to include improved voice and data communications as well as a reduction in credit-card approval times to around four or five seconds.

In a key strategic move – which began joining the dots between stores and Walmart's logistics network – the Douglas, GA, DC began operations in January 1986 using a UPC barcode laser scanning system similar to that used in stores, enabling a faster and more accurate flow of merchandise. Walmart again reiterated that all stores and DCs would be converted to this system by mid-1987. The system enabled store staff to receive and price-mark products using a handheld scanner, therefore bypassing the previously onerous paperwork.

UPC scanning in-store, in addition to the previously cited benefits for both retailer and shopper, had allowed the retailer to install a new 'Data Collect' function. This function allowed store managers to gather and analyse sales on an item-specific level, better enabling them to maintain an in-stock position on bestsellers and minimize shrink by providing greater visibility into the capture and recording of mark-downs.

Walmart revealed in 1986 that the trial of the UPC barcode laser scanning system in the Douglas, GA, DC had been a success and that all other DCs would be retrofitted with the system. The benefits of the system for stores were said to include more efficient paperless billing and automated receiving, the latter of which was said to provide a time saving of around 60 per cent compared to previous systems. In-store Series One computers matched the receipts against shipments and processed the necessary claims; all data were then transmitted via satellite to head office.

It becomes clear in this narrative that so many things that retailers and shoppers now take for granted were fairly innovative as recently as 25 years ago. For instance, it was only in 1987 that Walmart stated that the removal of price tags from items – replaced by on-shelf labelling – was being trialled in five stores and could represent significant cost savings if rolled out.

The year 1987 was something of a keystone year for Walmart's emergence as one of the most tech-savvy retailers on the face of the planet: the roll-out of in-store scanning was completed, as was the installation of the WSN, the largest private satellite network in the United States. WSN, scanning, automated receiving and the Telxon merchandising reordering were combined by Walmart as the foundation of future applications and systems development.

Walmart continued to pursue technological enhancements to its operations throughout the 1990s. In 1996, the retailer revealed how its in-store operations were being improved by the use of 'magic wands' (handheld computers) that enabled in-store employees to manage the 70,000 or 90,000 SKUs carried in a discount store or Supercenter, respectively. The handhelds were linked by a radio-frequency network to in-store terminals, enabling in-store associates to track inventory on hand, backup merchandise and deliveries. 'What it's really about is putting information in people's hands', said Randy Mott, Senior Vice President and Chief Information Officer at the time. 'We're careful not to get too enamoured with all the bells and whistles of technology. It's there to support people.'

Around this time, Walmart revealed that it had an annual technology and communications budget of $500 million and an information systems staff of 1,200. For the sake of context, that budget was equivalent to around 0.5 per cent of turnover. The average retail IT budget is around 4 per cent of sales now, but often only around 2 per cent of sales for grocers. 'With this technology, we're getting better, quicker and more accurate information to manage and control every aspect of our business', Mott said. 'Walmart has always been intensely conscious of holding down expenses, because that's another way we can have lower prices, better merchandise and service for our customers and better returns for our investors. We may be talking about state-of-the-art computer systems, but the way we manage them is pure Walmart.'

As we've seen in the previous chapter, the combination of forward-looking technology and Walmart's burgeoning expertise in logistics was a killer strength for the business, enabling it to brush aside its competitors in its march to world supremacy. By the late 1990s, Walmart was able to tell investors that it 'leads the retail industry with its version of a "just in time" supply system in which computers track every product and automatically alert warehouses when it's time to restock the shelves'. The company provided an example of how its operational improvements directly contributed to returns for investors: despite a 12 per cent increase in sales in 1998, the company saw only a 4 per cent increase in inventories, saving about $1.4 billion. Rather than blindly slashing inventory, Walmart used the data gathered by technology to make more inventory available in the key items that customers wanted most, while reducing inventories overall. The retailer added that, by 'data mining' the massive supply of information on customer shopping habits that its information technology systems provided, it was able to refine its store layouts and design, so that new and remodelled stores served shoppers more effectively.

As we noted earlier in this chapter, Walmart's (possibly undeserved) reputation for being a reluctant pioneer in technology, data and information placed the company in a great position to capitalize on its technology-enabled flow of data to become a better retailer. In 1998, Walmart stated that its emphasis on information stemmed from Sam Walton, quoted as stating that: 'People think we got big by putting big stores in small towns. Really we got big by replacing inventory with information.'

While much of the benefit realized by Walmart from technology related to behind-the-scenes advancement in efficiency, logistics and inventory management, the company was also able to generate competitive advantage through a better understanding of its shoppers. With regard to the shopper insight that its IT systems generated in the late 1990s, Walmart noted that its systems were able to gather information on exactly what any given shopping cart contained: 'The popular term is "data-mining," and Walmart has been doing it since about 1990.'

The retailer added that the resultant output was an enormous database of purchasing information that enabled it to place the right item in the right store at the right price. Walmart's computer system was said to receive 8.4 million updates every minute on the items that shoppers took home and, vitally, the relationship between the items in each basket: 'The computerized transmission of transactions to our systems, which keep track of what merchandise is needed where, is a key tool as Walmart merchants work to serve our customers.'

With Domesday theorists predicting the Y2K meltdown of the global network at the turn of the Millennium, 2000 was a key year for the international IT fraternity as much as it was for Walmart: the company announced that its computer system was the most powerful in the corporate world, with only the US government operating a larger computer network. Walmart's philosophy of building 'people-supportive' systems, it said, had 'given us a competitive edge that has and will be instrumental in the company's success'.

By 2004, Walmart was telling its investors that, thanks to over 75,000 associates in Logistics and in its Information Systems Division (ISD), it had 'the firepower' behind its retailing strategy that strived to achieve the Holy Grail for retailers: to have what the shopper wants, when the shopper wants it. Walmart noted that, with a data warehouse storage capacity of over 570 terabytes – larger than all of the fixed pages on the internet at the time – it had a remarkable level of real-time visibility into its merchandise planning. In a fantastic real-life example of how this influenced the retailer's merchandising, Walmart recalled how 'when Hurricane Ivan was heading toward the Florida panhandle, we knew that there would be a rise in demand for Kellogg's Strawberry Pop-Tart toaster pastries. Thanks to our associates in the distribution centres and our drivers on the road, merchandise arrived quickly.'

To ensure greater supply chain visibility, satellite-based tracking technology was being installed in the company's entire fleet of over-the-road trailers. The data generated by the system increased productivity, reduced costs and enhanced security. Construction of an Innovation Lab was also under way. This centre was intended to showcase leading-edge technology and demonstrate how it could lead to future products, as well as better ways to serve shoppers.

Opening the inner sanctum: Walmart's use of third-party IT suppliers

Until 2007, Walmart was famous for its in-house IT strategy and development: it had traditionally developed, maintained and operated its own systems in Bentonville and elsewhere through its ISD. This approach was possibly reinforced by the fact that vendors were usually more than willing to adapt to the systems used by Walmart, in many cases their biggest customer, at the same time as using standard third-party solutions for dealing with their other major retail customers.

Furthermore, Walmart clearly benefited from creating and shaping its own systems around its retailing and logistics functions rather than adapting its business to use off-the-shelf solutions from external hardware or software providers. Another factor is at play here: Walmart likes being independent and self-reliant and has not traditionally welcomed in third-party advisers or suppliers to interfere in its key trading systems.

Until five or six years ago, Walmart was wary of opening up to third-party software companies, consultancies and service providers, perhaps fearful that they have been known to develop systems and best practice at one company and then turn around and implement similar systems at a competitor. 'This is why we try to avoid working with software vendors and consultants in IT', a vice president IT of Walmart said in 2003.

Another benefit of the self-reliant approach was the fact that this strategy enabled centralization. 'Performance is crucial for us', a senior Walmart executive explained. 'The company loses $1,000 per hour per cash register that is down. And we get a better performance in China by managing our data in Bentonville.'

In keeping with the all-pervasive EDLP model that is the very DNA of Walmart's strategy, in-house technology development had the added advantage of being relatively cheap (as opposed to lining the pockets of external technology providers). According to a Walmart board member in the 1990s, the IT spending of the retail behemoth was 'significantly under' 0.5 per cent of its turnover. It is likely that other retailers have historically spent well over 1 per cent of sales on sourcing IT solutions and services from external providers.

Merchandising systems – often at the very heart of a retailer's operations – were a key area developed in-house by Walmart. Walmart's efforts in this regard dated back to the 1970s and were mainly based on IBM tools, when Walmart developed one of the first merchandising systems in the world, programmed in Cobol (central) as well as IBM 370 Assembler (store network), using IBM's CICS transaction processing system.

Nevertheless, in 2007, Walmart started to shift away from its strategy of self-reliance and isolation. The two most important vendors of enterprise applications, Oracle and SAP, were some of the first through the door. Firstly, Walmart introduced two software solutions from Oracle Retail. The first solution, Profitlogic, was implemented to help Walmart to optimize prices during mark-downs of seasonal apparel. The second solution was a merchandise planning solution for the buyers. In October 2007, Walmart decided to replace its legacy accounting and controlling systems with SAP Financials, a decision that provided conclusive evidence that Walmart's technology strategy had been opened up to packaged applications. We should be clear that purchasing packaged business applications doesn't mean that Walmart will necessarily have implemented what's known as a 'vanilla' solution. All complex business applications require configuration – which can make one company's implementation very different from another's – and in addition, Walmart might well have completed bespoke development on top of this.

The SAP implementation was followed in 2008 by a very decisive and comprehensive move: Walmart's selection of the Oracle Business Intelligence Suite Enterprise Edition Plus to provide comprehensive data intelligence and analysis from across all of Walmart's operations. Walmart planned to use the system to administer its logistics, transportation, category management, finance, human resources, real estate, merchandising, store and club operations and other business resources, within Walmart and Sam's Clubs. Oracle stated at the time of the deal: 'Information Technology has long been regarded as a core strength that enabled Walmart to reduce costs and improve operational efficiency.' From Walmart's perspective, Rollin Ford, Executive Vice President and Chief Information Officer, stated that 'Technology and analytics are essential to help us be more responsive and effective in serving

Walmart customers and Sam's Club members. The Oracle solution is very robust and it integrates well with our other applications, particularly as our business continues to grow in scale and complexity.'[10]

In June 2009, Walmart decided to implement another piece of standard software into its planning processes. Space optimization software provider Galleria Retail Technology Solutions was the recipient of Walmart's next move in its ongoing shift to utilizing third-party solutions. The retail giant had successfully completed a user acceptance and extensive scalability testing of Galleria's configured store and merchandise planning software system and stated that it would implement the solutions into its assortment, allocation and space planning process.

Of course, before this overt change of strategy, Walmart had already deployed hardware, components and services into its own systems from external technology vendors. Before the 2007/08 glasnost, names such as Teradata, IBM, SAS, Microsoft and Hewlett-Packard were already to be found within Walmart's internal technology architecture. But Walmart's data volumes, query requirements and stringent requirements for precision made it hard for an off-the-shelf product to be slotted in. So core solutions like merchandising systems, HR systems and logistics management had been developed in-house by the ISD.

Data warehousing: helping Walmart drink from a hosepipe of information

We have already described how Walmart has an embarrassment of riches in terms of data: 'We keep everything! Data is the great enabler', a Walmart board member stated in 2006. Data warehousing is the term for the organization and storage of this data in order that Walmart might benefit from identifying some of the trends and implications within it. Teradata is the provider of Walmart's data warehousing function, 'increasing its lead as the largest retail data warehouse in the world'. In addition to the application activities used in servicing Walmart's shoppers, the Teradata warehouse at Walmart is the foundation for the company's Retail Link decision-support system used by Walmart and its suppliers. As we've already noted, Retail Link allows suppliers to access large amounts of online, real-time, item-level data that can help those companies improve their operations.

In August 2007, HP announced that Walmart had selected the HP Neoview data warehousing platform to power complex analysis of data collected across its 4,000 US stores. The announcement took industry experts by surprise as Walmart had already built up one of the largest data collections in the world using NCR's Teradata technology. In January 2011, HP announced the discontinuation of its Neoview product and Walmart once again turned to Teradata technology, expanding its data warehouse capacities.

In late 2010, Walmart decided to upgrade and enhance its Teradata data warehouse environment. The expansion included a data warehouse technology refresh programme which ensured that Walmart's data warehouse was once again at the leading edge of technology. The agreement also included a research and development relationship. The Teradata technology had the additional benefit of a 50 per cent reduction in floor space required and a 40 per cent reduction in energy consumption required to run the data warehouse.

'As this partnership is expanded, we will be able to leverage scalability, processing power, and storage capacity, along with software enhancements', said Jose Hernandez, Walmart's Chief Technology Officer and Senior Vice President of Infrastructure. 'Consistent with our sustainability initiatives, this expansion will result in a significant reduction in our data centre power and cooling footprint.'[11] Walmart's Teradata Data Warehouse is now the second-largest civilian database behind eBay. The retailer keeps each POS transaction for two years and then it is paged out to a second tier of storage. This vast reservoir of data has been an invaluable asset for Walmart: 'This automated process has made it possible for Walmart stores to be in stock consistently and minimize the dollars invested in inventory at the same time – that equals superior service for the customers and reduced capital commitment from the company'.[12]

Retail Link: a new era for Walmart and its suppliers

Like 1987, 1990 was a monumental year for Walmart's technology-enabled rise to supremacy: it was the year that the retailer announced Retail Link to its vendors. Retail Link was described as 'an aggressive step to further our partnership relations by moving beyond electronic data sharing. We desire to provide our vendor partners the quality of information concerning sales trends and inventory levels to facilitate genuine partnering in our mutual goal to serve our customers.' The system was said to be intended to capitalize on existing barcode and satellite capacities 'to bring our suppliers closer to our individual stores'.

By 1996, the Retail Link system was being touted as a key component of Walmart's technological advantage, providing sales data – by item, by store, by day – to vendors. The system was therefore said to save vendors time and expense in planning production and distribution, translating into lower product prices at Walmart.

Walmart was at pains to reiterate the importance of Retail Link in its relationship with vendors in the late 1990s. Starting from the basic information compiled at the checkout, at the shelves, and gathered by associates equipped with handheld computers, Walmart used technology to manage its supplies and inventories not only in the stores, but all the way back to the original source. Through Retail Link, Walmart granted its suppliers access to some of its data, which enabled them to know exactly what was selling, and to plan their production accordingly. This not only helped Walmart keep inventories under control, but also helped the supplier deliver the lowest-cost product to the customer.

With sales and in-stock information transmitted between Walmart and its suppliers in seconds over the internet, buyers and suppliers were privy to the same facts and were thus able to negotiate based on a shared understanding – saving a significant amount of time and energy over more traditional, low-tech systems. Buyers were said to benefit from the supplier's product knowledge, while the supplier benefited from Walmart's experience in the market.

In an update to investors in 2000, Walmart once again underscored the fact that Retail Link was one of the core enablers of its success. It was keen to point out its fundamental belief in building a collaborative environment with its suppliers in which both parties worked together to grow both businesses and provide lower retail prices for customers: 'While some retailers have been reluctant to share sales or other proprietary data with suppliers, Walmart has allowed suppliers this type of access since early 1991. This system evolved into a web-based product called Retail Link.' It allows the company and suppliers to track merchandise to study how products sell in any store by region or by individual unit. They can also review inventory levels, returns and inventory adjustments. 'We think sharing information with suppliers allows for better input from them about how to maximize sales and profits. We can then implement best practices and pass the savings on to customers', Kevin Turner, the company's Chief Information Officer, said.

Retail Link continues to be an important – and global – cornerstone of Walmart's success. Suppliers, both big and small, are given a user ID and password to access the system. Retail Link is used to get reports regarding the sales of products, complete online supplier agreements and obtain information about how to do business with the retailer. In the words of Don Soderquist in 2005, 'No other retailer to date has replicated this system, which is another way that technology has aided Walmart in developing a significant strategic advantage in the marketplace'.[13]

The false dawn of RFID

It was in 1992 that Walmart first publicly brought up the topic of radio frequency identification (RFID). The advent of RFID put many suppliers (in general, not just those that supplied to Walmart) in a tailspin. On paper, RFID had the potential to revolutionize the world of distribution and retail: the system enabled communication through the use of radio waves to exchange data between a reader and an electronic tag attached to an object, for the purpose of identification and tracking. At the time of its nascent introduction by a variety of retailers, RFID was commonly perceived as having the potential to transform the world of commerce in the way that the barcode did several decades before.

Theoretically, RFID made it feasible for vendors and/or retailers to give each product, or pallet of products, its own unique identifying number to track its whereabouts or progress through the supply chain. For retailers in particular, RFID technology made it theoretically possible to locate pallets in DCs or in the storage rooms at individual stores. Even in this day and age, it is remarkable to what extent retailers can rely on manual checking of stock, opening up the possibility of human error and entire pallets of goods being misplaced.

While barcodes are rightly hailed as one of the greatest developments in the history of the distribution of consumer goods, they are not without their limitations. Barcodes have to be 'shown' to readers in close proximity; either by being passed in front of a static reader (such as a pallet being sped past a barcode reader on a conveyor belt in a DC) or, in a scenario familiar to us all, being manually passed over a checkout reader by a member of staff in a retail store. In other words, barcodes rely on proximity and a line of sight between label and reader, and scanners are generally only able to read one barcode at a time. RFID, therefore, marked a huge advantage over barcodes: they can be 'read' from a distance; they can be read from within cartons; and they can be read hundreds at a time.

While RFID has become widely used in other areas of life (motorists using turnpikes in the United States will be familiar with the E-ZPass system; commuters in London will need no reminding of the ubiquity of Oyster cards; and other – more esoteric – uses of RFID include tracking high-value casino chips and monitoring livestock), its anticipated impact in the world of FMCG and retail has turned out to be something of a damp squib.

In 1992, Walmart stated that the aim of RFID technology was to achieve 'the simplification of what we do, elimination of waste and access to more meaningful information'. The retailer added that the advent of RFID enabled it to access better sales and inventory information, thus leading to a better in-stock position.

In February 2004, Walmart received the first pallets tagged with RFID labels in its Fort Worth, TX, distribution centre. They were shipped from Procter & Gamble, Gillette, Unilever, Kraft, Johnson & Johnson, Kimberly-Clark, Nestlé Purina and Hewlett-Packard. At this time, seven Supercenters, supplied by the Fort Worth distribution centre, were involved. Writing around this time, Don Soderquist posited that 'I am convinced that RFID will become a major breakthrough technology in the years ahead. And Walmart is out in front'.[14]

Two years later in 2006, Walmart told investors that 'innovation is taking place in a number of areas. Nowhere is this more evident than in the application of RFID technology. Walmart has been a critical catalyst that has brought this technology to business use and now is helping to foster worldwide RFID standards.'

On the back of this – and despite problems with RFID reading owing to the influences of metals and liquids in grocery distribution – Walmart was striving to roll out the technology at pallet and case level in the United States. Even though Walmart was expressing an aspiration at this stage that single items would be tagged with RFID chips, there were very few, if any, implementations at Walmart of this more granular tagging.

In 2007, the RFID strategy leader at Walmart, Ron Moser, said that the retailer could increase sales by $287 million by fixing just a small portion of its inventory problems using RFID technology. As of late 2007, around 2 per cent of all lost sales were due to the simple fact that a store had run out of an item, but 41 per cent of lost sales were due to inventory problems, according to Moser. He expected RFID to have a bigger impact on the company than barcodes did when that technology was introduced in 1984. With RFID, Moser expected inventory accuracy to improve tremendously. He believed that products would get to shelves faster, thereby reducing lost sales, and that lost or missing merchandise would become a phenomenon of the past. Going forward, the company planned to work more closely with suppliers on RFID. By October 2007, 600 of Walmart's top suppliers had started using RFID tags at their own expense, in order to comply with Walmart's initiative. Some of these suppliers had found their own inventory cost savings, but others had not, according to Moser: 'We have seen suppliers that are getting no benefit out of RFID and use it only because we told them to. We've got to work with these suppliers to help them find cost savings and other benefits from the technology.'[15]

In July 2010, Walmart started to sell menswear such as jeans tagged with RFID labels in an effort to gain easier control of its inventory. This initiative marked the start of the retailer's new approach to RFID technology after some of its past projects were discontinued. The clothes were RFID-tagged by the suppliers at the point of manufacturing with EPCglobal's second-generation ultra-high-frequency (UHF) RFID standard tags. The new programme concentrated on those types of products that have multiple SKUs and are, therefore, a challenge to manage from an inventory perspective, according to Myron Burke, Walmart's Director of Store Innovation, who was leading the retailer's electronic product code (EPC) programme in the United States. 'We are addressing the opportunity to improve inventory accuracy and inventory availability', Burke said. 'We have been working collaboratively with suppliers on a strategic basis to make this part of our systems.' Unlike previous efforts, in which Walmart required suppliers to tag items by a certain date, the retailer was working with suppliers collaboratively to incorporate EPC data into their warehouse management systems, the *RFID Journal* reported. In order to address the substantial privacy concerns (Walmart employees were not removing or deactivating the RFID tags when items were sold), Walmart stated that it expected that its customers would cut off and discard the tags prior to wearing the items, as they customarily would for other non-RFID labels and hangtags. Walmart added that it would not be reading the tags at checkout, so the EPCs will not be associated with any personally identifiable information, to protect consumer privacy.[16]

By 2009, Sam's Club required some suppliers to tag single items with RFID tags. The edict applied to 5,000 club-sized bulk packs, rather than conventional store items. By the same deadline, Sam's Club expected all suppliers to tag all deliveries at the pallet level for all 17 Sam's Club distribution centres as well as for direct store deliveries with RFID. Suppliers failing to meet those requirements were being charged $2.50 per pallet.

The globalization of technology in Walmart

An additional benefit of Walmart's self-sufficient approach to technology was the ability to use similar systems as it globalized. The world's largest retailer is rightly proud of the harmonization of its IT architecture around the world: according to a Walmart VP in 1997, about 90 per cent of all IT systems were the same in all countries.

This strategy is one pioneered by Walmart, although retailers such as Tesco (which developed an international back-office package called Tesco in a Box) have been following suit by standardizing technology across their international markets. Walmart was quick to establish a common technology strategy for all of its global operations: since 1995, Walmart's ISD has been using one common merchandise system for all of its cross-border retail operations. 'The common system, centrally managed, is our competitive advantage at Walmart', one of its vice presidents claimed.

Walmart continues to pursue this approach – exploiting best practice from the United States and elsewhere in all of its new and existing international markets. Walmart is expected to roll out its systems quickly in South Africa, for example, while it has already adopted this strategy in India. In 2008, Walmart decided to provide technology systems to its Indian joint venture partner Bharti, not only for the partners' jointly operated cash & carry business but also for Bharti Retail, Bharti's wholly owned subsidiary that operates easyday supermarkets and easyday Market compact hypermarkets. Both companies have entered into a franchise agreement whereby Walmart provides technical support to Bharti Retail.

Technology and private label development

Another key area where Walmart has been looking to third parties for technological enhancement has been in private label development – inherently a complex side of the business since many Walmart private brands are sourced from a disparate mix of low-wage economies and the end-products are sold through Walmart stores across the world.

Since 2008, Walmart has been working with Agentrics' product lifecycle management (PLM) platform to support the collaborative development of its private brand products, with initial efforts focusing on the Great Value grocery range. Agentrics' PLM features a web-based, collaborative, end-to-end work process, database and production environment to drive speed, innovation and consistency across the product lifecycle. Agentrics rebranded the Walmart system, which is now referred to as Walmart Aspect across the retailer's network. Walmart and more than 500 suppliers began using Agentrics PLM to support the redesign and re-branding of the Great Value line.

Walmart also deploys the collaborative design software Odin from Sun Brand Technologies for the brand management of its private label products. The online tool is accessed by Walmart staff, suppliers and external agencies to develop artwork. Brand guidelines and briefs are available, as well as the status of projects in progress. Asda in the UK was the first Walmart division to use the tool. Asda initially deployed the system for its own-brand food ranges, where the design-to-print cycle was cut from 18 to 12 weeks, before rolling the solution out to its non-food private labels. In 2009, Walmart US installed the brand management software across its Marketside range of fresh produce and its Equate health and beauty portfolio.

A similar process was implemented for George, the Asda-developed global fashion brand available in Walmart stores across the world. George, based in the UK, deployed an online collaboration portal from British internet specialist Concrete to serve the Walmart apparel businesses around the world. George implemented the solution to cut the costs of producing products for sale internationally, as well as to provide consistency in how George products are sold across Walmart International. Walmart's national retail divisions can browse all product designs and download artwork for those they wish to sell from George's head office in the UK. Before the portal was introduced, this artwork was being redrawn in each country for local suppliers to work from.

Price optimization

As we've already seen, price optimization (an analysis of factors such as price elasticity to ensure that demand and margins are maximized) was one of the first functions for which Walmart looked beyond its own capabilities and secured input from an external supplier, installing the Profitlogic solution from Oracle in 2007 to optimize mark-downs for seasonal apparel.

Since then, Walmart has deployed other, more general, price optimization solutions across its business. By mid-2010, DemandTec's price optimization solution was already live in seven of the retailer's markets. In the United States, Walmart uses DemandTec's price optimization for all of its retail operations, including Sam's Club.

Bean counting and number-crunching

In October 2007, Walmart decided to replace its legacy accounting and controlling system with SAP Financials. Walmart has since been rolling out the package from the German software maker globally in phases. By early 2010, Walmart had completed the implementation of SAP Financials at Asda in the UK. The retailer stated that the implementation 'went exceptionally well'. Walmart has since implemented the system in most of its international markets, meaning that virtually all of the retailer's operations have deployed the standard accounting and controlling system. The retail giant stated in its annual report that: 'this new financial system is a significant component of our internal control over financial reporting. We will continue to implement it in stages, and each implementation may become a significant component of our internal control over financial reporting.'

Walmart has commented that it does not anticipate any significant year-on-year cost increases for the implementation of the SAP financial system. SAP modules work hand-in-hand with in-house accounting and consolidation tools. According to Walmart, it purchased SAP Financials to 'support the retailer's global expansion and its need to efficiently respond to changes in the business and regulatory landscape. We believe SAP's experience in helping global companies with their financial systems will bring more flexibility and scalability to our growing business.'

In-store technology

Having provided some colour around Walmart's strategy and progress in establishing best practice in back-office technology, we can turn to the increasingly important issue of in-store technology. As shoppers, assisted by the proliferation of mobile devices, become more tech-savvy and as social media become more embedded in influencing shopper behaviour, Walmart has been on the front foot in terms of utilizing the latest technologies to optimize the shopping experience. This optimization stretches from the mundane (cash registers) to the more fanciful, but Walmart has proven time and time again that technology is a vital component of its effort to remain a core shopping destination for shoppers across the globe.

Walmart is proud of running the same POS software solution at most of its checkouts around the world. It is based on the relatively elderly IBM 'supermarket application' (IBM SA) but has been heavily modified by Walmart's in-house ISD in Bentonville.

An exception can be found in Walmart Japan, where Walmart was not able to reconcile the local language coding with its central POS solution. Because of its 'mature' POS technology base, Walmart's common POS system is not able to support the standard Unicode which helps to run software in all letters and language codes of the world.

Walmart has installed NCR's Selfserv Checkout (formerly Fastlane) in most of its stores in the United States and the UK. In a Walmart Supercenter in the United States, there are usually four self-checkouts and eight Express-Checkouts for smaller baskets added to an average of 26 full checkouts. Although Walmart predominately deploys self-checkouts from NCR, some stores are equipped with self-checkouts from IBM.

Walmart is the world's largest user of NCR's self-checkouts. The retail giant was also one of the first retailers to use this technology: after testing four different self-checkout systems in 2001, Walmart decided in 2002 to embark on a roll-out of NCR's NCR Selfserv system. Since then, every new and remodelled store has been equipped with self-checkouts. The retrofitting of existing stores proceeded quickly: in June 2004, around 840 stores had the system and by April 2005, 1,325 stores were running NCR Selfserv. In 2007, most Supercenters in the United States were running self-checkouts.

In the UK, Asda has installed NCR Selfserv in almost all of its stores. In May 2009, Asda completed the roll-out which it started in 2006. Most Asda stores now have either four or eight self-checkout systems. In June 2009, Asda opened a new store in Keighley which is the first Asda store with more self-checkouts than manned tills: the store comprises 22 self-service and 14 traditional checkouts.

With the colossal number of shoppers that enter its stores each week, both Walmart and its suppliers have been quick to realize the potential of Walmart – and its in-store TV network – as a valuable way of communicating to US consumers. In 2009, about 150 million Walmart shoppers viewed the chain's digital TV network each month. At this time, most Walmart Supercenters in the United States already had plasma screens in key departments, such as home electronics as well as health and beauty. By early 2010, the retailer had installed additional 15-inch screens at its checkouts.

In September 2008, Walmart US presented a revised in-store TV concept to agencies and marketers. It was called Walmart Smart Network (Smart) and was facilitated by Thomson's Premier Retail Networks (PRN). Smart was the result of two years and $10 million in research and development used to identify the optimal locations, applications and programming for reaching the millions of consumers who visit the retailer's stores each week. Walmart completed the chain-wide deployment with 27,000 screens in early 2010. The new concept, which was developed with the support of the consultancy DS-IQ, involves moving TV screens or digital signage closer to eye level. The screens are now part of product displays and create interactive virtual assistants to provide product information to shoppers or refine choices in key categories.

Custom programming on the network is provided by Studio2, a newly formed company led by key advertising executives who are experts in in-store communications and who were involved in the development and testing of the new network. Network operations, implementation, advertising sales and high-definition television (HDTV) wall programming are provided by PRN. Response measurement, learning and message optimization technologies are provided by DS-IQ, which supplied analytical insights for the network pilot in 2010.

With the revised in-store TV, Walmart is the first retailer in the United States to roll out a next-generation retail media network using Internet Protocol television technology that allows the retailer to monitor and control more than 27,000 screens in more than 2,700 stores across the country. The Walmart Smart Network also deploys response measurement and message optimization technologies to enable delivery of the most relevant content to shoppers – by store, by screen, by day and by time of day. All of the content on the Walmart Smart Network is customized, designed to deliver product information to consumers at the point of decision when and where they need it in the store.

In February 2010, Walmart stated that its Smart digital signage network was a huge success compared to its predecessor, Walmart TV. At the Digital Signage Expo in Las Vegas, Walmart's creative director Andy Johnson said that the Smart Network had been successful in the past 18 months, as it had demonstrably increased sales for many of the products that were advertised on it. A Nielsen survey said that 40 per cent of Walmart shoppers noticed the network, 32 per cent recalled an ad on the network and 64 per cent reported a 'positive experience' from the network. Walmart sells what it calls triple play, where a campaign is shown on a large welcome screen at the entrance of the store, a category screen in departments and endcap screens on each aisle. According to Johnson, it takes 21 seconds for a shopper to move from the door of the store to the greeting area where the welcome screen is placed. 'We know what content is played on what screens at what stores at what times', Johnson said. 'And simultaneously we know what was sold at those times.'[17]

Like many retailers the world over, Walmart has implemented kiosk-based solutions to bring its shoppers value-added services. Principal among these services are redbox DVD rental and Coinstar coin-counting machines. Both services are operated by Coinstar, for whom Walmart accounted for 18.6 per cent of 2010 revenues.

In late 2009, Walmart started to install new photo kiosks from HP in its US stores. The roll-out of the 'Prints in Minutes' terminals was completed by summer 2010. The HP kiosks are replacing solutions from Eastman Kodak, which had been deployed at Walmart since 2006.

'Our computer really does give us the power of competitive advantage'

Walmart has justifiably been lauded as a retailer that owes much of its success to its early and rapid adoption of state-of-the art technology and, indeed, its own in-house technological development to create its own solutions when off-the-shelf alternatives were too costly, unsuitable or simply did not exist.

One aspect of the advantage that this prowess in technology gave Walmart was an advantage in terms of information. As Sam Walton noted, Walmart's forensic knowledge gleaned through Retail Link 'makes it tough for a vendor to know more about how his product is doing in our stores than we do. I guess we've always known that information gives you a certain power, but the degree to which we can retrieve in our computer really does give us a competitive advantage.'[18]

Retail Link still remains a key competitive advantage for Walmart and it remains a vital platform for the retailer and its suppliers all around the world. Indeed, when Walmart announced its intention to enter the African market, we were struck by the urgency with which local suppliers approached us for information and insight concerning Walmart's expectations regarding issues like Retail Link and other technological matters.

That said, we believe that Walmart's competitive advantage derived from technology has been eroded in recent years. Many retailers (in the United States and in other key Walmart markets such as the UK and Canada) have effectively caught up with the Bentonville giant, developing their own iterations of the Retail Link concept. In fact, many retailers, such as Tesco in the UK, have overtaken Walmart in technological terms, particularly in areas such as e-commerce and shopper insight systems. We've seen in another chapter how Walmart's relative lack of shopper insights led to some serious missteps in its SKU rationalization programme, especially in contrast to Tesco which was able to conduct its own assortment editing process with fewer mistakes thanks to the data and learning from its dunnhumby shopper insights data.

The adoption by Walmart of standard systems (Teradata, SAP etc) also signals that Walmart may have relented somewhat on its more insular and independent approach to technology development and implementation. This might well make economic sense for Walmart, particularly as it enters more foreign markets where suppliers will be unable or unwilling to adapt to the Walmart way of doing things when they have much bigger customers to supply in markets such as the UK, South Africa and Japan. In the United States, where Walmart is the biggest game in town, the incentive for suppliers to adapt to Walmart's requirements is more substantial.

Technology might just be one of very few areas where Walmart has ceased to be a leader and has become a follower. Not a terminal condition to be in, but certainly an uncomfortable realization for the boffins in Arkansas. Although it's worth remembering the words of former executive vice president and chief information officer at Walmart, Linda Dillman: 'We don't want to be famous for our technology. We want to be famous for what our technology allows us to do.'

Internal technological excellence has been one of the key attributes that Walmart has been able to capitalize on. With e-commerce, mobile commerce and social media becoming all the more important as Walmart's multi-channel strategy evolves, Walmart's shopper-facing technological development is becoming increasingly important. We turn now to assess the importance of online retailing, along with other growth opportunities such as smaller store formats, for the future of the world's number-one retailer.

Notes

1 Soderquist, D (2005) *The Wal-Mart Way: The inside story of the success of the world's largest company*, Thomas Nelson, Nashville, TN, pp 138–139

2 Ortega, B (1999) *In Sam We Trust: The untold story of Sam Walton and how Wal-Mart is devouring the world*, Kogan Page, London, p 129

3 Lichtenstein, N et al (2006) *Wal-Mart: The face of twenty-first-century capitalism*, The New Press, New York, p 91

4 Walton, S with Huey, J (1992) *Sam Walton: Made in America*, Doubleday, New York, p 271

5 Walton, p 285

6 Walton, pp 109–111

7 Walton, p 270

8 Soderquist, p 143

9 Walton, pp 270–271

10 http://www2.prnewswire.com/cgi-bin/stories.pl?ACCT=104&STORY=/www/story/07-21-2008/0004852304&EDATE=

11 http://dssresources.com/news/3177.php

12 Soderquist, p 146

13 Soderquist, p 147

14 Soderquist, 144

15 http://www.pcworld.com/businesscenter/article/138391/walmart_eyes_287_million_benefit_from_rfid.html

16 http://www.rfidjournal.com/article/view/7753

17 http://www.digitalsignagetoday.com/article/159854/DSE-Walmart-reveals-18-month-results-for-SMART-Network

18 Walton, p 285

Facing up to a multi-channel future

10

Growth in sales... growth in profitability... growth in customers... growth in number of stores... growth in distribution centers... growth in markets... growth in associates... growth in market share... growth in shareholders... growth in suppliers... growth in financial strength. No word better describes Walmart than does growth.[1] WALMART

This is an excerpt from Walmart's 1982 annual report, the year that sales reached $2.5 billion. Today, it's more like half a trillion dollars.[2] The word growth has certainly been an accurate depiction, if not understatement, of Walmart for the past 30 years, but the big question on everyone's minds is – just how much of it is left?

From Little Rock to Big Apple

Going back to the early 1980s, Little Rock, Arkansas and Joplin, Missouri were among Walmart's largest metropolitan areas.[3] At that time, Walmart was still focused on its small-town strategy, targeting the rural areas of America that its competitors had originally considered too small to support a store of Walmart's size: '... the first big lesson we learned was that there was much, much more business out there in small-town America than anybody, including me, had ever dreamed of', Mr Walton wrote.[4] While discounters such as Kmart believed that a catchment area of 50,000 people was the minimum needed to support a discount store,[5] Walmart proved them wrong by opening its first store in Rogers, Arkansas, a town of fewer than 10,000 inhabitants.[6] In fact, back in the early Walmart days, Mr Walton's wife Helen refused to live in towns with more than 10,000 people.

Walmart may have broken all the rules of traditional retailing but its initial small-town strategy wasn't about avoiding the competition – it was about serving those who were being underserved, something that still rings true for Walmart today, albeit in a different form. Today, Walmart's influence across the US heartland is unmatched, and now the retailer is looking to prove its competitors wrong once again by reaching out to a new, unconventional consumer: the city dweller.

With approximately 3,000 domestic Supercenters and another 700 discount stores, today there is one big-box Walmart store for approximately every 85,000 people.[7] This compares to one Target for every 175,000 people or one Kroger for every 125,000 people. Walmart has recognized that the end is nigh for its larger US formats, which is forcing the retailer to shift its focus towards smaller stores in US urban areas and so-called food deserts.

At the same time, it's important to remember that US consumers are rapidly changing the way they engage with retailers, utilizing technology and social media to help make purchasing decisions and increasingly transacting online. It's fair to say that a 'one size fits all' cookie-cutter approach to retailing is simply no longer valid: a multi-channel strategy encompassing both proximity-led formats and e-commerce will be key for future growth.

Before we get into how the Walmart of 2020 may look – the king of small? the urban pioneer? the new Amazon? – it's important to look back at what Walmart has achieved in its first 50 years of retailing.

The Supercenter and Walmart's rise to grocery domination

The world's largest retailer has never been ashamed of stealing a good idea. Its self-service discount stores were based on the success of early discounters such as Ann & Hope and Spartan's.[8] Its Sam's Club format was a carbon copy of Price Club. Referring to a dinner he had with Price Club founder Sol Price in 1983, Sam Walton writes in his autobiography: '... We dropped down to have dinner with Sol and his wife Helen at Lubock's. And I admit it. I didn't tell him at the time I was going to copy his program, but that's what I did.'[9] Today, Sam's Club is a $50 billion business.[10]

What eventually became the Walmart Supercenter concept (Hypermart preceded the Walmart Supercenter as the company's foray into hypermarket retailing) was the result of Sam Walton travelling the globe and borrowing ideas from hypermarkets overseas. Walton became inspired by these big-box formats in Europe, South Africa, South America and Australia, with a particular admiration for Carrefour in France and Brazil. 'I argued that everybody except the United States was successful with this concept and we should get in on the ground floor with it. I was certain this was where the next competitive battlefield would be.'[11]

This was the late 1980s, and back at home there was a tremendous amount of consolidation taking place in the US grocery sector. As a result of the lack of competition, food prices rose as the supermarkets cushioned their bottom lines. In fact, the price of food sold at supermarkets nationwide grew at twice the rate of the producer-price index from 1991 through 2001. This meant that Walmart could come in and reduce prices by up to 15 per cent and still remain profitable.[12]

And so they did. Walmart began adding food to the mix in the late 1980s, as discussed previously, and by 2001 they had taken the throne to become the largest seller of food in the United States.[13] It is amazing to think that Walmart achieved all of this in a space of just over a decade, quite a remarkable feat considering how long the existing competition had been around. A&P, once the United States' biggest supermarket, dates back to 1859.[14] In fact, it has been referred to as the 'Walmart before Walmart', having invented the modern-day supermarket, launching *Women's Day* magazine, sponsoring A&P radio hour and owning the world's best-selling coffee brand at one time. In the 1930s, A&P had approximately 16,000 stores and more than $1 billion in revenue.[15] Kroger – the largest traditional supermarket chain today – has been trading since 1883 when Barney Kroger opened his very first grocery store in downtown Cincinnati.[16] It would be over 100 years before Walmart would even consider getting into the food business, yet once it did there would be no turning back.

Today, Walmart commands a 15 per cent market share of the US food sector, which may sound low compared to Tesco or Carrefour's share in their domestic markets, but it's important to remember that the US grocery sector is vast and still quite regional despite the bouts of consolidation that have occurred over the past few decades. In fact, Walmart's 15 per cent share translates to over $100 billion of sales (food, consumables and HBC[17]) and, in some areas, often lower-income mid-sized cities, Walmart plays a much more dominant role with more than 30 per cent market share in certain cases.[18]

It's important, however, to remember that not everything Walmart touches turns to gold. Hypermart, the large-box concept that preceded Walmart Supercenter as the company's foray into hypermarket retailing, was a total flop. In an unusual twist, a concept that originated in Europe was deemed too big for US shoppers. With over 200,000 sq. ft, Hypermarts aimed to combine everything under one roof – groceries, clothing, electronics, banking, photo-processing etc. A 'mall without walls' as described by Walmart.

Since its launch in the early 1960s, the hypermarket concept had been a hit across the Atlantic; however, circumstances were very different in the US retail market. Shopping malls and big discount stores were already well established. The market was very competitive, with category specialists such as Toys 'R' Us dominating the non-food arena and supermarkets winning on location. Although some US retailers were finding success with this larger format – namely Meijer and Fred Meyer – Walmart found it too difficult to manage a store the size of four football fields (during Carrefour's brief stint in the United States, employees in its 330,000 sq. ft Philadelphia store wore roller skates to navigate the aisles).[19] Concerns over both profitability and manageability led to Hypermart's discontinuation in 1990 in favour of the smaller, more profitable Supercenter concept.[20] Throughout its history, Walmart also experimented with other formats such as Dot Discount Drug Stores – a chain of drugstores in Kansas, Missouri and Iowa which was sold in 1990;[21] Save-Co Home Improvement (divested in the 1970s);[22] and Helen's Arts and Crafts Store which was sold off to the United States' largest crafts retailer, Michael's:[23]

Supercenter conversions have fuelled Walmart's phenomenal growth in the food retailing sector. Aside from acquisition, how else could a retailer go from zero to 3,000 stores totalling over a half billion sq. ft, the equivalent of four times its closest competitor, in the space of just over a decade?[25] Walmart's existing fleet of general merchandise discount stores provided the retailer with a vast network to convert to the more profitable Supercenter format. Adding groceries to existing stores – versus organic expansion with a new format – was a relatively straightforward, non-capital-intensive project that enabled Walmart to drive shopper frequency and increase basket size.

> More than cost cuts or technology – or even Wall Street schmoozing – it's
> the Supercenters that are likely to carry Walmart into the next century.
> (*Fortune*, 1998)[24]

During the 1990s, Walmart converted nearly 600 discount stores to the Supercenter concept as it looked to make its rapid incursion into the $425 billion US grocery industry.[26] At the time, the hugely fragmented super-market sector was almost three times the size of the discount segment, where Walmart was one of three retailers that, when combined, controlled over 80 per cent of the market. In the grocery sector, however, the top five retail-ers accounted for less than a quarter of the market.[27] As recent as the early 1990s, the leading supermarket chains still included companies like A&P (filed for Chapter 11 in 2010), Winn-Dixie (filed for Chapter 11 in 2005) and American Stores (merged with Albertsons, now part of SuperValu, in 1998). Walmart certainly ignited change in the industry.

The format was such a success that during the next decade (2000s), Walmart converted more than twice as many (over 1,200) discount stores to the Supercenter concept.[28] The weighted square-footage average of a big-box Walmart store (ie including discount stores and Supercenters) grew from 125,000 sq. ft in 2000 to 169,000 sq. ft in 2010 as Walmart embarked on the most significant food-retailing conversion process in US history. And Walmart wasn't alone: supermarkets were also getting bigger. In fact, the Food Marketing Institute estimates that over the past 15 years, the average US supermarket has grown by 24 per cent to 46,000 sq. ft.[29]

But going back to Walmart Supercenters, these stores introduced low prices and broad ranges to rural or low-income areas. The value-led, no-frills concept exposed the high cost structure of traditional supermarkets, particularly when it came to the always touchy subject of labour relations. Walmart employs over 2 million associates worldwide, 1.4 million of whom are in the United States. Not only is Walmart one of the largest private employers in the United States, but it is also the largest in Mexico and one of the largest in Canada. In the United States, and to a slightly lesser extent Canada, the retailer has faced years of backlash for its anti-union stance. This, of course, has contributed to Walmart's ability to undercut traditional supermarkets on price, given that labour – primarily unionized – is typically the largest single expense item for retailers.

It is a classic case of Walmart doing what it does best – getting rid of the middleman, stripping out inefficiencies and passing the savings on to customers in the form of lower prices. As discussed in the previous chapters, its scale, lean cost structure and EDLP policy makes it impossible for the majority of supermarkets to compete with Walmart on price. Those that aim to take Walmart head on often find themselves digging an early grave, and as witnessed in markets such as Canada, retailers with a high non-food share will typically be more exposed to the Walmart threat. Therefore a far healthier approach is to play to Walmart's weaknesses, which up until recently have been product quality, store environment and convenience:

> Supercenters effectively serve a large trade area, but we think there may be some business that we are not getting purely because they may not be as close to the customer or convenient for small shopping trips.
>
> (David Glass, 1998)

Today, the Supercenter concept remains the backbone of Walmart's business, both at home and abroad, with Planet Retail estimating that approximately three-quarters of Walmart's global sales were generated through this format in 2010. Looking ahead, emerging economies are ripe for large-format development (ie Brazil, South Africa, China and India, foreign direct investment (FDI) permitting), which will enable Walmart to drive growth – a proven formula abroad (albeit with some local tweaks and infrastructure challenges as we'll discuss in the next chapter). However, for the American Supercenter, time is quickly running out.

We expect Walmart to have completed the conversion of its discount stores to Supercenters by 2020 (see Figure 10.1). These conversions have fuelled Supercenter growth since inception, yet over the next decade there will only be a few hundred opportunities for conversions.[30] In fact, 2009 was the first year in Walmart's history that it did not open any new discount stores.[31] It is a format nearing extinction and once it does, organic expansion with the Supercenter format is also expected to dry up for three reasons.

Firstly: saturation – Walmart already holds a market-leading position in the vast majority of US trading regions. There are Supercenters in every US state except for Hawaii and Vermont.[32] Secondly: population growth in

FIGURE 10.1 Number of US Walmart Supercenters, 1990–2030f

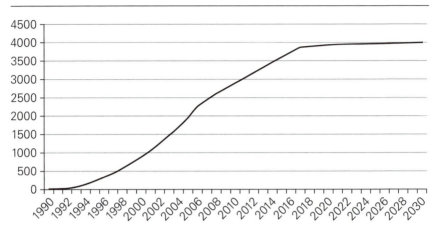

SOURCE: Company reports; Authors' forecasts

the United States will not be fast enough to sustain a significant number of new Supercenter openings: the US population is expected to increase by less than 1 per cent on a compounded annual basis over the next decade.[33] And thirdly: consumers are rapidly shifting their shopping patterns owing to technological and societal changes. The growth of e-commerce alone will result in a degree of cannibalization of bricks-and-mortar stores, all the more incentive to slow Supercenter growth. The bottom line is that Walmart is coming to an end of an era. It is reaching saturation with a format upon which the company has built its success. We expect Walmart Supercenters to hit saturation in the US market at approximately the 4,000 mark, leaving one last decade of meaningful growth with the format.

But Walmart has never been one to rest on its laurels, so the world's largest company is now on an ambitious path to discover new avenues of growth. Supercenters will continue to play a key role in Walmart's future, but it must also explore the two most obvious untapped segments in its domestic market – small-box stores and e-commerce.

In an exclusive interview with the authors, Bill Simon, President and CEO of Walmart US, commented: 'We believe there is tremendous opportunity for growth here in the US. The growth will come from additional penetration into more metropolitan markets, as well as from new formats and stronger integration with the online business. We will move toward a three-format portfolio, which will drive expansion to urban markets and small towns, as well as fill in gaps in existing markets.'

The final frontier: getting bigger by going small

You can't just keep doing what works one time. Everything around you is changing. To succeed, stay out in front of change. (SAM WALTON)[34]

When most people think of Walmart, the image of a 185,000 sq. ft Supercenter looming over US highways is typically what comes to mind: big stores in the 'burbs with shelves piled high with cheap merchandise. This is how Walmart has established itself in the United States. In fact, an old annual report proudly states that 'since its beginning, the Walmart concept was based on the theory that a quality discount store could open profitably, and even thrive, in a small community'. They've done this – in fact, they mastered it – but the question today is can they survive in a 'big community'?[35]

The Walmart of the future will feature a whole new dimension – the 15,000 sq. ft store. A fraction of the size of a Supercenter, the Walmart Express concept was rolled out in 2011 and marks a whole new era of retailing for the Bentonville giant. The stores feature between 11,000 and 12,000 SKUs, with grocery items accounting for around 70 per cent of the assortment.[36] The store's entire range may be equivalent to that of a small department in a Supercenter, but it's important to point out that it is catering to three unique trips – quick, fill-in and stock-up. Despite its edited assortment, Walmart Express still offers three times the number of products found in a typical Fresh & Easy outlet (more on that to follow).

The store concept was developed in less than six months. To put that into perspective, Walmart's previous new-store format took three years to complete.[37] However, it's no secret that Walmart was losing market share to the dollar stores – and losing it quickly. Walmart Express therefore can be seen as a defensive mechanism towards both the rise in dollar stores and alternative food formats, yet it is also very much an offensive move as it will grant Walmart a better chance of tapping into underpenetrated urban areas in the United States.

Although Walmart will exert a fair degree of caution with regard to a broad-scale roll-out, it is fair to say that there could be hundreds of these small-format stores in operation within just a few years. While price continues to play a key role with this new condensed format, quality and convenience are also vital ingredients, requiring a major strategic shift for the world's largest retailer.

It's not just the micro stores that will help Walmart reach untapped consumer markets. Walmart's three-format portfolio, unveiled in late 2010, includes Supercenters and small formats (under 30,000 sq. ft) as discussed but also a mid-sized store ranging from 30,000 to 60,000 sq. ft.[38] This mid-sized store, very much in line with the size of an average US supermarket trades as Walmart Market and Walmart Neighborhood Market, a move signifying that Walmart is looking to emulate the single-brand, multi-channel approach which has been so successful for European retailers such as Tesco. It's about extending the Walmart brand, realizing synergies and ensuring a consistent shopping experience across multiple formats. Averaging 42,000 sq. ft, Walmart Market will work in tandem with Express to penetrate those difficult urban settings where a 185,000 sq. ft store would be deemed impossible, too expensive or irrelevant.

In an exclusive interview with the authors, Anthony Hucker, Vice President of Strategy and Business Development at Walmart US, commented: 'Supercenters are still our highest ROI-generating vehicle, so we start with the largest box we can, according to what's appropriate in the particular trade area, and use a sequencing technique which, simply put, goes from large, to medium, to small which takes into account the politics permitting and economics that either enable or inhibit that particular opportunity.'

If we look back to just five years ago, Walmart would have been in no position to launch its small-format assault. Despite the fact that Walmart Market (then Neighborhood Market) has been trading since the late 1990s, it was never a priority for the company given their focus on more profitable growth through Supercenter conversions. Fresh, high-quality food is a key ingredient for small-format stores, an area where Walmart has traditionally struggled. However, as discussed in the private label chapter, the overhaul of the Great Value line and other improvements in grocery have helped to reposition Walmart's quality perception, instilling trust among consumers. Equally, Walmart today is able to use its smaller stores as distribution points for online orders, making the store size and lack of non-food assortment less of an issue than it would have been just five years ago when the notion of ordering online and picking up in-store was virtually non-existent:

> Where we weren't five years ago is a place where we were willing to put small stores into urban areas. What we have to do is deliver the brand to customers in those markets, and the brand can come in a small format.
>
> (Bill Simon, 2011)[39]

Walmart may have made its name with big stores, but this isn't to say that they hadn't considered small-box in the past. In the late 1980s, Walmart tested a handful of convenience stores positioned next to existing Supercenters and Sam's Clubs. However, that only lasted a few years before Walmart sold the nine stores to Conoco.[40] A decade on in the late 1990s, Walmart tested yet another concept, this time aimed at taking the grocers head on. The 40,000 sq. ft stores were tentatively billed as Wal-Mart Food & Drug Express,[41] not far from the branding Walmart has gone for in its most recent drive for small-box. In fact, looking back at Walmart under David Glass's leadership, we see that certain strategic initiatives 15 years ago bear a striking resemblance to the Walmart of 2012 – primarily the drive to tap into urban settings with a food format. Wal-Mart Food & Drug Express never made it to launch; instead the stores opened as Neighborhood Market. At the time of launch, the *Wall Street Journal* wrote:

'The new stores could let Walmart add stores in small towns and urban markets that aren't right for the large Supercenters... The smaller size could appeal to customers who don't want the hassle of braving the mammoth parking lots and extensive aisles of Supercenters.'[42] So why, since its launch, has the company opened an average of just 13 Walmart Market stores per year?[43]

The answer is simple: it had its hands full opening nearly 200 Supercenters annually (from 1998 to 2010; includes conversions). It's clear to see where Walmart's priorities were. Supercenters are inherently more profitable owing to their size and non-food assortment, but as we know by now, that growth potential is nearing an end, which means that Walmart has no choice but to make one last push for smaller stores.

The icing on the cake

As we hope we have demonstrated so far, Walmart is not a believer in complacency. Just as they recognized the potential in European hypermarkets – albeit with a few tweaks – the same can be said for their smaller stores. In the United States, the average supermarket measures 46,000 sq. ft.[44] There are very few operators who have cracked the 20,000 sq. ft range and below and for good reasons. Firstly, there is little incentive to go small when real estate is cheap and land is plentiful. The same cannot be said in Western Europe where high-rent, densely populated and saturated markets such as the UK have led all of the major supermarkets to launch smaller formats (including Walmart's own Asda which acquired the Netto discount chain in 2010). Secondly, going small is trickier than it sounds. Getting the assortment right is vital. Since shoppers typically won't be able to complete a full basket in this setting, getting the right brands, SKUs and categories is a must. It has to be relevant and local to be successful and this is where access to shopper data comes into play.

Generally, these scaled-down stores should feature a heavy amount of private label items in order to push profits (in urban areas in particular the cost of doing business is greater, which puts pressure on margins). Walmart Express is arguably too brand-led in its current state; however, given the retailer's failures with regard to rationalizing its SKU base, going heavier on brands versus private label is a much safer bet.

Labour, as discussed, is one of the largest expenses for retailers, and therefore achieving a cost-effective labour model is vital in a smaller box. Although there are, of course, fewer staff per store in a Walmart Express, for example, it's important to bear in mind that these stores must be replenished more frequently owing to their smaller size – which inevitably adds cost into the business. 'The EDLC model is the only way to operate these smaller stores', Mr Hucker told us. 'Getting the store economics right is crucial in order for this format to succeed.' One of the largest elements of labour is the front-end (and this therefore explains why Tesco's Fresh & Easy went for self-checkouts only). It is a difficult balance of managing costs and customer service.

Shopper data and demand forecasting are key in order to keep stock at the right levels. Finally, these stores must be located within relatively close proximity to larger Supercenters in order to achieve economies in the supply chain (which enables Walmart to offer low prices in a smaller-format setting). As such, there is certainly a degree of self-cannibalization. This has been a problem in China in particular where poor infrastructure has put even greater pressure on retailers to co-locate their stores, particularly for Walmart which must achieve EDLC in order to invest in EDLP. It's no coincidence that the company's first compact hypermarket in Zhangshu is located near to six Walmart Supercenters, and its Smart Choice discount stores are also within close proximity to larger formats.

This all sounds like quite a hassle, especially when you consider that it would take 500 smaller stores to deliver the same benefit as 10 superstores, as former Asda CEO Andy Bond pointed out. 'Convenience stores are not the cake, they are the icing', he said back in 2007.[45] However, the cake can't get much bigger in markets like the UK and the United States where, as we have discussed, Supercenter growth is nearing saturation. Time to focus on the icing.

The British are coming

In the United States, small-box development was spurred on in 2007 when Britain's Tesco, the world's third-largest food retailer, entered the market with a completely new concept: Fresh & Easy. Tesco broke all the rules of US food retailing (something that hasn't gone unnoticed judging by its financial results – Tesco is unlikely to turn a profit in the United States until 2013).[46] Everything about the concept was different at the time of launch. At 10,000 sq. ft, Fresh & Easy is around a quarter of the size of a traditional supermarket. With 4,000 SKUs, its breadth of product choice is similar to limited assortment retailers such as Costco. Half the offering is private label (twice as much as found in a typical supermarket). None of these factors were deal breakers. In fact, there have been similar alternative formats that have successfully struck a chord with US shoppers. Trader Joe's, the limited assortment, mainly private label supermarket chain owned by Germany's Aldi, has a cult-like following in the United States. With sales per square foot of $1,750, store productivity levels are twice that of Whole Foods Market.[47]

So what went wrong at Fresh & Easy? Well, some of it simply comes down to bad timing. Tesco entered the United States months before the economic crisis struck. The Southwest, where Fresh & Easy set up shop, was one of the hardest-hit regions during the recession. High home-foreclosure rates and unemployment levels actually led to negative population growth – many of America's boom cities on the West Coast, once growing by 6–7 per cent, were suddenly declining by 10 per cent year-on-year.[48] In fact, about a quarter of US foreclosures in 2008 were derived from just eight counties in Arizona, California, Nevada (all three of which are on Fresh & Easy turf) and Florida.[49]

At the same time, Tesco had set up the infrastructure to service thousands of stores (former CEO Terry Leahy had originally envisioned 10,000 outlets[50]), but the economic gloom stunted store expansion plans and after three years of trading fewer than 200 stores were in operation.[51] At the time of writing, losses plus initial investment amounted to roughly £1 billion.[52]

While some of Tesco's misfortune has been out of its control, there have also been some fundamental problems with its store concept. The efficiency-driven, sterile store environment initially failed to connect with US shoppers. They may have been used to shelf-ready packaging and products displayed on pallets (both of which are reminiscent of the warehouse club channel, which is hugely popular among US families), but shoppers weren't ready for pre-packed fruit and vegetables or a self-checkout-only option. There is no counter service, which adds to the clinical feel, and, unlike the Brits, US consumers have a strong preference for freshly cut deli meats.

The stores did not initially accept loyalty cards, despite the fact that Tesco operates what is arguably the most successful loyalty scheme in the world. This held Tesco back, not only from rewarding shoppers for their custom but also from gathering the essential shopper data that have enabled the retailer to tailor its merchandising and marketing efforts in 12 other markets around the globe. In the United States, dunnhumby is a joint venture with Kroger, which initially put Fresh & Easy in an awkward and limiting position. Sharing a shopper database with the competition was unlikely ever to happen (although Fresh & Easy finally managed to launch a loyalty scheme, using dunnhumby UK, in 2011). In any case, despite Tesco's initial fumbles and greater concerns over the long-term viability of Fresh & Easy, it has certainly been successful in one thing – igniting change in the industry.

Since Fresh & Easy debuted on US soil, there has been a proliferation of small-format launches across the nation. Walmart itself rolled out its first new format in a decade – Marketside, the four-store, 15,000 sq. ft concept debuted in the Phoenix area a year after Fresh & Easy's launch. Despite always referring to Marketside as a pilot, Walmart said from the start that the concept could evolve to up to 1,500 stores with annual sales of more than $10 billion.[53] Things clearly didn't go to plan; however, it sparked similar reactions by other retailers looking to experiment with scaled-down versions of their larger stores, including Target (CityTarget), Ahold (Giant), Safeway (Vons), Price Chopper, Hy-Vee, Schnucks, SuperValu and Giant Eagle.

Although Marketside failed to move beyond its pilot phase, it served as a very valuable experiment for Walmart in terms of both operating a store of that size (hence the Walmart Express launch three years later) and improving its grocery offering. Also, the Marketside private label is now offered across Walmart's Supercenters, giving it far greater visibility than when it was a range limited to a handful of stores in Arizona, and helping to improve Walmart's quality perception on freshly prepared foods.

In another move towards diversification, Walmart launched its first Hispanic format in 2009. Converting a 39,000 sq. ft Neighborhood Market store, the retailer's first Supermercado de Walmart concept opened its doors in Houston, Texas in April that year. The 13,000 products on offer included a wide assortment of national brands from the United States and Mexico, fresh tropical fruits and vegetables, and a bakery offering more than 40 traditional sweet breads and fresh corn tortillas. Speciality meats included milanesa, diezmillo, fajitas, chuleta de cerdo, carnes marinadas and arrachera, all targeted towards the local Hispanic customer.[54] Walmart was able to draw on its expertise in Latin America, Mexico in particular, in order to ensure local relevance to Houston's vast Hispanic population.

You have to applaud Walmart for moving away from one size fits all in an attempt to cater to America's fastest-growing consumer group. In fact, by 2050 the country's Hispanic population is expected to triple to 132.8 million, at which point nearly one in three US residents will be Hispanic. Although places like Texas and California are already majority-minority states, by 2042 the entire United States is expected to transition to a majority-minority country.[55] Clearly, retailers and manufacturers need to be thinking about how to better serve this increasingly important demographic.

Unfortunately, however, like Marketside, Supermercado de Walmart is unlikely ever to move beyond the experimental phase. The concept was arguably *too* specialized, catering more towards Latin-American-born consumers versus the millions of second- and third-generation Hispanics in the United States. The vast majority of the latter group would surely prefer a traditional US store, perhaps tailored to offer more localized ranges, but not an entire shopping experience similar to what you would find south of the border:

> We have lots of learnings around the world from Walmart in small formats. Our group in Mexico and Central America and Latin America operates small formats very well and very profitably, and we are going to beg, borrow, steal and learn from them as quickly as we can, because it is important for our urban strategy.
>
> (Bill Simon)

Yet, as demonstrated by new concepts such as Marketside and Supermercado, Walmart as an organization is becoming far more versatile with regard to its formats. As we'll discuss in the next chapter, it's becoming less about broadcasting plans from a Bentonville base and increasingly a two-way conversation with international operations, particularly when it comes to format development. This is true of cash & carries where Walmart has exported learnings from Brazil to India. '... We're flexible, and we can look at a market and think about where we put a specific format so that we can grow the overall share and increase profitability by being more than one dimensional as it relates to formats', Doug McMillon said in 2010.[56]

Compact hypermarkets, which are about half the size of a Walmart Supercenter but generate similar returns on investment, have been copied and pasted from Mexico to China, where, as mentioned previously, Walmart opened its first compact hypermarket in 2010.[57] The UK team is helping to share their e-commerce expertise with the rest of Walmart's operations, particularly in the United States where the company began testing an online grocery offering in 2011.[58] And going back to its next era of small-box retailing in the United States, Walmart has been heavily inspired by the success of its Latin American bodegas. Walmart Express may have been 'created with a US lens', as Mr Hucker puts it, but it most certainly draws on the likes of Todo Dia in Brazil, Bodega Aurerra Express in Mexico and Changomas in Argentina. 'We run small formats all over the world,' said Bill Simon, 'and these small boxes are among the most profitable businesses that these countries run.'[59]

Grandma, the Manhattanite and fraternity boys

Smaller stores will play a pivotal role in the next phase of retail evolution in the United States. By 2050, one in five Americans will be over the age of 65. The United States' elderly population is expected to more than double (based on 2010) to 89 million people.[60] That is almost the equivalent of the size of Germany today.[61] Retailers are right to begin thinking about how to cater to this cash-rich emerging demographic. These shoppers will certainly prefer proximity over bulk buying.

At the same time, US consumers are increasingly leading fast-paced lifestyles – there are a rising number of single households as well as time-sensitive working moms, both of which are factors that bode well for a small-box format. The acceleration of Walmart Market and Express will allow the retailer to continue to fill in markets where they already have a Supercenter presence, such as Dallas and Las Vegas, as well as potentially enter new urban areas such as New York and Los Angeles.

Reaching the untapped and potentially extremely lucrative urban shopper would be Walmart's final jackpot. The top 15 metro areas in the United States represent a huge multi-billion opportunity for the retailer compared to the market share they have in the rural United States.[62] 'These cities could almost be viewed as countries in and of their own right, when we size the prize of food deserts and customers either being badly served or underserved', Mr Hucker told us.

> Most people would think that our base in America is probably people who've historically self-identified themselves as conservative voters. So now we only have one segment left – people who self-identify themselves as liberals.
>
> (Leslie Dach, Walmart's Executive Vice President of Corporate Affairs and Government Relations, 2010 (on Walmart's urban strategy))[63]

Now Walmart has had a notoriously difficult time gaining approval from city councils, mainly owing to strong union opposition, who fear Walmart's arrival will result in the demise of neighbourhood shops, job losses, the erosion of downtown districts and continued retail homogeneity. And it's not only cities – it can take up to seven years to open a Supercenter in the state of California.[64] Walmart too has had its fair share of frustrations with urban development, so much so that former CEO Lee Scott infamously said that New York City was simply not 'worth the effort'. He told *New York Times* reporters in 2007: 'I don't care if we are ever here.'[65] Not only was Walmart facing fierce opposition from labour unions but it also found that doing business in New York came with a hefty price tag. Despite its mammoth buying power, even Walmart finds it more challenging to buffer its profit margins in an urban setting, owing to higher property costs. Pricing needs to be consistent with its larger stores so that Walmart can stick with its golden rule of selling national brands cheaper than competitors do. This will be one of the biggest challenges for Walmart in urban areas given that real-estate costs can be more than double that of their rural locations ($40–50/sq. ft versus $20/sq. ft):[66]

> Every Day Low Prices can happen in 15,000 square feet.
>
> (Bill Simon, 2011)[67]

But Walmart hasn't given up on the city that never sleeps, and recently the company has drastically shifted gears in a final bid to tap into the Manhattanite's wallet. Walmartnyc.com was launched in 2011 as a way to raise awareness of the benefits that Walmart can bring to a city of over 8 million so-called underserved consumers. According to the retailer, nearly three-quarters of New Yorkers want Walmart to open. City residents are already spending nearly $200 million at its stores outside the five boroughs, which amounts to enough sales to support three Supercenters. Despite, or indeed because of, a lack of physical store presence, New York City is Walmart's largest US market for its online division.[68,69] It would be the retailer's last and largest domestic prize.

But it's not just about the lucrative New York market. Mr Simon told the authors that he believes there are 'plenty of opportunities' to serve more consumers in the United States. 'This is especially true in places like Chicago and Washington, DC with large populations of residents who are underserved, need convenient access to fresh, affordable food, and live in communities that are in need of new jobs and economic growth.'

More than 23 million US consumers, including 6 million children, currently lack access to supermarkets and fresh foods, living in so-called food deserts. As part of Michelle Obama's initiative to bring healthy foods to these impoverished neighbourhoods, Walmart, along with SuperValu and Walgreens, has committed to expanding in these underserved areas. By 2016, Walmart will open up to 300 stores in such areas, while SuperValu has committed to opening a similar number. Meanwhile, at least 1,000 Walgreens stores will open or be converted to include food over the next several years. Currently, almost half Walgreens stores are located in areas that do not have easy access to fresh food.[70]

Walmart has come a long way in cities like Washington, DC, and Chicago thanks to improvements in food quality, labour relations, healthier food strategy and environmental initiatives which have helped to improve its reputation among both consumers and city councils. Walmart has since won approval to open its first stores in Washington, DC, which will debut in late 2012, bringing fresh groceries, a full-service pharmacy and a variety of general merchandise to areas that have traditionally been underrepresented by chain retailers. Once again, Walmart has been the primary beneficiary of a weak US economy. With high levels of unemployment and many urban consumers lacking access to fresh, low-priced groceries, the same local governments that previously shunned Walmart are now having a change of heart. In Washington, DC, Walmart will create 1,200 jobs.[71] In Chicago, where Walmart has faced severe public opposition for years, it won approval in 2011 to open six stores which will create 10,000 jobs by 2015.

'When I met with Walmart [in 2010], I encouraged them to take an approach that addressed the needs of the urban shopper if they truly wanted to make a difference in our underserved neighbourhoods', said Chicago's Mayor Richard Daley. The six Chicago stores include Supercenters, Express stores and Walmart Markets.[72] This flexible, multi-channel approach is how Walmart will crack America's cities.

Meanwhile, there is one other untapped consumer segment that has caught the Bentonville giant's eye. This group has historically gone unnoticed by US retailers given their general lack of purchasing power and consequent love for Ramen noodles and Kraft Mac & Cheese – the American college student. As part of its broader small-format strategy, Walmart opened its first Walmart on Campus store in 2011. Like most pilot formats, the campus store was tested close to home at the University of Arkansas. Replacing a university-run pharmacy, the 3,500 sq. ft Walmart on Campus store is the retailer's smallest to date, featuring a full-service pharmacy, groceries and a selection of general merchandise. The authors visited the store soon after opening and were impressed once again with Walmart's growing flexibility with regard to store layout and merchandising – this is quite possibly the only Walmart store with entire endcaps devoted to Ramen noodles. Despite the fact that college kids may not be the most cash-rich group to target, there are more than 20 million nationwide[73] – many of whom are currently limited with regard to retail operations on campus – not to mention the staff, faculty, visitors and community members who will also benefit from a Walmart opening. We view this as a fantastic life-stage opportunity to connect with future consumers. At the time of writing, the concept was exceeding company expectations and there has been much interest from other colleges and universities. Watch this space.

The kings of convenience: US drugstores

We are going to be adding hundreds of these in the coming years and maybe even more depending on how they work out.

(BILL SIMON ON SMALLER FORMATS IN THE UNITED STATES, 2011)[74]

Given Walmart's ambitious growth plans with a smaller format, the authors can't help but wonder if an acquisition could be on the cards. Although there are cases against it (Walmart has traditionally opted for organic over acquisitive growth in the United States, small-box development could occur quickly enough on an organic basis and, of course, there would likely be regulatory barriers), an acquisition would give Walmart a foothold in the convenience market essentially overnight. And they certainly have the cash.

So who might they consider? Well, as we said earlier, not many traditional supermarkets have cracked the 20,000 sq. ft and under range, so more likely than not Walmart would be looking at a drug or dollar store primarily from a real-estate perspective. The main US drugstore chains – Walgreens, CVS and Rite Aid – have an astonishing reach with a combined 20,000 stores.[75] In fact, nearly three-quarters of the US population live within five miles of a Walgreens and 6 million shoppers visit their stores on a daily basis.[76] Powerful stuff.

The drugstores are now looking to capitalize on their advantageous real estate by adding more fresh foods to the mix. For example, Walgreens has added nearly 800 new food items, including fresh fruits and vegetables, frozen meats and fish, pasta, rice, beans, eggs and whole-grain cereals, to some of its stores.[77] CVS is in the process of adding food to about 300 urban stores in Boston, New York, Washington, Detroit and Philadelphia. One-fifth of its 7,000 stores could eventually be reconfigured.[78] Rite Aid is also looking to get in on the action, having partnered with SuperValu's Save-A-Lot discount chain to launch a hybrid format combining grocery and drug (which, call us crazy, almost sounds like... a supermarket). The drugstores have also been busy revamping their private label assortment so as to grab a larger share of the grocery pie more profitably while at the same time driving shopper loyalty. In 2011, Walgreens launched the Nice! range while CVS debuted its Just the Basics brand.

Although the drugstore channel on the whole is smaller than traditional supermarkets, food sales are growing far more rapidly in the drugstore channel. This is a clear indication that their strategies are paying off and that there is genuine demand for low-priced, quality foods in a convenient setting. According to SymphonyIRI, in the 52 weeks to June 2011, drugstores experienced a 6.9 per cent increase in beer sales to $1.1 billion, versus supermarket growth of just 1 per cent in the category to $8.4 billion. Frozen dinners is another booming category: the drugstores saw a 15.9 per cent increase in sales while supermarkets recorded a mere 0.09 per cent rise. In some categories, such as dog food, the drugstores have grown sales by close to 20 per cent while supermarkets have actually lost share:[79]

> Going small prevents us from losing the milk, bread and eggs trip to the drugstores... but we're still a long way from perfecting this.
>
> (Walmart executive)

The drugstores win on convenience. They win on shopper frequency, particularly when catering to shoppers with repeat prescriptions, of which there will be many more in the coming decade. However, there is one area where they let shoppers down – price. Because groceries are not the drugstores' core offering, they tend to buy and store food less efficiently than supermarkets, which is noticeably reflected in their prices. In Brooklyn, for example, a Siggi's yogurt at a Duane Reade costs $3.19, but can be purchased for just $2.75 at a nearby corner store. 'There is a cost of convenience, because we are on some of the best corners in America', said Walgreens' chief merchandising officer, Bryan Pugh.[80] We can think of one retailer in particular that is ready to challenge that statement.

That is not to say that Walmart shouldn't be worried, particularly given the projected growth in over-65s as discussed earlier in the chapter. A one-stop shop – food and pharmacy – in a small, convenient setting has a long, healthy future in store. So we believe that Walmart could look to make a drugstore acquisition as part of its smaller-format strategy. Not only would it enable the company to stamp out the growing grocery business in existing drugstore chains, but Walmart would also benefit from the expertise of a smaller chain as they look to capitalize on the United States' ageing consumer base. To our mind, based on current valuations and distribution of stores, Rite Aid would be the ideal candidate.

Living off Walmart's crumbs

An acquisition would also enable Walmart to battle another thorn in its side – the dollar stores. Currently worth $45 billion, the US discount sector is expected to more than double in the next decade to reach $100 billion, according to Planet Retail. And as much as it may pain Walmart to admit it, the dollar stores in particular have been eating into its market share over the past several years.

Kantar Retail's shopping behaviour analysis, ShopperScape, indicates that many shoppers have defected from Walmart to conventional supermarkets and Target. However, parsing the data by income market shows that less affluent shoppers are most likely to divert trips to dollar stores – evidence that leakage to dollar stores has the potential to derail Walmart's efforts to reassert its EDLP price leadership position among a core shopper segment.

As discussed in the pricing chapter, taking its eye off EDLP was a major opportunity for the dollar stores to flaunt their pricing credentials. And while these stores used to cater primarily to low- and fixed-income groups, today they are seeing more affluent, bargain-seeking shoppers coming through their doors. Consequently, average spend per store has increased. The dollar stores are now making major improvements in terms of store design, merchandising (like the drugstores, they are adding more groceries to the mix) and, crucially, improvements in location. Owing to the high number of property vacancies and sudden demand for value among consumers, these discount-led stores have been able to get into higher-traffic and higher-income sites which, as a result, has helped to raise their awareness among new consumer groups.

As discussed earlier, the dollar stores and Walmart have traditionally not gone head to head. Given the small size of a typical dollar store, merchandising assortment is extremely limited, which means that shoppers can't complete a full weekly basket. Yet, given the strong overlap in shopper demographics, the dollar stores benefit from the amount of traffic generated by Walmart. 'You can't out-Walmart Walmart', Family Dollar CEO Howard Levine said in 2011. 'The dollar stores are not going after the same trip Walmart is going after. We're going after the fill-in trip. We live off the crumbs they leave us.'[81] The roll-out of Walmart Express will surely change Levine's view about sharing a similar trip. Express will enable Walmart to reach those rural consumers in a new, convenient setting. It is not only fighting back on the value front (with comparable Supercenter prices) but it differentiates from the dollar stores with in-store pharmacies, cheque cashing and other financial services, and its site-to-store initiative.

> Based on our analytical modelling, we believe we still have approximately 12,000 opportunities for new stores.
>
> (Richard Dreiling, CEO of Dollar General)[82]

However, up until now, living off the crumbs has not been a bad strategy, given the high growth levels we have seen from this sector over the past decade. Dollar General, the largest of the bunch with roughly 10,000 stores, has opened an average of 450 stores annually over the past decade.[83] Growth has been phenomenal and there are certainly no signs of slowing down: at the end of 2010, Dollar General told investors that there is room for an additional 12,000 new stores, of which 8,000 will be in existing markets.[84] Private equity ownership has fuelled Dollar General's growth, and this is a trend we continue to see throughout the sector.

The addition of perishable groceries, a clear pricing model, rapid expansion plans, store remodels and better sites are all reasons why the dollar stores are keeping Walmart up at night. During the recession, while Walmart was reporting quarter after quarter of negative comparable store sales growth, Dollar General was posting high single-digit increases. With little sign of this sector slowing down, Walmart will have to get serious about going small.

Digital evolution

A new retail world is evolving and Walmart is ready to embrace it.

(EDUARDO CASTRO-WRIGHT, 2011)[85]

Just as small stores were never a priority in the past, e-commerce was also a back-burner topic for Walmart for many years. Its stores may attract 10.5 billion consumers around the globe each year, but in cyberspace Walmart attracts roughly one-tenth of that figure.[86] In terms of revenues, e-commerce accounts for a mere 2 per cent of Walmart's total sales, despite the retailer's 15+ years' presence on the world wide web.[87] So why have they been so late to the game?

As discussed earlier in the chapter, for the past decade the company was – justifiably to a certain degree – more concerned with growing its Supercenter estate during this time. Supercenters were highly profitable, in demand, and far less risky than growing a dotcom business. 'The internet has some very interesting aspects and will definitely serve a growing market as we move into the 21st century', Chairman Rob Walton noted back in 1999. 'However, very few, if any, internet retailers have made a profit, and issues like the cost of delivery, merchandise returns and data security all have to be resolved before this business model is validated.'[88]

Internet retailing used to be confined to buying books and music from a desktop computer. Today, smartphones let us customize our grocery list while waiting for a bus. Today, thanks to augmented reality, clothes can be tried on virtually before placing an order. Today, we don't have to wait in for a delivery – we can order online and pick up at a local store at our convenience. By 2015, the US e-commerce market is expected to be worth $279 billion, a statistic that Walmart can no longer ignore.[89]

But it's not just about transacting online – the internet has truly empowered consumers. Today, we are armed with product and pricing information. We thrive off transparency. We use social media to interact with retailers and brands (and, crucially, to be heard when something goes wrong). We use the internet to share deals and recommend products. We find both value and excitement through flash sales and group buying. E-commerce today is instant, engaging and relevant. And Walmart has been missing out.

Democratization of technology

'It's fair to say that up until about a year ago, when Mike Duke defined what we call the next generation of Walmart as a major initiative for the company, probably we were not as keenly devoted to creating the kind of shopping experiences across all channels as we are doing today', said Eduardo Castro-Wright,[90] who took the helm of the company's online division in June 2010.

Walmart has been slow to jump on the digital bandwagon, in part because its core shoppers have not been the earliest adopters when it comes to new technologies. In 2007, Walmart closed down its movie and TV show download service with Hewlett-Packard just 10 months after launch.[91] Three years earlier, Walmart launched a digital music download service in a bid to catch up to iTunes and Amazon's MP3 store, but that too failed to resonate with shoppers, and was eventually shut down in 2011.[92]

A survey by Gallup showed that in 2005, households with annual income of $100,000 or more were three times as likely to buy online compared to households with income under $35,000 and 33 per cent more likely than households with income of $75,000–$100,000.[93] Back in 2005, lower-income households (ie core Walmart shoppers) were less likely to own a computer, which at the time was the only way to shop online. Fast-forward to today and not only has there been significant price deflation in the PC category, but consumers can now purchase goods from their smartphones[94] (which one-third of Walmart shoppers now own) as well as other new media such as lower-priced netbooks as well as tablets. Online shopping has been democratized.

It's also important to remember that Walmart's shopper base has broadened over the past several years, with many higher-income, tech-savvy consumers trading down during the recession in a bid to find better value at the shelf. Many of these shoppers see Walmart as a way to save a few bucks on weekly groceries, but when it comes to downloading music, not to name the elephant in the room, but surely there are more obvious choices.

Yet it wasn't just a lack of consumer demand: Walmart was also late to the e-commerce arena because of structural reasons. According to a former Walmart.com executive, many store managers initially feared that making a push for e-commerce would cannibalize their in-store sales (and consequently their bonuses). This approach, not exactly customer-centric or sustainable, was not unique to Walmart. Across the Atlantic, Germany's Media-Saturn suffered from the same fears and it was only in 2011 that Europe's largest consumer electronics chain finally succumbed to demand with plans to launch a transactional website.

In any case, e-commerce is the fastest-growing retail channel today and Walmart has no choice but to embrace the new digital world, not only because it is a long-term consumer-driven trend but also because, as we have discussed, Walmart must find alternative avenues for growth in its domestic market:

> If I had to guess, social commerce is the next area to really blow up.
>
> (Mark Zuckerberg, founder of Facebook)

In support of this new strategic focus and to serve the digital consumer more broadly, Walmart has made a number of key investments over the past few years, including the acquisition of online movie service Vudu which is enabling it to go head to head with the likes of Netflix and iTunes, the launch of a beta online grocery service in San Jose, the nationwide expansion of its Pick Up Today programme, and notably the $300 million acquisition of social media technology platform Kosmix. The purchase of Kosmix, which has been integrated into a division called @WalmartLabs, was very un-Walmart and took many analysts by surprise; however, it could only be viewed as a step in the right direction as it is helping Walmart to tackle two key areas where it had virtually zero experience – mobile and social commerce.

By 2015, shoppers around the globe are expected to spend $119 billion on goods and services purchased through their mobile phones. It's important to point out here that much of this growth will come at the expense of traditional e-commerce, but still represents a fast-growing sector nonetheless. Meanwhile, the global social commerce market, virtually non-existent in 2010, is expected to reach $30 billion by 2015. Half of this will come from the United States.[95]

It may sound fluffy to some, but companies can genuinely drive sales socially. Take Gap, for example. The struggling apparel retailer rang up sales of $11 million in just one day by partnering with Groupon.[96] Going forward, we will see many more retailers pursue flash sales and group buying. Not only does it create a sense of urgency and excitement among shoppers, but it also enables retailers to genuinely translate the promotional experience online and shift stock where needed.

Social media on the whole is rapidly changing the way consumers engage with brands and retailers and, if used correctly, can also provide companies with a wealth of information about their customers. The challenge, however, is transferring the sheer amount of data and feedback into actionable insight.

Within Walmart, Asda has been the pioneer in this field. By monitoring real-time customer input from social media sites such as Twitter, Facebook, YouTube and other online forums via its Online Reputation Booth (ORB), it has been able to respond quickly to customer queries and get feedback on specific products. For example, Asda once noticed a flurry of (unrelated) social media users discussing how their Bourbon biscuits suddenly tasted differently. Asda fed those comments back to its biscuits buyer who confirmed that the retailer had in fact recently changed suppliers. Thanks to the feedback from customers, Asda made the decision to change quickly back to its original biscuit supplier. 'Social media is a free, massive focus group, taking place in real time. And it is taking place with or without your permission', said Rick Bendel, Walmart's global chief marketing officer, who is based in the UK.[97]

Consumers today want to share, they want to be heard, and retailers are missing a trick if they are not listening. 'It was clear to us that word-of-mouth marketing had been elevated to a new level. Fed by the rise in technology and ease of access to the web, peer-to-peer endorsement was now turbo-charged', Bendel noted.[98] Asda was able to further capitalize on this general shift in consumer mind-set when it came time to re-launch its private label line, now known as Chosen By You. This was the largest-ever private label re-launch in UK history and proof that retailers can go a long way by simply listening to their customers. All 3,500 of the original products had been blind-tasted by at least 50 consumers and more than two-thirds of those had to approve the product.[99]

Prior to the re-launch, the range was generating annual sales in excess of £8 billion (or 85 per cent of Asda's private label sales) and being purchased by 92 per cent of Asda shoppers, so all in all it wasn't a bad idea to ask the people buying it before making any changes.[100] The result? Not only did shoppers notice a quality improvement across the board but Asda uncovered valuable item-related preferences (ie toffee-flavoured ice cream and lemon cupcakes), which led to NPD and consequent sales increases. The message is simple – retailers must get customers involved, both online and in person.

It's important to bear in mind, however, that the UK is a nation of 62 million consumers, whereas the United States is home to nearly five times as many people. Asda therefore will find it much easier to involve customers in the decision-making process, to monitor feedback, and even to use social media to track competitive activity. During heavy snow, Asda was able to respond to customers experiencing delays to their grocery home-shopping order, prompting the business to communicate more quickly with affected customers. This would be much harder to do in the United States where the volume of activity is much, much greater.

However, Walmart is recognizing the need to harness data and get closer to its shoppers in the process, and, again in a very un-Walmart fashion, created a Consumer Insights Division in 2011. If this were any other retailer, such an announcement would be deemed relatively insignificant. But this is Walmart – the retailer who has traditionally shunned such initiatives for being too fluffy and adding unnecessary cost into the business. So why the change of heart? After two years of comparable sales declines, Walmart has finally recognized that it needs to do a better job when it comes to leveraging shopper insights. Like Asda, Walmart US is listening to shoppers via social media: at the time of writing, Walmart had 6 million Facebook fans, half a million of whom were providing feedback on transactions.[101] The challenge is ensuring that the right people within the Walmart organization receive that feedback and respond to it. 'In the future, we will dramatically expand the opportunity to listen to and engage with our customer', said Cindy Davis, who heads the Consumer Insights Division.[102] As part of that process, Walmart lifted a decade-long ban on data sharing in 2011, and is now working closely with market research firms like Nielsen and SymphonyIRI in a bid to gain deeper insights into shopper purchases. As Sam Walton always said, 'There is only one boss – the customer. And he can fire everybody in the company from the chairman down, simply by spending his money somewhere else.'

Amazon – 'the Walmart of our era'

Looking back to the early success of Walmart Supercenters, and hyper-markets in general, the concept won based on three principles. Firstly, the convenience of buying everything under one roof. Secondly, the lowest prices around. And thirdly, the broadest assortment you could imagine. Does that sound familiar? Yes, that sounds a lot like e-commerce today.

'In global e-commerce, we will not just be competing. We will play to win', Mike Duke told investors at the company's 2011 Shareholders Meeting. There is only one company in the world unlikely to be losing sleep over those comments – Amazon.

In fact, it's far more likely that Amazon is keeping Bentonville awake at night. Despite a number of key differences between the two companies – Amazon's best-selling item is the Kindle, Walmart's is the banana[103] – they are finding themselves closer competitors by the day. The future is digital and Amazon is extremely well placed to cater to it. Walmart's e-commerce sales are estimated to be around $6 billion, which is peanuts next to Amazon's $34 billion.[104] By 2024, Amazon is expected to overtake Walmart as the largest retailer in the world.[105]

So how is it doing it? Ironically, it is beating Walmart at its own game – pricing and assortment. Pricing is far more transparent online, although bricks-and-mortar retailers are increasingly making use of price comparison apps and other forms of price guarantees in order to bridge the gap. A 2011 study by Wells Fargo found that Amazon was up to 19 per cent cheaper than Walmart on a basket of goods (or about 9 per cent cheaper when you factor in shipping costs).[106] This opens up a debate on whether online retailers should be subject to paying sales tax but, regardless, it is a dis-advantage to Walmart, whose internet prices are generally comparable to those found in-store.

In terms of assortment, pure-play online retailers are not constrained by shelf space. Amazon offers approximately 14 times the number of products that Walmart does. In electronics, for example, Amazon offered 2,016 types of digital camcorders versus the 96 found on Walmart.com.[107] Two months after the initial Wells Fargo study, the firm compared prices once again and found that not only did Amazon have more products in stock than its competitors, but it increased its prices by an average of 10 per cent com-pared to the first study on products that were sold out at rivals.[108]

Morgan Stanley's Scott Devitt wrote in 2011: 'Amazon.com is the Walmart of our era but it's better, in our view – Amazon.com is the com-bination of a technology and logistics company, allowing it to participate in a transition of physical to digital retail supported by a store-less (in Seattle) business model that leads to higher long-term economic returns.'[109]

The future looks bright for Amazon, and more challenging for Walmart.com. Unlike Walmart, Amazon has a massive opportunity to expand simply by growing sales with existing customers (ie stealing share from competitors such as Walmart itself). Amazon's 121 million shoppers spend an annual average of $275 whereas Walmart's 300 million shoppers spend $750 per year.[110] If we factored in the money spent on groceries and at Sam's Club, the gap would be even more astonishing.

Going global.com

In terms of international growth, pure-play online retailers such as Amazon are able to penetrate new markets more quickly than those with a bricks-and-mortar presence. It is far less risky and cost-intensive to launch a new website compared to investing in a chain of stores. Since inception, it took 46 years for Walmart's International division to account for 25 per cent of total sales. For Amazon, it took eight.[111]

Looking ahead, we cannot rule out Walmart taking a leaf from Amazon's book by entering a new market purely with a domain name. Fashion retailers and department stores are spearheading this trend, with Macy's, Bloomingdales, Saks, Next, John Lewis and Marks & Spencer all prime examples. This is a fantastic way to test demand for a brand and to generate awareness, perhaps before a physical launch. A Saks website without store support is still offering something new to the market. However, a Walmart website without store support is surely just a smaller and potentially more expensive version of... well, Amazon.

Walmart therefore needs to leverage its thousands of physical stores to support its e-commerce strategy. This is how they can compete against pure-play online retailers. While online is without a doubt an increasingly important aspect of retailing today, let's not forget that a very small percentage of shoppers today buy only online. They still want the physical in-store experience and, of course, Amazon cannot offer this (although there have been rumours of Amazon launching physical stores for years now). Walmart will not win in e-commerce – Walmart will win in multi-channel.

Mr Simon told the authors: 'We want our customers to be able to shop at Walmart whenever, wherever and however they want by integrating the shopping experience between bricks-and-mortar stores and e-commerce. This also reflects the continued integration of customers using web-based devices to shop our stores and to research and shop online, as well.' With initiatives such as Site-to-Store and Pick Up Today, the retailer is certainly heading in the right direction.

Globally, there are plenty of opportunities for Walmart to grow e-commerce sales. They have been ramping up investment in Asia and Latin America, having quietly launched transactional sites in Brazil, China, Mexico and Chile over the past several years.

China in particular is poised for an e-commerce boom – by 2016, it is expected to overtake the United States to become the world's largest e-commerce market. Currently, one in four of the world's internet users live in China; this is equivalent to 460 million which is greater than the entire US population.[112] This hasn't gone unnoticed in Bentonville.

Walmart has ramped up online activity in China by launching a transactional site for its Sam's Club operation as well as acquiring a minority stake in Yihaodian, a fast-growing online supermarket. Yihaodian distinguishes itself from bricks-and-mortar retailers by offering a broad assortment of 100,000 SKUs compared with the 20,000 found in a typical Chinese supermarket. Prices are 3–5 per cent cheaper than those found in bricks-and-mortar retailers, making it an attractive fit for Walmart.[113]

Most Chinese e-commerce retailers specialize in a single product line; however, Yihaodian has found success selling across a multitude of categories. Its core lines make up the broader grocery category, although products in the baby care, consumer electronics and apparel categories are also featured. Nonetheless, given the country's poor infrastructure, achieving economies of scale in the supply chain will be Walmart's biggest challenge in China.

Brazil, which is home to 40 per cent of Latin America's internet users, is another market to watch.[114] Walmart's Brazilian e-commerce operations offer 10 times the assortment available in-store and have been growing at double the market rate in recent years.[115] The country's burgeoning middle class will continue to support this growth: according to Forrester Research, the market is expected to grow at an 18 per cent annual rate with total sales expected to reach $22 billion by 2016, nearly three times more than in 2010.[116]

Looking ahead, Walmart will expand its reach in more markets and categories, and it will grow mobile commerce in emerging markets, given that in many of these countries there are far more mobile phones than internet connections. According to the Boston Consulting Group, in 2010 there were 610 million regular internet users in the BRICI markets (Brazil, Russia, India, China and Indonesia) compared to a whopping 1.8 billion mobile phone connections.[117]

But online growth will not be restricted to emerging economies; it is also a priority in more mature, sluggish markets such as Japan where the retailer plans to grow e-commerce sales twentyfold over a five-year period to 2016. Customer count is expected to grow tenfold during that time. Walmart has had an online presence in Japan for over a decade, yet only 47 stores are used as picking centres for home delivery. By the end of 2013, this will grow to 350 stores.[118] Despite a stagnant economy, shrinking population and ongoing contraction of the broader retail sector, Japan's e-commerce sector continues to grow at approximately 10 per cent annually.[119]

One would have expected the densely populated, tech-savvy nation to be a goldmine for e-commerce. Yet, compared to the rest of the world, Japan has been surprisingly late to embrace this channel – particularly for fruit and vegetables as many consumers still prefer to see, touch and feel before buying. However, the recession has changed the way consumers behave, research and ultimately purchase goods. More people staying at home have created opportunities for the sector, and retailers such as Walmart are now looking to capitalize on this trend. However, Walmart will face some strong domestic competition as it looks to expand its online operation: two-thirds of the 90 million internet users in Japan shop via Rakuten, the country's largest online shopping mall.[120]

Growth in e-commerce, both at home and abroad, will undoubtedly impact the way Walmart – and all retailers for that matter – operate their physical stores. In the next decade, as more consumers around the world gain access to online shopping, there will be a need for retailers to create a more compelling in-store experience. Shopping is still a pastime in most countries, developed and emerging, and physical stores can capitalize on this as a means of differentiating from the encroaching online channel. Price and assortment can be replicated too easily; instead, retailers will need to ramp up their efforts in areas such as ancillary offerings (ie in-store daycare, spas, social areas) and retail theatre, and, crucially, invest in customer service.

Notes

1 Walmart 1982 Annual Report, p 4. **http://media.corporate-ir.net/media_files/irol/11/112761/ARs/1982AR.pdf**

2 2011 net sales $419 bn. **http://www.sec.gov/Archives/edgar/data/104169/000119312511083157/dex13.htm**

3 Walmart 1981 Annual Report, p 4. **http://media.corporate-ir.net/media_files/irol/11/112761/ARs/1981AR.pdf**

4 Walton (1992), p 64

5 *Progressive Grocer*, Driving Wal-Mart's growth engine: a dramatic shift in strategic assumptions has propelled the retailer's spectacular expansion since the death of founder Sam Walton, 1 February 2004

6 **http://www.rogersarkansas.com/museum/rogershistory.asp**

7 All based on US population divided by 2010 store numbers from 10ks

8 Walton (1992), p 54

9 Walton (1992), p 256

10 As per 2011 10k (2010 numbers) p 9. **http://www.sec.gov/Archives/edgar/data/104169/000119312511083157/d10k.htm**

11 Walton (1992), p 254

12 *The Wall Street Journal*, Price war in aisle 3 – Wal-Mart tops grocery list with Supercenter format; but fewer choices, amenities, Patricia Callahan and Ann Zimmerman, 27 May 2003

13 *Supermarket News*. **http://www.pbs.org/wsw/tvprogram/drbulreportwmt.pdf**

14 **http://www.aptea.com/company.asp**

15 *The Wall Street Journal*, A&P heading to the checkout counter? Dave Kansas, 10 December 2010. **http://blogs.wsj.com/marketbeat/2010/12/10/ ap-heading-to-the-checkout-counter/**

16 **http://www.thekrogerco.com/corpnews/corpnewsinfo_timeline.htm**

17 Planet Retail

18 *Supermarket News*, Aldi fires up value fight in Dallas market, Jon Springer, 5 April 2010. **http://subscribers.supermarketnews.com/retail_financial/ aldi-fires-up-value-0405/**

19 Philly.com, Carrefour seeks N.J. outlet. French retailer picks Voorhees site, Susan Warner, Inquirer Staff Writer, 24 October 1990. **http://articles.philly.com/ 1990-10-24/business/25891701_1_carrefour-french-retailer- shopping-center**

20 *Discount Store News*, Hypermart USA units get SuperCenter-type facelift – Wal-Mart Supercenter combination stores; Hypermart USA hypermarkets, Arthur Markowitz, 9 April 1990

21 *Arkansas Business*, Arkansas consumers soon will test Wal-Mart's new supermarket concept, David Smith, 28 September 1998

22 Walmart 1979 Annual Report, p 1. **http://media.corporate-ir.net/ media_files/irol/11/112761/ARs/1979AR.pdf**

23 PR Newswire, Michaels Stores consummates acquisition of Helen's Arts and Crafts Stores from Wal-Mart, 2 May 1988. **http://www.highbeam.com/ doc/1G1-6635339.html**

24 *Fortune*, Nelson D. Schwartz, 16 February 1998. **http://money.cnn.com/ magazines/fortune/fortune_archive/1998/02/16/237707/index.htm**

25 Walmart 2011 Annual Report and Kroger 10k. Kroger total sq ft is 149m

26 The 600 conversions statistic was based on author research from Walmart 10ks.$425 statistic source: Walmart 1997 Annual Report, p 3. **http://media.corporate-ir.net/media_files/irol/11/112761/ARs/ 1997_annualreport.pdf**

27 Walmart 1997 Annual Report, p 3. **http://media.corporate-ir.net/ media_files/irol/11/112761/ARs/1997_annualreport.pdf**

28 Author research/Walmart 10k

29 Food Marketing Institute. **http://www.fmi.org/facts_figs/keyfacts/? fuseaction=storesize**

30 Author research based on Walmart 10ks

31 2010 10k

32 Walmart, as of August 2011

33 Census. **http://www.census.gov/population/www/projections/ usinterimproj/natprojtab02a.pdf**

34 **http://www.knowledgeatwharton.com.cn/index.cfm?fa= printArticle&articleID=1420&languageid=1**

35 Walmart 1978 annual report. **http://media.corporate-ir.net/media_files/ irol/11/112761/ARs/1978AR.pdf**

36 Walmart/Walmart contact/Planet Retail

37 Walmart contact

38 **http://investors.walmartstores.com/phoenix.zhtml?c=112761&p=irol-newsArticle&ID=1482363&highlight=**

39 *The Wall Street Journal*, With sales flabby, Wal-Mart turns to its core, Miguel Bustillo, 21 March 2011. **http://online.wsj.com/article/ SB10001424052748703328404576207161692001774.html**

40 **http://news.google.com/newspapers?id=-VJSAAAAIBAJ&sjid= mzYNAAAAIBAJ&pg=3688,3873785&dq=walmart+sells+convenience+ stores+to+conoco&hl=en**

41 *The Wall Street Journal*, Wal-Mart to build a test supermarket in bid to boost grocery-industry share, Emily Nelson, Staff Reporter, 10 June 1998

42 *The Wall Street Journal*, as above

43 Author research based on Walmart 10ks

44 Food Marketing Institute. **http://www.fmi.org/facts_figs/?fuseaction= superfact**

45 *Independent,* Asda plans move into convenience stores, Susie Mesure, Retail Correspondent. **http://www.independent.co.uk/news/business/ news/asda-plans-move-into-convenience-stores-437360.html**

46 *Independent*, US business will make money in three years, Tesco predicts, James Thompson, 6 October 2010. **http://www.independent.co.uk/news/ business/news/asda-plans-move-into-convenience-stores-437360.html**

47 *Fortune*, The rise of the grocery co-op, Beth Kowitt, writer-reporter, 19 September 2010. **http://money.cnn.com/2010/09/16/news/ companies/grocery_coop_Brooklyn.fortune/index.htm**

48 Planet Retail

49 *USA Today*, Most foreclosures pack into a few counties, Brad Heath, 6 March. **http://www.usatoday.com/money/economy/housing/ 2009-03-05-foreclosure_N.htm**

50 *Supermarket News*, Next Tesco CEO: Fresh & Easy future uncertain, 20 September 2010. **http://supermarketnews.com/news/fresh_easy_0920/**

51 164 as per FY 2011 annual report. **http://ar2011.tescoplc.com/overview/ tesco-around-the-world.html#null**

52 *Guardian*, Tesco perseveres with Fresh & Easy, Nils Pratley, 19 April 2011. **http://www.guardian.co.uk/business/2011/apr/19/viewpoint-tesco**

53 *Financial Times*, Wal-Mart sees Marketside as $10bn chain, Jonathan Birchall, 7 August 2008

54 **http://walmartstores.com/pressroom/news/9106.aspx**

55 Census, *Note based on 2008 figures. **http://www.census.gov/newsroom/releases/archives/population/cb08-123.html**

56 17th Annual Meeting for the Investment Community – Day 2 – Final, 13 October 2010

57 *Financial Times*, Walmart slims down stores for China, Jonathan Birchall, 1 December 2010

58 *New York Times*, Wal-Mart tests service for buying food online, Stephanie Clifford, 24 April 2011

59 WalMart Stores, Inc. at Bank of America Merrill Lynch Consumer Conference – Final, 10 March 2011

60 Census. **http://www.census.gov/population/www/projections/summarytables.html**. Table 2: Projections of the Population by Selected Age Groups and Sex for the United States: 2010 to 2050

61 81m according to **http://www.google.co.uk/publicdata/explore?ds=d5bncppjof8f9_&met_y=sp_pop_totl&idim=country:DEU&dl=en&hl=en&q=population+of+germany**

62 Hucker

63 *New York Times*, Wal-Mart tries a refined path into New York, Elizabeth A. Harris, 25 March 2011. **http://www.nytimes.com/2011/03/26/nyregion/26walmart.html**

64 Hucker

65 *New York Times*, Wal-Mart chief writes off New York, Michael Barbaro and Steven Greenhouse, 28 March 2007. **www.nytimes.com/2007/03/28/business/28retail.html**

66 Hucker

67 Miguel Bustillo, as note 39

68 **http://www.observer.com/2011/real-estate/wal-mart-and-lesson-betamax**

69 *The Wall Street Journal*, Wal-Mart bids to break into Gotham, Charles Fishman, 12 February 2011. **http://online.wsj.com/article/SB10001424052748704132204576136190865458376.html**

70 *International Business Times*, Michelle Obama, Walmart to Bring Healthy Choices to 'Food Desert', 20 July 2011. **http://www.ibtimes.com/articles/183847/20110720/michelle-obama-walmart-bring-healthy-food-to-food-desert.htm**

71 **http://walmartstores.com/pressroom/news/10479.aspx**

72 **http://investors.walmartstores.com/phoenix.zhtml?c=112761&p=irol-newsArticle&ID=1539962&highlight=**

73 College enrollment was a projected 20.6 million in fall 2010. **http://nces.ed.gov/programs/digest/d10/**

74   WalMart Stores, Inc. at Bank of America Merrill Lynch Consumer Conference – Final, 10 March 2011

75   Company reports

76   Walgreens 2010 10k. **http://www.sec.gov/Archives/edgar/data/104207/ 000010420710000098/fy2010_10k.htm**

77   **http://news.walgreens.com/article_display.cfm?article_id=5328** launched in 2010

78   Bloomberg Businessweek, Big retail chains market groceries to inner cities, Carol Wolf, 28 October 2010

79   **http://supermarketnews.com/viewpoints/new_proof_drug_0815/**

80   *New York Times*, Big retailers fill more aisles with groceries, Stephanie Clifford, 16 January 2011. **http://www.nytimes.com/2011/01/17/ business/17grocery.html?pagewanted=all**

81   *TIME*, Dollar stores: getting more bang from the buck, Sean Gregory, Charlotte, Sunday, 2 January 2011. Read more: **http://www.time.com/ time/magazine/article/0,9171,2036156,00.html#ixzz1UjSsQzwd**

82   *Supermarket News*, DG market primed for expansion, Jon Springer, 13 December 2010. **http://supermarketnews.com/retail_financial/ dg-market-primed-expansion-1213/**

83   Author research based on company reports

84   Jon Springer, as note 82

85   Walmart Shareholders Meeting, June 2011

86   Walmart Shareholders Meeting, June 2011 – ECW states that online attracts 1.5bn people globally vs. 10.5 instore

87   Bloomberg Businessweek, Wal-Mart's rocky path from bricks to clicks, Matthew Boyle and Douglas MacMillan, 21 July 2011. **http://www.businessweek.com/magazine/ walmarts-rocky-path-from-bricks-to-clicks-07212011.html**

88   Walmart Annual Report

89   Forrester Research. **http://www.forrester.com/ER/Press/Release/ 0,1769,1367,00.html**

90   Matthew Boyle and Douglas MacMillan, as note 87

91   *New York Times*, Wal-Mart is buying Vudu movie service, Dealbook, 22 February 2010. **http://dealbook.nytimes.com/2010/02/22/ wal-mart-is-said-to-be-buying-vudu-movie-service/**

92   *New York Times*, After 7 years, Wal-Mart closes its MP3 store, Ben Sisario, 9 August 2011. **http://mediadecoder.blogs.nytimes.com/2011/08/09/ after-7-years-wal-mart-closes-its-mp3-store/**

93   **http://www.internetretailer.com/2005/12/22/ likelihood-to-shop-online-goes-up-with-income**

94 ABI Research. **http://www.abiresearch.com/press/1605-Shopping+by+ Mobile+Will+Grow+to+%24119+Billion+in+2015**

95 Booz & Company. **http://www.booz.com/media/uploads/BaC-Turning_ Like_to_Buy.pdf**

96 **http://www.zdnet.com/blog/btl/groupons-11-million-gap-day-a- business-winner-or-loser/38259**

97 *Retail Week*, Tried and trusted, 6 May 2011

98 As above

99 **http://your.asda.com/2010/9/21/asda-unveils-new-quality-mark- across-3-500-products-chosen-by-you**

100 *The Wall Street Journal*, Asda tries to revive food line-up, Simon Zekaria, 22 September 2010

101 Comment from Cindy Davis at Walmart Shareholders Meeting, June 2011

102 As above

103 **http://mashable.com/2011/06/21/amazon-walmart-infographic/**

104 Matthew Boyle and Douglas MacMillan, as note 87

105 **http://mashable.com/2011/06/21/amazon-walmart-infographic/**

106 Matthew Boyle and Douglas MacMillan, as note 87

107 Matthew Boyle and Douglas MacMillan, as note 87

108 *The Wall Street Journal*, Retailers struggle in Amazon's jungle, John Jannarone, 22 February 2011

109 *Wired*. **http://www.wired.com/epicenter/2011/07/amazon-out- walmarts-walmart/**

110 ZDNet, Amazon: On track for $100 billion in revenue in 2015, Larry Dignan, 4 January 2011. **http://www.zdnet.com/blog/btl/amazon-on-track- for-100-billion-in-revenue-in-2015/43124**

111 Morgan Stanley source via ZDNet, Amazon, as above

112 Comments from Walmart at its 2011 Shareholders Meeting

113 **http://www.chinadaily.com.cn/business/2011-07/11/content_12875084.htm**

114 *Tokyo Times*, Japan to push e-commerce in Brazil, China, 8 June 2011. **http://www.tokyotimes.jp/post/en/1945/Japan+to+push+e- commerce+in+Brazil+China.html**

115 Walmart

116 *Tokyo Times*, as above

117 **http://www.bcg.com/media/PressReleaseDetails.aspx? id=tcm:12-59401**

118 Walmart. **http://walmartstores.com/pressroom/news/10524.aspx**

119 *The Economist*, E-commerce takes off in Japan: Up and away, 10 June 2010. **http://www.economist.com/node/16322651**

120 *The Economist*, as above

11

Going global: Walmart's international retail leadership

While Walmart's US operations give the retailer huge scale and power, the limitations on growth in that market and the exciting growth prospects elsewhere mean that Walmart International has massive potential and is therefore rightly regarded in Bentonville as of colossal strategic importance. Indeed, 2010 was the first year when Walmart International's stores outnumbered those that the retailer operated in its domestic market.

Exposed to growth-opportunity markets like China, Brazil and India (Russia is the only BRIC country where Walmart has yet to enter – it closed its Moscow market research and evaluation office in 2011), the long-term potential for Walmart International is immense. Leaving aside any new acquisitions or market entries, Walmart can potentially access nearly 4 billion consumers across the world, of whom 'only' 311 million are in the retailer's domestic market of the United States.

Taken in isolation, Walmart International was, at the time of writing, the world's third-largest retailer (behind Walmart US and Carrefour, and ahead of Tesco and Metro); however, it is expected to have become the second-largest retailer by 2012 as its growth is juxtaposed with Carrefour's divestments. In addition to opening up new avenues for growth, Walmart International has been fulfilling other valuable functions for Walmart – providing 'reverse synergies' in terms of personnel, small-format expertise, private label, marketing, grocery merchandising and e-commerce.

Notably through acquisition, Walmart International has grown extremely quickly and – against the backdrop of an uncharacteristically subdued Walmart performance in the United States – has become perhaps the most encouraging component of the broader Walmart business in terms of sales and profitability growth over the past couple of years. It should be noted that Walmart International has also been the scene of some dismal failures (Germany is the prime example here, although the list also includes South Korea, Indonesia and Hong Kong), so it would be wrong to regard the organization as a flawless beast that has progressed without any serious setbacks.

With a truly multi-format, multi-banner, global raft of operations, Walmart International serves millions of customers every week in North America, Latin America, the UK, Africa and Asia. Benefiting from being part of a larger retail group, many of Walmart's international operations are growing at an extremely rapid rate and still have significant potential in areas such as further market entries, channel development, e-commerce, private label and financial services.

Walmart International's market entry strategies

The choice of market entry mode is one that faces every retailer and Walmart International is no exception. As we show in the timeline in the appendix, it has used a variety of methods around the world – with varying degrees of success, it must be noted – and we can group them into three main types here:

1 Organic: Walmart enters a country by opening its own stores from scratch and developing its own supply chain and back-office capabilities.

2 Joint venture: Similar to organic market entry, but with the key differential and benefit of opening in conjunction with a local partner that (theoretically) has an in-depth knowledge of the country or broader region.

3 Acquisition: The full or partial acquisition of an existing retailer already trading in the target market.

The acquisition route could be further subdivided into two components: what we would call the land grab and the laissez-faire. Land-grab acquisitions are those in which Walmart has bought a chain of stores with no other intention than to convert them into a Walmart concept. This process was in evidence in Canada, Germany and South Korea. It is notable that two of these collapsed into rather ignominious defeat. Laissez-faire acquisitions have seen Walmart acquire another retailer but largely retain local brand identities and store formats, with only modest changes in consumer-facing aspects such as private label. Where Walmart has made changes in these cases is in back-office areas such as procurement, systems and logistics. This second type of acquisition has generally been more successful.

Table 11.1 plots Walmart's market entry strategies and subsequent growth phases for all of its international markets past and present. Walmart

TABLE 11.1 Walmart: market entry and development strategy by country

Country	Market entry	Phase II	Phase III
Argentina	Organic	Organic/acquisition	Format development
Brazil	Joint venture	Organic/format dev.	Acquisition
Canada	Acquisition	Organic	Format development
Chile	Acquisition	Organic	
China	Joint venture	Organic/acquisition	Format development
Costa Rica	Acquisition		
El Salvador	Acquisition		
Germany	Acquisition	Withdrawal	
Guatemala	Acquisition		
Hong Kong	Joint venture	Withdrawal	
Honduras	Acquisition		
India	Joint venture	Organic	
Indonesia	Joint venture	Withdrawal	
Japan	Acquisition		
Mexico	Joint venture	Acquisition	Organic/format development
Nicaragua	Acquisition		
Puerto Rico	Organic	Acquisition	Format development
S Africa	Acquisition*		
S Korea	Acquisition	Withdrawal	
UK	Acquisition	Organic/format dev.	Acquisition

* Includes stores in over a dozen African markets.
SOURCE: Authors

International's strategy is similar to that of retailers like Tesco, who have overwhelmingly favoured joint ventures and acquisitions over organic entry as a vehicle to trading in new markets. What is clear is that there are no hard and fast rules over the efficacy or otherwise of each market entry strategy: both acquisitions and joint ventures have had a mixed record, although we would suggest that laissez-faire acquisitions have been much more successful than the flag-planting land grabs. A more detailed narrative is provided below.

Argentina: Walmart entered Argentina organically through the opening of a Sam's Club in Avellaneda in 1995, a development followed up later in the same year with the unveiling of a Supercenter in the same region. An arduous and fairly fruitless period of organic growth followed until 2000 when Walmart decided to jettison Sam's Club in the market. Supercenters plodded along at a snail's pace until 2007 when the retailer acquired three former Auchan stores for conversion to the Supercenter format. Supercenter growth has remained slow, but Walmart is finding much faster success with the Changomas and Changomas Express discount-style concept that is being expanded rapidly.

Brazil: Walmart entered Brazil in 1995, initially through a 60/40 joint venture with the major general merchandise retailer Lojas Americanos (ironically now a bitter rival). Initially trading through the Supercenter and Sam's Club concepts, Walmart augmented organic growth through the design and roll-out of the Todo Dia discount-led concept. Greater scale, and a broader geographic spread, was achieved through two major acquisitions: in early 2004, Walmart Brazil acquired Bompreço's 118 stores in the northern region from Ahold, a deal followed by the late 2005 purchase of Sonae's 140 stores in the southern region. Since then, virtually all formats have been expanded organically, although there has been a strategic skew towards low price and cash & carry concepts.

Canada: Walmart Canada was established through the acquisition of the Woolco Canada chain of 122 stores in 1994. Woolco was the chain of large discount department stores operated by the F.W. Woolworth Company. The stores were rapidly rebadged to the Walmart fascia, although the company took longer than expected to reach profitability. The next major development came in 2003 when Walmart opened its first four Sam's Club warehouse outlets in Canada. This development – which pitched it against the established might of Costco – was fairly short-lived, the stores closing in 2009. More successful was the launch of the Supercentre chain in Canada. The first stores opened in late 2006 and the expansion of the chain has been rapid, exerting a strong impact on grocery competitors in the market. The launch of e-commerce in Canada followed in June 2011 when the retailer launched a site selling computer games, since augmented by a number of other categories.

Chile: Walmart debuted in Chile in 2009, through the acquisition of a majority stake in D&S. According to Craig Herkert, Walmart EVP and CEO of the Americas at the time, 'Partnering with D&S, with its strong brands and its position as Chile's largest food retailer, is an important step in implementing Walmart's international strategy. We continue to focus on portfolio optimization, global leverage and winning in every market.' With net revenues in excess of US~$3.8 billion, D&S operated more than 180 stores, 10 shopping centres and 85 PRESTO financial services branches at the time of the acquisition.

China: Walmart opened its first superstore (Luohu district) and Sam's Club (Futian) in Shenzhen in 1996. By necessity, these stores were opened through local joint ventures. Walmart went on to open its Neighborhood Market concept in China and followed up with the acquisition of a majority stake in hypermarket chain Trust-Mart in 2006 (there has since been a convoluted process that has seen Walmart edge towards taking full control of Trust-Mart). A more recent development has been the opening of the low-price proximity-format Smart Choice and the launch of a compact hypermarket, also under the Smart Choice brand.

Costa Rica, El Salvador, Guatemala, Honduras, Nicaragua: Walmart's entry into Central America was completed in late 2005 when Ahold sold its indirectly owned stake of 33.33 per cent in CARHCO, its Central American joint venture, to Walmart. CARHCO owned an 85.6 per cent stake in La Fragua, a discount store, supermarket and hypermarket company in Guatemala, with a presence in El Salvador and Honduras. CARHCO also fully owned Corporación de Supermercados Unidos (CSU), a discount store, supermarket and hypermarket operator in Costa Rica, Nicaragua and Honduras. In late 2009 Walmart Centroamérica was acquired by Walmex. Walmex said it would pay $110 million in cash and would issue around 593 million new shares to compensate minority investors in the Central American retail chain who agreed to be paid in shares. By 2009, Walmart owned 51 per cent of Walmart Centroamérica, with the remainder in the hands of local investors, and the deal gave it control in Central America as the US parent company also has a majority share in Walmex.

Germany: Walmart entered Germany in late 2007 through the acquisition of the 21-store Wertkauf hypermarket business, followed over a year later by the purchase of the 71-strong Interspar hypermarket chain. After a nightmarish period of heavy losses, no small amount of controversy and constant under-delivery, Walmart 'sold' its operations to Metro Group, although subsequent regulatory filings revealed that Walmart effectively paid Metro to take its German business off its hands.

Hong Kong: By no means the horrific ordeal that Germany was, Walmart also failed to find success in Hong Kong. In 1993, Walmart established a partnership with Charoen Pokphand (CP), the Asian business conglomerate. The venture was extremely short-lived, with the market exit coming just three years after entry. The stores traded as Value Club and were warehouse club outlets targeted at small businesses. It is understood that the stores suffered from poor locations and a somewhat misguided assortment. There was also speculation that Walmart and CP clashed often over strategy, with each side blaming the other for demanding too much control.

India: Walmart became active in India in 2007 when Bharti Enterprises and Walmart signed an agreement to establish Bharti Wal-Mart Private Limited, a joint venture (JV) for wholesale cash & carry stores and back-end supply chain management operations in India. The JV is now trading through a chain of Best Price Modern Wholesale stores and Walmart also supports the activities of Bharti Retail, the operator of easyday supermarkets and compact hypermarkets. Owing to the onerous restrictions on foreign retailers, Walmart is currently unable to operate its own retail activities in the Indian market, although – at the time of writing – there are limited indications that these restrictions might be at least partially relaxed.

Indonesia: As in Hong Kong, poor locations and assortment were accusations also levelled at Walmart's ill-fated presence in Indonesia. It entered the country in 1996, after signing a franchise agreement with Lippo Group the previous year to open Walmart stores. Weak trading was compounded by the fact that one of its stores in Jakarta was looted and burnt during the 1997–98 riots. A *Business Week* story in early 2008 reported that Walmart was seeking to end the franchise agreement with Lippo after claims that Lippo violated the agreement when, without Walmart's prior knowledge, it bought a controlling stake in rival discounter Matahari, with Walmart fearing that the acquisition would give its rival access to proprietary information. 'There was a clear non-compete clause' in the franchise agreement, said a Walmart spokesman, adding that Lippo owed Walmart millions of dollars in franchise fees.

Japan: While there are no signs that Walmart is considering quitting Japan, its activities in the country have become another arduous tale of losses and struggles to rejuvenate operations in a very crowded and competitive market. It first acquired a minority stake in Seiyu in 2002, before gaining a majority stake and making Seiyu a subsidiary in 2005. The business struggled to gain market share or turn a profit, despite Walmart implementing many initiatives around systems, supply chain, private label and pricing. A gradual turnaround now appears to be in place, however, with business picking up after Walmart implemented its hallmark EDLP positioning.

Mexico: Walmex has been a phenomenal success for the retailer. It enjoys a colossal market leadership in the country and continues to grow at a breakneck pace, notably through its Bodega Aurrera family of banners. Walmart entered Mexico in 2001 through a JV with Cifra and the opening of a Sam's Club. Walmart acquired a majority stake in Cifra in 2007. Thanks to this acquisition it operates a diverse portfolio of operations, including restaurants and clothing stores alongside its grocery activities. Walmex acquired Walmart Centroamérica in late 2009 in a move that created significant growth potential and synergies.

Puerto Rico: Now included in the Walmart US business unit, activities in Puerto Rico have featured a familiar combination of organic growth, acquisition and new-format development. The retailer opened its first stores in Puerto Rico in 1992 and 10 years later announced the acquisition of Supermercados Amigo, the country's leading supermarket chain with 35 outlets (a few stores had to be divested to meet regulatory requirements). More recently (late 2008), Walmart opened a new chain under the Super Ahorros brand. It is a bodega discount format, similar to the Bodega Express chain operated in Mexico.

South Africa: Walmart announced its move into South Africa in September 2010 through a $4 billion offer for Massmart. At the time of the announcement, Massmart traded through nearly 300 stores in 13 African countries. The deal was approved by regulators in June 2011. Massmart operates four operating divisions, comprising: Massdiscounters (Game discount stores and Dion Wired electronics stores); Masswarehouse (which comprises the Makro cash & carry chain), Massbuild (a variety of home improvement retail concepts including Builders Warehouse, Builders Express and Builders Trade Depot); and Masscash (a portfolio of grocery wholesale, retail and symbol group activities that trade as CBW, Jumbo Cash and Carry, Shield, Thaba Cash & Carry, Sunshine, Cambridge and Astor).

South Korea: Walmart's presence in South Korea lasted from 1998, when it acquired a handful of stores from Makro, until 2006, when the retailer announced the sale of its 16-store chain in South Korea to Shinsegae for $882 million. The company had failed to achieve enough scale to compete effectively in the market and had misread local tastes, and its stores also suffered from poor locations.

UK: Alongside Mexico, the UK is the most important overseas market for Walmart International. Walmart acquired Asda in mid-1999 and has developed the business ever since, despite the difficulty it has encountered in opening big-box outlets. Although its initiatives such as George clothing stores and Asda Essentials failed, it has found greater success through Asda Living and e-commerce. Its 2010/11 acquisition of Netto saw its supermarket division increase from around 30 to 170 stores.

By the numbers

As already noted, Walmart International has been one of the fastest-growing components of the broader Walmart business, and Table 11.2 highlights the development of the unit in terms of store-count, tracking the company from the handful of stores in Mexico to the true multinational giant it is today.

A similarly impressive trajectory can be seen when one considers the growth of sales from the Walmart International segment since 1995 (the first year that sales for the segment were split out). See Table 11.3.

TABLE 11.2 Walmart International, store count 1991–2010

Year	Stores
1991	4
1992	5
1993	14
1994	163
1995	191
1996	227
1997	601
1998	715
1999	1,004
2000	1,071
2001	1,170
2002	1,288
2003	1,355
2004	1,587
2005	2,285
2006	2,734
2007	3,098
2008	3,615
2009	4,112
2010	4,557

SOURCE: Authors, from Walmart filings

TABLE 11.3 Walmart International, sales 1995–2010 ($ m)

Year	Sales
1995	3,712
1996	5,002
1997	7,517
1998	12,247
1999	22,728
2000	32,100
2001	35,485
2002	40,794
2003	47,572
2004	56,277
2005	62,719
2006	76,883
2007	90,421
2008	98,645
2009	100,107
2010	109,232

SOURCE: Authors, from Walmart filings

Walmart International in context

As already noted, Walmart International has become a colossal retail enterprise in its own right and, as a standalone company, is among the largest retail operations in the world (Table 11.4).

TABLE 11.4 Top 10 global retailers, net sales (2010, $m)

Walmart US	260,261
Carrefour	126,739
Walmart International	109,232
Tesco	93,173
Metro Group	87,714
Kroger	78,834
Costco	78,394
Schwarz Group	76,339
Seven & I	70,959
Home Depot	68,002

SOURCE: Company reports; author's estimates

Walmart International performance

Faced with an extremely sluggish performance in the United States, attributable to strong competition, ongoing travails in terms of consumer confidence and at least a few self-inflicted tactical errors, Walmart US suffered something of a slump between 2009 and 2011 in terms of comparable sales growth. Importantly, the business remains hugely profitable and has made stellar progress on areas such as inventory reduction and efficiency, but it is fair to conclude that the US unit is being overshadowed to an extent by Walmart International as the star performer and growth engine of the future.

The years 2009 and 2010 were not so great for Walmart International based on top-line sales data, but a brief look behind the top line shows a much more encouraging picture of the business living up to its own impressive growth standards. If currency effects are stripped out of the 2009 and 2010 sales performances, the growth rates appear much more impressive. Indeed, Walmart is often vocally proud of the performance exhibited by its International division: as Mike Duke, the CEO of Walmart, asked investors after a particularly gruelling quarter: 'Let me ask all of you a question.

How many of you know a $100 billion dollar business that grew top-line sales by 12 per cent and grew profit by 19 per cent in this very difficult economic environment during this fourth quarter? I know you're thinking about it, but, let me go ahead and name one for you. The name – Walmart International.'

The scope and scale of Walmart International

Contrary to popular belief (a perception perhaps fostered by the bad old days of the retailer slapping down Walmart Supercenters in markets as diverse as Argentina, Germany and South Korea), the Walmart International of 2012 is an immensely diverse business trading through over 60 different store concepts. Furthermore, thanks to the acquisition of many different banners – and the humility to preserve local brand equity – well over three-quarters of the stores within Walmart International trade through a non-Walmart banner.

The Walmart International business is spread across five main territories, although two of these are effectively single-country operations. In North America, Walmart International trades in the form of Walmart Canada. South American operations are effectively split in two, with Walmart de Mexico taking control of Walmart Centroamérica in late 2009. The remainder of Walmart's operations in the region (Argentina, Brazil and Chile) are overseen by Walmart Latin America. Walmart Asia comprises activities in Japan, China and India, while – following the divestment of stores in Germany – the hope of developing a European division was effectively shelved, leaving Asda as something of a metaphorical and literal island (although hopes were raised of a return to European ambition in June 2011 when reports in the UK suggested that Walmart was establishing a research team near Heathrow Airport to evaluate new European market entries). The final territory, Africa, was established through the acquisition of a majority stake in South African-based retailer Massmart in 2011.

Walmart is currently active in 28 markets (27 excluding the United States) in terms of the markets in which it, or its JVs, operate stores. Markets in which it is no longer active comprise Hong Kong, Indonesia, Germany and South Korea.

Channel strategy

While Walmart International becomes an ever more esoteric and diverse business, it is fair to suggest that there are some common trading formats that form the backbone of the global business unit.

Walmart is active across a large number of channels and store types. In grocery, it trades through all channels with the exception of convenience stores. Convenience retailing is unlikely to feature on Walmart's radar anytime soon owing to its unwillingness to sacrifice its EDLP stance and preference for national pricing across all of its markets (many grocers like Tesco will typically charge higher prices in their convenience stores in order to cover off the higher operating costs of staffing and servicing these smaller outlets).

On a global level, Walmart is reliant on hypermarkets (Supercenters) for the majority of its revenues, with its other key channels comprising warehouse clubs/cash & carries and general merchandise discount superstores (or discount stores as they are known by Walmart US). As discount superstores in North America are transitioned to Supercenters, the discount superstore channel will decline in importance, with regular grocery supermarkets and superstores likely to be the third-largest sales channel by 2015.

Hypermarkets/Supercenters

As already noted, Supercenters and hypermarkets (54,000 sq. ft +) are the backbone of Walmart's global business, thanks in part to the scale of the channel for Walmart in the United States. The channel is also key for Walmart International, with Walmart Supercenters trading in Argentina, Brazil, Canada, China, Costa Rica, Guatemala, Honduras, Mexico and Puerto Rico. Other hypermarket concepts include Big and Hiper Bompreço (Brazil); Hiper Lider (Chile); Trust-Mart (China); Livin and Seiyu (Japan); Bodega Aurrera (Mexico); and Asda Walmart Supercentre (UK). Hipermas (Costa Rica) and Hiper Paiz (Guatemala and Honduras) stores were converted to the Supercenter concept in the summer of 2011.

The hypermarket concept is key for Walmart as the stores enable the retailer to exhibit its strong credentials in general merchandise, particularly in areas such as toys, electronics and apparel, as well as being able to offer a full grocery assortment and auxiliary services such as photo-processing, pharmacy and financial services. However, Walmart faces limits on the potential growth of these larger formats, particularly in saturated markets like the UK and Japan, and also in smaller markets such as certain Central American territories where there is a limit to the number of major cities that can sustain these large-format stores.

Superstores

With many of its international acquisitions Walmart has picked up a significant presence in the superstore (27,000–54,000 sq. ft) channel. These stores still offer a non-food range in many cases, but are more akin to regular grocery stores. Walmart's presence in this channel comprises Changomas

(Argentina); Bompreço (Brazil); Mas-x-menos (Costa Rica); Hiper Paiz (El Salvador); Seiyu (Japan); Bodega Aurrera (Mexico); Amigo (Puerto Rico); and Asda (UK).

Supermarkets and neighbourhood stores

Again largely through acquisition, Walmart has picked up a raft of supermarket (less than 27,000 sq. ft) operations around the world, including: Changomas Express (Argentina); Bompreço, Nacional and Mercadorama (Brazil); aCuenta and Express de Lider (Chile); Neighborhood Market (China); La Despensa de Don Juan (El Salvador); Maxi Bodega (Costa Rica, Honduras and Guatemala); Supertiendas Paiz (Guatemala and Honduras); Seiyu, Seiyu SSV; Food Magazine, Sunny and Seiyu The Food Factory (Japan); Superama, Bodega Aurrera Express and Mi Bodega Aurrera (Mexico); La Union (Nicaragua); and Asda Supermarket (UK). Please note that some of these concepts could also be classified as discount stores or proximity concepts – more of which below.

Discount superstores

On the one hand, these stores are something of a dwindling legacy. In both the United States and Canada, Walmart discount superstores are plummeting in number as they are expanded or relocated to become Supercenters. Walmart also operates the Walmart discount superstore concept in Puerto Rico. In the UK, however, the Asda Living general merchandise superstore concept is poised to become a significant growth channel: the retailer has a medium-term goal of trading through 150 such units. This type of activity was bolstered through the 2011 acquisition of Massmart in South Africa – enabling the Game discount store chain to be welcomed into the Walmart global family. It should be noted that the addition of FoodCo departments to the Game store concept might see them transition into more of a hypermarket or superstore concept in the fullness of time.

Discount stores

Although a similar size to supermarkets, these stores can be characterized as discount stores thanks to sharing characteristics such as a limited assortment, high private label penetration, a fairly Spartan in-store environment and a focus on low prices. Another way to describe this type of store is 'proximity discount' – small stores offering low prices near to where people live and work. Stores in this category include Todo Dia (Brazil); Smart Choice (China); Ekono (Chile); Pali (Costa Rica and Nicaragua); Super Ahorros (Puerto Rico); and Despensa Familiar (El Salvador and Honduras).

Warehouse club/cash & carry

Walmart has long been a dominant global participant in this segment thanks to its Sam's Club business in the United States. However, Sam's Club has proven less portable than other Walmart concepts, having been closed down in Canada and Argentina. That said, Sam's Club still trades successfully in China, Mexico, Brazil and Puerto Rico. Walmart also has the rapidly growing Maxxi Atacado cash & carry chain in Brazil, the two-store ClubCo business in Guatemala and the Best Price Modern Wholesale operation in India. Again, this segment of the Walmart International business was augmented through the acquisition of Massmart in South Africa: the deal added operations including Makro, Jumbo Cash & Carry and Thaba Cash & Carry.

Others

While we have covered the main components of Walmart International's empire, it is worth mentioning that Walmart's acquisitive expansion has endowed it with a legacy of all kinds of activities around the world. These include: Vips and El Porton restaurants in Mexico; a single Hiper Magazine bookstore in Brazil; the Suburbia clothing chain in Mexico; the Wakana delicatessen business in Japan; Dion Wired electronics stores in South Africa; and the Builders Warehouse, Builders Express and Builders Trade Depot home improvement retail chains in the same country. A more recent proactive initiative was the news that Asda was seeking a franchise partner to open standalone fashion stores in the Middle East.

Small-box development

Although Walmart International is dominated by bigger-box grocery retailing, many of Walmart's international divisions are embracing a shift towards smaller boxes that are focused on offering consumers smaller assortments, low prices, an extensive range of private labels and a degree of convenience. This shows us that Walmart is realizing that – particularly in emerging markets – many shoppers are keen to see stores that are close to them and that offer a quick and easy shop that also provides good value for money.

This shift to 'proximity' retailing is proving to be highly successful in markets such as Mexico, and other countries such as China, the UK, Puerto Rico and even the United States are looking to follow suit. Indeed, as we discussed in the multi-channel chapter, Bill Simon, President and CEO of Walmart US, was quick to point towards Walmart International's success in proximity retailing as an inspiration for Walmart's planned assault on urban retailing in the United States through the Walmart Express concept.

The winning formula hit upon by Walmart is the combination of true convenience without the premium prices traditionally associated with proximity retailing. One other significant plus-point for the retailer is that these smaller concepts open up a whole new world of growth potential. While there is a clear growth ceiling for big-box development in many markets, the progression of these smaller concepts means that a large number of smaller towns and cities are now on Walmart's radar.

For suppliers, the strategic shift to small-box retailing by Walmart International will undoubtedly have a number of implications. There might well be some margin pressure as Walmart's small boxes heap further pressure on the informal retail sector and Walmart's increasing focus on low-price, narrow-assortment proximity retailing will mean that suppliers in certain markets will have to innovate in terms of pricing, value and pack sizes to win a place on the shelf.

Walmart International has either acquired or organically developed proximity store concepts in markets around the world, and below we present the concepts and some of their key features.

Changomas Express & Mi Changomas (Argentina)

Changomas Express and Mi Changomas are smaller-footprint versions of the main Changomas chain. All of the concepts are based on the Bodega Aurrera concept from Walmart de Mexico. Changomas itself is a bodega-style concept trading from around 48,000 sq. ft. The chain introduced the smaller Changomas Express concept in late 2008 and Mi Changomas in late 2009. These concepts largely sell groceries without the non-food assortment of their larger equivalents. Private labels are featured extensively, with Great Value, Equate and Ol' Roy present in the grocery assortment.

Todo Dia (Brazil)

While many of the Toda Dia stores are fairly hefty and come in at over 20,000 sq. ft, many of the stores are as small as 300 sq. ft (the size of a typical convenience store) and are located in populous areas, serving as a neighbourhood discount store. They trade as soft discounters with the look and feel of a warehouse, with concrete floors, no air-conditioning and products displayed in pallets or open boxes. Todo Dia stores sell food and household items at prices which are 5 per cent less than neighbouring family-owned supermarkets and drugstores (and even 2 per cent less than Walmart's own Supercenters). Along with Maxxi Atacado, Todo Dia is one of the fastest-growing chains in the Walmart Brazil stable.

Ekono (Chile)

Ekono was a new concept that was developed by D&S prior to its acquisition by Walmart. Nonetheless, the chain is growing quickly and very much models the ethos of proximity retailing seen elsewhere in Walmart International. Launched in January 2007, D&S presented Ekono as a brand new 'discount' format in Chile. This format basically offers food and is located in highly populated areas, for top-up shopping because of its quick and easy access at low prices. It also offers a broad range of own-brand products, which account for a 30 per cent share of total sales, and it has a low-price policy owing to the reduced costs of running the store. It has a product range of approximately 1,500 items and its sales floor is 3,800 sq. ft on average, with a maximum of 4 checkouts and 11 employees per store.

Smart Choice (China)

The relatively new stores – designed to attract value-conscious consumers in the economic slowdown – were loosely designed to be a small-box equivalent to Sam's Club, trading from around only 3,000 sq. ft in size. Smart Choice sells only groceries and there are around 2,000 SKUs in the store. The concept epitomizes a low-cost retail model: its small size saves on rent and the unit is decorated in a fairly Spartan fashion. The units feature deep shelving and there is a strong focus on shelf-ready packaging. Many products are in multi-buy packages with further discounts and the retailer tells consumers clearly how much they can save. As for private labels, Smart Choice has not introduced its own but has some taken from the Walmart Supercenter chain, such as Mainstays, SIMPLYBASIC, and Great Value.

Pali (Costa Rica and Nicaragua)

Established in Costa Rica and since expanded into Nicaragua, Pali is a simple operation, based on economy and efficiency. Stores are fairly austere and offer a limited range. The stores offer an extensive range of private brands, including global Walmart brands such as Equate.

Despensa Familiar (El Salvador, Guatemala and Honduras)

These hard discount stores are located in high-traffic locations, carrying between 8,000 and 9,000 SKUs. These are primarily dry groceries, although stores also carry a non-food section including clothing, footwear and stationery. Around 800 SKUs are private labels, which account for some 30 per cent of total sales.

Mi Bodega Aurrera and Bodega Aurrera Express (Mexico)

Mi Bodega Aurrera units are smaller-format grocery stores, designed to help Walmart Mexico compete more extensively with independent neighbourhood retailers and c-store chains. The stores have a selling space of between 4,000 and 5,000 sq. ft, around a tenth of the size of a traditional Bodega Aurrera unit. Stores sell a mix of grocery items, c-store impulse lines and other FMCG staples.

Bodega Aurrera Express is said to have surpassed expectations in productivity and profitability. It is a new prototype – a discount and convenience store all rolled into one – that targets income levels D and E in markets ranging from 12,000 to 20,000 inhabitants and allows Walmart to meet the replenishment needs of customers at Bodega Aurrera prices.

Super Ahorros (Puerto Rico)

This is a bodega discount format, similar to the Bodega Aurrera Express chain operated in Mexico. The first store opened for business in mid-November 2008 in the municipality of Villalba. The new concept offers an extensive selection of private labels, with the product category mix standing at 80:20 in favour of groceries.

Asda Supermarket (UK)

While far removed from the bodega retail operations in Latin America, it is worth pointing out that smaller-footprint stores are very much on the agenda for Asda in the UK. The impetus behind small-store development was ratcheted up in 2010 with the acquisition of most of the Netto discount chain in the UK. In converted stores, customers see a much broader range of products. As part of the Netto to Asda Supermarket conversion programme, the number of products rose from an average 1,800 up to around 10,000, with up to 12,000 in the larger stores.

Cambridge Foods (South Africa)

Cambridge Foods, a small cash & carry-style retail store developed by the Masscash division of Massmart, is likely to be the subject of intense acceleration following the takeover of the South African retailer by Walmart. Walmart has confirmed that Cambridge will be the focal point of investment, with the concept deemed ideal for serving those lower-income shoppers currently underserved by the modern retail trade in South Africa and beyond.

Walmart International: the good, the bad and the ugly

While Walmart International has become a formidable presence in its own right, dwarfing other leading global retailers, its progress has by no means been a flawlessly executed rise to glory. Indeed, some of Walmart International's misadventures have epitomized the very worst in clumsy commercial colonialism and breathtaking arrogance and stupidity. At the same time, Walmart's entry and leadership in other markets have been virtual case studies in how to expand successfully overseas. Why the contrast? Simply put, Walmart learnt some extremely hard lessons in some markets in the first couple of phases of its international expansion.

The 1997 quote earlier in the appendix from Bob Martin, then president of the Walmart International division, provides some of the reasons why Walmart International did not fare so well in some markets. While it was true that 'the Walmart name is better known outside the United States than any of us imagine', it did not necessarily follow that trading as Walmart in foreign markets was the right move. In some Asian and European markets, the Walmart brand did not resonate in the slightest and smacked of the Americanization of global society that many consumers have proven to be so distrusting of.

Furthermore, some of the hideous failures undergone by Walmart International proved that the Walmart Supercenter store model, so beloved in the United States, was something of a lame duck in certain international territories. In markets with different shopper behaviours, different transport systems and different successful domestic retailers, the Supercenter concept was quickly exposed as cookie-cutter retail colonialism gone awry. The Walmart Supercenter is one of the most pivotal and successful concepts in the history of commerce; but that does not mean it is one of the most portable.

Martin's assertion that Walmart stood for 'low cost, best value... to customers everywhere' was also a debatable premise. While Walmart's EDLP stance, enabled by its scale and high efficiency, ensured that it succeeded against less efficient local competitors in a market like Mexico, the same could not be said for markets like South Korea and Germany. In South Korea, Walmart was a relative minnow compared to the might of Lotte and Shinsegae. As we demonstrated in the chapter on procurement, FMCG buying is still largely a local affair, and Walmart's lack of scale in the South Korean market meant that its EDLP model was stretched beyond breaking point. In Germany, Walmart was pitting itself against the likes of Aldi, one of the most brutally efficient low-price retailers in the world of retailing. By taking EDLP to the home of EDLP, Walmart was effectively embarking on an unwinnable war. There were other factors at play in the German market that turned the odds against the US interloper (such as gentlemen's agreements between both retailers and suppliers to hamper Walmart's progress), but the fact that Walmart could never be the lowest-price retailer while still making money in Germany was apparent to external observers from the outset.

Walmart International's evolution over the past 20 years can be broadly split into four phases. The first phase, between 1991 – when Walmart first kicked off its trading in Mexico – and 1999 was an era of flag-planting colonization. Within the space of 10 years, Walmart embarked on a rapid flurry of JVs, acquisitions and organic market entries into a mix of mature and emerging markets. The distinction between mature and emerging markets is an important one: Walmart's greatest successes have come in emerging markets, where the retailer's state-of-the-art logistics and EDLC philosophy have enabled it to outmanoeuvre and undercut local chains, meeting with a great reception from less affluent shoppers. On the flip side, Walmart's most humbling failures have taken place in mature, modern retail sectors where Walmart International squared up to an established local hegemony.

The decade saw Walmart International embark on a fairly scattergun approach with a seemingly high tolerance for loss-making ventures. It is also worth remembering that this era was one in which Walmart exhibited an almost total insistence on using the Walmart brand in many of its international ventures. Attempts at achieving synergies in this era, which saw Walmart enter Mexico, Brazil, Argentina, Canada, Puerto Rico, Indonesia, Hong Kong, China, the UK and Germany, are best described as hesitant and inconsistent. As already noted, the entries into Hong Kong and Indonesia were aborted in fairly short order.

The period was also one of learning for Walmart International: it was slowly coming to grips with the fact that the cookie-cutter approach was not a wise one. For example, in Argentina, Walmart noted that it did not anticipate the heavy customer traffic, which temporarily overwhelmed its stores' relatively narrow aisles. It also made mistakes in product selection in categories such as jewellery and meat. Walmart was forced to adjust its offer to cater for what it called 'cultural nuances', offering Argentine shoppers specialized cuts of meat and simple gold and silver jewellery ranges in retooled stores with wider aisles.

Walmart International's John Menzer acknowledged at the time that:

> it wasn't such a good idea to stick so closely to the domestic Walmart blueprint in Argentina, or in some of the other international markets we've entered, for that matter. In Mexico City we sold tennis balls that wouldn't bounce right in the high altitude. We built large parking lots at some of our Mexican stores, only to realize that many of our customers there rode the bus to the store, then trudged across those large parking lots with bags full of merchandise. We responded by creating bus shuttles to drop customers off at the door. These were all mistakes that were easy to address, but we're now working smarter internationally to avoid cultural and regional problems on the front end.

The next phase – 2000 to 2005 – can be characterized as Walmart attempting to build global scale for local advantage. The nascent Walmart International business unit, formed in 1993, was making progress in constructing a global management structure to accelerate local development, with Bentonville exporting best practice in private label, IT systems and supply chain to global markets. At the same time, Walmart was expanding through organic growth in key markets like China, completing in-fill acquisitions in key markets (Brazil and Central America) and acquiring businesses in new markets (Japan).

The period from 2006 to 2008 saw Walmart lose patience with its loss-making ventures that had little or no hope of achieving scale and/or profitability. By jettisoning its businesses in South Korea and Germany, Walmart had shifted its strategy to 'major on the majors': the retailer had enacted a more stringent evaluation of international operations, deciding that it would exit certain geographies if sufficient profitability and scale was not a feasible outcome. For its other markets, Walmart was exercising perpetual vigilance for acquisition or new-format opportunities in existing markets and acquisition opportunities in adjacent or high-growth potential markets. It is notable that no new markets were entered in this phase.

The final – and current – phase in Walmart International's development has taken place very much under the banner of 'serving the underserved'. Walmart International has placed its strategic focus on serving less affluent (often rural) shoppers, entering new 'emerging' markets, developing small-box proximity stores to take custom from informal retail, using price and private label to deliver value for money and enacting a renaissance of cash & carry within the world of Walmart. In this phase, Walmart has entered markets like Chile, India and South Africa.

Walmart has very much learnt some hard lessons from its failures in markets such as Germany. That failure – which ranks alongside Tesco in France, Sainsbury's in Egypt and Carrefour in Russia in terms of risibility – really drove home to Walmart the importance of local brand equity; the absolute need for humility; and the advantage of driving change (and bringing to bear Walmart's global scale) behind the scenes of an acquired international business. Indeed, a key theme emanating from Bentonville, and from the global operating companies themselves, is that each country's business unit is a local retailer 'powered by Walmart'. While no-one but the most vigilant shopper might notice that Walmart was the owner of stores in, say, Chile or South Africa, the benefits of Walmart's scale will be felt through lower prices and enhanced private label offerings.

Where next?

One of the joys of being an analyst who covers Walmart is the constant stream of speculation one encounters, particularly with regard to the countries or regions that Walmart might enter next. Over the years, there have been very few parts of the world that have not been touted as a possible destination for Walmart International, ranging from the logical (further markets in Latin America) and the improbable (Scandinavia) to the commercially suicidal (France).

One question that needs asking here is whether or not Walmart actually needs to enter new markets. Put another way, is there not enough potential in its existing markets to satisfy even the most ambitious retailer? Walmart certainly has enough to be getting on with in its existing global operations. The retailer told investors and employees at its 2011 shareholders meeting that there was, over a five-year time period, a $2.4 trillion growth opportunity in existing markets (compared to what could loosely be described as a relatively modest $800 billion opportunity in the United States over the same time period.) As the retailer's Cathy Smith said at the meeting: 'There's not a single Walmart market that is even close to saturation.' Considering that statement included extremely crowded markets like the UK, the ambition inherent in Smith's statement is manifest.

There is undoubtedly huge scope for Walmart to expand in its existing territories. The addition of Massmart's African empire (including a presence in Nigeria, regarded with great anticipation as a potentially huge untapped market by FMCG suppliers) has increased the number of potential shoppers and consumers that Walmart can theoretically reach from 3.48 billion to 3.85 billion. Markets like China and India (should the Indian government ever deregulate the retail sector) have colossal scope. Indeed, such is the strength of local retailers in the market – coupled with the virtually limitless scope for new-store growth in the market – Doug McMillon told investors in 2011: 'I don't know if we'll ever be the largest retailer in China.' Walmart is aggressively expanding into e-commerce in China, which should hasten its growth there, although word reaches us from within Walmart China that the ongoing integration of the Trust-Mart chain in the country is turning into something of a living hell for both parties, which doesn't bode well for the overall health of the business in that market.

Walmart has established a holding company structure in Japan that has been expressly designed to completed M&As – a necessity if Walmart wishes to gain any sort of genuine scale in a market widely regarded as an ultra-competitive bloodbath.

Elsewhere, the prospects and the sentiments are altogether more ebullient. Although performance in the UK might not have been quite where Walmart would want it, there are growth opportunities in food (through acquisitions such as Netto as well as e-commerce) and non-food (an acquisition of Homebase and Argos owner Home Retail Group has been a frequent rumour on the financial pages). In Canada, Walmart continues to grow at a rapid rate, while in markets such as Chile, Central America, Brazil and Argentina there is still plenty of headroom for further acquisitions and organic expansion. Further acquisitions are particularly likely in Brazil and Argentina, with a senior figure from Carrefour telling us that Walmart had been actively pursuing both Carrefour and CBD in the Brazilian market. In Chile, Walmart plans to double the size of business to $10 billion by 2018, and a postponed entry by Walmart's Chilean business D&S into Peru is also likely to be revived.

Perhaps the brightest growth prospects lie in Africa. Through its acquisition of a majority stake in Massmart, Walmart has accessed a presence in a wide variety of African markets and an impressive portfolio of food and specialist non-food retail formats. Cambridge Foods is the concept that has Walmart International licking its lips with anticipation, although – perhaps counter-intuitively – officials within Walmart International have communicated to us that they are also extremely excited by the potential of Massmart's DIY retail activities. The African housing market is poised for a boom, and a presence in home improvement retailing puts Walmart International on the cusp of a potentially very lucrative wave.

The question remains: where next? The only gap remaining in the so-called BRIC economies of Brazil, Russia, India and China is Russia. In what must have been a fairly expensive episode of shooting blanks, Walmart operated a well-staffed development office in the Russian market, tasked with evaluating opportunities – both acquisitive and organic – in the market. After the best part of three years, the office closed without yielding any progress.

The issue appears to us to have been one of culture rather than any other: there is no shortage of possible acquisition targets in the market (although the price tags attached to them might be considered eye-watering) and it was surely not beyond the wit of Walmart International to open its own stores. However, the potential risks must have substantially outweighed the possible rewards. The Russian market is notoriously corrupt and foreign retailers have been incessantly and infamously targeted by shady government officials looking to make a fast buck (or several hundred thousand fast bucks if some of IKEA's revelations about doing business in Russia are to be believed). Given Walmart's zero-tolerance policy towards the use of brown envelopes in business, it seems as though the retailer will await a commercial environment that is somewhat more chaste before it decides to entertain its entry into the Russian market. Walmart has reiterated its long-term interest in Russia, but there are several more sizeable fish to fry at present.

Hot on the heels of the BRICs are the more exotically feline group of countries that are being portrayed as the red-hot investment destinations: the CIVETS. Sharing some attractive characteristics for retailers (large and young populations; diverse and rapidly growing economies; relative political stability and reasonably well-regulated financial systems), Colombia, Indonesia, Vietnam, Egypt, Turkey and South Africa have been held up as the next batch of rising stars.

Walmart has already chalked up a presence in South Africa via its Massmart deal, while Colombia is thought to be next in line – along with Peru – for market entry in Latin America. That said, there is still a sizeable opportunity for backfilling operations in markets like Brazil, so Walmart International might be able to afford to be patient and/or opportunistic when it comes to Colombian market entry.

With regard to Indonesia, a market that left Walmart with a discernibly bitter aftertaste, the retailer has been linked as a potential investor in, or strategic partner to, local retailer Matahari. Press reports in late 2010 linked Walmart to a possible bid for Hypermart, Matahari's hypermarket chain, although subsequent reports in early 2011 suggested that Matahari was instead looking for a 'global strategic partner' to help it develop the business. At the time of writing, there have been no further updates, but it seems fair to conclude that Indonesia is still very much a market on Walmart's shortlist.

Vietnam is a market that Walmart has already been briefly and tangentially active in already: its Japanese arm Seiyu operated a franchised department store in Hanoi while Walmart was building its stake in the Japanese business. Although Walmart has been putatively linked to an entry into Vietnam, there has been nothing more substantive than idle tittle-tattle to suggest that Walmart is considering entering the Vietnamese sector, and indeed Vietnam has not been mentioned to us by Walmart International personnel as an immediate priority.

Egypt also appears off limits for the time being. Although Asda will be setting up franchised stores in the Middle East, there has been nothing to so far suggest that North Africa is on the radar. While we cannot rule out an eventual expansion into the North African market from the south via Massmart, it would appear unlikely that the Egyptian market is very high up Walmart's wish list in the immediate future, particularly in light of the unrest that afflicted the country in early 2011 (Metro Group reported that both its Makro stores in Cairo were damaged, with one store, which was set on fire, having had to be rebuilt).

Of more interest will be the Turkish market. Walmart is the only one of the global retail pioneers not yet present in the Turkish market, with Carrefour, Tesco and Metro Group already firmly entrenched in the sector. The most likely entry mode for Walmart would be an acquisition of, or joint venture with, Migros Ticaret, a leading retail business majority controlled by investment vehicle MH Perakendecilik. This vehicle is controlled by Moonlight Capital, which itself is controlled by private equity firm BC Partners. The retailer – once the Turkish offshoot of leading Swiss retailer Migros – trades through over 700 Migros, Tansaş, Macro Center and 5M stores in Turkey and 27 Ramstore stores in Kazakhstan and Macedonia. The group disposed of its 1,244-strong hard discount chain Şok in 2011. With private equity typically looking to spin off or exit its investments after a period of five or so years, it seems reasonable to suggest that Migros could be an acquisition opportunity for the likes of Walmart in 2013 or, indeed, earlier.

The establishment of a European M&A office in London is understood to have been completed, with staff now in place to evaluate potential deals across Europe. There has been some reasonably substantive speculation linking Walmart with two possible transactions. Press reports in 2011 put Walmart in the frame for a somewhat implausible, if not impossible, return to Germany through an acquisition of the Real hypermarket chain from Metro Group. The reports suggested that Metro Group was planning to spin off the Real division having successfully turned around the performance of its hypermarket chain, which trades through around 320 stores in Germany and around 110 stores in Poland, Romania, Russia, Turkey and Ukraine. While Walmart would be understandably reticent about returning to the scene of its humiliation in a German market that has only got more competitive since the retailer left, it is understood that the ability to forge a presence in Poland, Romania, Russia, Turkey and Ukraine might be a sufficient sweetener for Walmart to contemplate a move for Real. As an aside, it is worth pointing out that Asda has also been linked as a possible suitor for Metro Group's UK cash & carry chain, Makro. Makro has been racking up losses for a number of years and speculation has suggested that, faced with a paucity of food retail acquisition opportunities, Asda might countenance a move into wholesaling by taking over Makro and turning it into a Sam's Club-style warehouse club operation.

A similar situation applies in the speculation that Walmart is casting its eye over the international discount store chain Dia, spun off by parent company Carrefour in 2011. The situation is similar as, while Walmart would not wish to enter the French market, Dia has other store networks that are of great strategic interest for Walmart. Dia, the world's third-largest discounter behind German stalwarts Aldi and Lidl, generates nearly €10 billion in sales through around 6,400 stores in France, Spain, Portugal, Turkey, Brazil, Argentina and China. It is the market-leading hard discounter in Spain, Brazil and Argentina, number two in Portugal and Turkey and number three in France.

As an attraction for Walmart, Dia can offer stores that are in Walmart's current sweet spot of proximity discount retailing, the business can offer sizeable expansion in markets like Brazil, Argentina and China (where the Dia brand could be retained, or the stores could be re-bannered to Todo Dia, Changomas or Smart Choice, respectively) and market entry in Turkey. Also of possible interest would be an opportunity for Walmart to enter the Iberian grocery market. The main drawbacks for Walmart would be its reluctance to enter the French market (Bentonville insiders have told us that the French labour laws are anathema to the company) and also the heavy skew of the Dia business towards franchised stores (over 2,000, or 32 per cent, are franchised units), which is at odds with Walmart's love of controlling its own stores.

There is no shortage of other potential acquisition targets for Walmart across Europe. Whether these are single chain operations in particular markets or regional retail conglomerates, Walmart clearly has the deep pockets and resolve to make more of a concerted effort to become a serious pan-European retailer. These European ambitions, alongside a strong strategic presence in North America, Latin America, Africa and Asia and a very realistic potential to expand successfully into the Middle East and markets like Australia (where Walmart could conceivably consider an acquisitive entry into a market already successfully penetrated by the likes of Aldi and Costco), will mean that Walmart International will almost certainly become the second-largest retailer in the world behind Walmart US. In all likelihood, there is no tangible reason why Walmart International will not become the largest retailer in the world.

Tomorrow's Walmart

12

At the very start of this book, we posed the question: Is Walmart the best-positioned retailer in the world? Like all companies, it has had its share of *failures*, whether that is failing to crack the German retail market or rationalizing their assortment to the point where shoppers are driven to the competition. They have had their share of *criticism*, whether that is bullying suppliers, being blamed for putting independent retailers out of business or treating their employees unfairly. And looking ahead, Walmart will certainly have its share of *challenges*, the most notable of which is without a doubt Amazon.

However, the world's largest retailer didn't get to the top position by chance and, for all its faults, Walmart has also been a force for good. It has improved efficiencies across the consumer goods sector, stimulated jobs at home and abroad, and generally raised the bar for the way retailing is done.

And, crucially for consumers, Walmart has lowered prices around the globe. Looking ahead, the retailer's role in the global economy will become all the more important as food resources become strained. Saving people money so they can live better. This is what Walmart is about and there is no denying that it will continue to bring efficiencies to regions like Central Asia and sub-Saharan Africa where a lack of cold-storage facilities and poor infrastructure currently prohibit retailers from offering low prices to consumers. Walmart has a proven track record of driving down inflation and therefore undoubtedly has a long, healthy future in store in emerging economies.

But what about the more developed markets where prices can't get much lower but consumers can get more demanding? The Walmart business was built on offering low prices on a wide assortment of brands in the rural United States. That strategy was still paying dividends up until Walmart reported its first-ever comparable store sales decline in 2009. Despite unprecedented levels of growth up until that point, the recession should have been a period of acceleration, not deceleration. It was a harsh reality check, showing what happens when Walmart veers away from its core.

There is no denying that Walmart must reconfigure for future growth. It needs to have a much stronger presence in the digital world. It needs to bring low prices to urban consumers. And it needs to have a format with which it can effectively bat off those pesky dollar stores. Yet as Walmart adapts its business model to cater to today's changing consumer and retail environment, it must be careful not to veer too far from its core business philosophy. Price and assortment are increasingly prerequisites for many shoppers, which will result in the further dilution of the Walmart proposition. The question that remains is: do they have what it takes to reposition for the next 50 years of growth?

The answer must be that Walmart has what it takes to succeed, but will need to be nimble, adaptable and innovative to reconfigure to the new realities of commerce. Retail is becoming faster, more digital and heavily influenced by shoppers as social and mobile technologies and media take hold. Stores are getting smaller, and arguably less relevant, as e-commerce tightens its grip on the future of retail. Walmart is aware of these facts and it would take a brave person to bet against the retailer as it adjusts to these new challenges.

APPENDIX
The development of Walmart International

Here, we depict a timeline of the development of Walmart International – from a couple of stores in Mexico to a $100 billion plus business that straddles the globe (a notable achievement in a little over 20 years).

1991

- Walmart enters a joint venture with local operator CIFRA to open two Club Aurrera units in Mexico. Club Aurrera was a version of the Sam's Club concept.

1992

- Walmart opens its first stores in Puerto Rico. The retailer states that it hopes the Puerto Rican stores will provide learning opportunities in cross-cultural merchandising and 'oceanic shipping'.
- Activities in Mexico are expanded to include Bodega discount stores and Aurrera combination stores. Walmart states that 1993/94 will see the opening of Walmart Supercenters in Mexico.

1993

- Formal creation of the Walmart International division to 'capitalise on dynamic growth opportunities'.
- Mexican JV is broadened to include Vips restaurants, Superama supermarkets and Suburbia clothing/department stores.

1994

- Walmart Canada established through the acquisition of the Woolco Canada chain of 122 stores.

- The retailer pledges to explore further international opportunities: 'While we will proceed cautiously in light of obvious cultural differences, we are confident that the Walmart concept is "exportable" in part because of our emphasis on providing the customer with quality, value and service.'
- Opening of three Value Clubs in Hong Kong in partnership with Charoen Pokphand.
- Canadian operations are loss-making for the whole year, but make a small operating profit in Q4.

1995

- Walmart Brazil begins operations with two Supercenters and three Sam's Clubs in the state of São Paulo in a JV in which Walmart has a 60 per cent interest. The remainder of the JV is owned by local retail group Lojas Americanas.
- Operations start in Argentina, with the opening of a Sam's Club in Avellaneda.
- Walmart signs an agreement with Lippo Group to open Walmart stores in Indonesia on a royalty basis.
- The Supercenter concept debuts in Argentina, opening in Avellaneda.

1996

- Walmart Canada is said to have achieved operating profitability and a discount market share of 40 per cent in 1995 (after seeing a doubling in sales per sq. ft compared to the acquired Woolco network). Initial results in Argentina and Brazil are said to be 'encouraging'.
- Walmart Mexico becomes the country's largest retailer.
- Walmart elucidates on its international strategy, stating that it is following a 'one store at a time strategy': 'From a core of several well-performing Sam's Clubs and Supercenters, Walmart International can trigger a more aggressive expansion when the opportunity strikes.'
- Walmart begins its retail operations in China with the opening of a Supercenter and Sam's Club in Shenzhen (both operated in partnership with local JVs).
- Opens first franchised store in Indonesia.
- Exits Hong Kong.

1997

- Bob Martin, President of the Walmart International division, provides some context on the potential scope of the global operation: 'The Walmart name is better known outside the United States than any of us imagine. We are a global brand name. To customers everywhere it means low cost, best value, greatest selection of quality merchandise and highest standards of customer service. It takes time to make money in these markets, but the fact that International has grown to $5 billion in sales in less than five years gives us an idea of how great the potential is. The Walmart culture has proven that it is transportable to other cultures worldwide. The international market is virtually unlimited, and the farther the Walmart "global brand" reaches around the world, the greater the opportunity for long-term growth.'
- Walmart acquires a majority stake in CIFRA in Mexico.
- Walmart acquires the 40 per cent minority interest in its Brazilian JV from Lojas Americanas.
- Acquisition of the 21-store Wertkauf hypermarket business in Germany.

1998

- Walmart highlights the opportunity of learning from its international operations: 'We are beginning to understand the true meaning and benefits of being a global company. The best in class from all over the world now set the benchmarks for our industry, whether domestic or international. "Speedy checkouts", "gravity walls" and new merchandise items are examples of ideas from international markets that we imported and applied to our domestic business.'
- Exits Indonesia after one of its two stores is looted and torched during riots.
- Entry into South Korea via the acquisition of Makro Korea.

1999

- Acquisition of the 71-strong Interspar hypermarket business in Germany.
- In the UK, Asda is acquired by Walmart.

2000

- In Mexico, Cifra changes name to Walmart de México (WALMEX).
- Sells the three-strong Sam's Club chain in Argentina.
- Dave Ferguson, former director of Walmart's Canadian operations, is named in fiscal 2001 as the new President and CEO of Walmart Europe.

2001

- Walmart China opens its first Neighborhood Market in Shenzhen.

2002

- Walmart announces the proposed acquisition of Supermercados Amigo, the leading supermarket chain in Puerto Rico with 35 outlets.
- Walmart acquires a 6.1 per cent stake in Seiyu in Japan.

2003

- Asda in the UK opens two pilot George standalone fashion stores.
- Walmart opens its first four Sam's Club warehouse outlets in Canada.

2004

- Walmart Brazil acquires Bompreço's 118 stores in the Northern region from Dutch-based international grocery retailer Ahold.
- Asda in the UK opens its first Asda Living general merchandise superstore.

2005

- Walmart acquires a 33.3 per cent interest in CARHCO from Ahold. CARHCO operates in Guatemala, El Salvador, Honduras, Nicaragua and Costa Rica.
- Walmart Brazil acquires Sonae's 140 stores in the southern region.

- Walmart acquires a majority interest in Seiyu in Japan, making Seiyu a Walmart subsidiary.
- Opens first MercaMás pilot small format discount store in Mexico.

2006

- February – Walmart increases its interest in CARHCO to 51 per cent and the name is changed to Walmart Centroamérica.
- March – In the UK, Asda opens its first pilot Asda Essentials store, a take on the hard-discount concept.
- May – Walmart announces the sale of its 16-store chain in South Korea to Shinsegai for US~$882 million.
- July – Walmart agrees to 'sell' its retail business in Germany to Metro.
- November – Walmart Canada opens its first Supercentres.
- In Mexico, the trial of the MercaMás pilot small-format discount store in Mexico is shelved, the five stores being converted to the Bodega Aurrera Express concept.

2007

- February – Walmart China purchases a 35 per cent interest in Trust-Mart.
- April – Walmart Argentina opens the Changomas concept in La Rioja Province.
- August – Bharti Enterprises and Walmart sign an agreement to establish Bharti Wal-Mart Private Limited, a joint venture for wholesale cash & carry and back-end supply chain management operations in India.
- October – Walmart Argentina acquires three Auchan stores in La Tablada, Quilmes and Avellaneda for conversion to the Supercenter format.
- December – Walmart completes tender offer for Seiyu in Japan, raising its ownership of Seiyu from 50.9 to 95.1 per cent.

2008

- February – In the UK, Asda closes the last of its Asda Essentials stores, converting the store to the regular Asda fascia.

- March – Asda closes its chain of George high-street clothing stores in the UK following a four-and-a-half-year pilot of the standalone clothing concept.
- April – Appointment of Dr Stephan Fanderl as President of Walmart Emerging Markets – East. Fanderl is appointed to lead the company's efforts to explore retail business opportunities in Russia and neighbouring markets. Office opens in Moscow.
- April – Walmart proceeds with steps to acquire all of the remaining shares in Seiyu in Japan, which results in the delisting of Seiyu shares. In June 2008, Seiyu became a wholly owned subsidiary of Walmart.
- December – Walmart Puerto Rico opens a new concept, Super Ahorros. It is a bodega discount format, similar to the Bodega Express chain operated in Mexico.

2009

- January – Walmart acquires a majority in D&S, a leading food retailer in Chile.
- February – Walmart Canada closes its Sam's Club chain.
- March – Walmart China begins trading through three Smart Choice small-format stores.
- May – In India, Walmart and JV partner Bharti open their first Best Price Modern Wholesale cash & carry in Amritsar.
- December – Walmex confirms an agreement to acquire Walmart Centroamérica, taking full control of the regional division of Walmart International.

2010

- January – Walmart Puerto Rico is absorbed into the Walmart US business unit.
- May – Asda announces plans to acquire the 193-strong Netto discount chain in the UK from Dansk Supermarked. The deal is referred to regulators to decide how many stores should be divested to maintain local competition.
- September – Walmart announces a $4 billion offer for South Africa's Massmart. At the time of the announcement, Massmart traded through nearly 300 stores in 13 African countries. The offer is referred to various local regulators.

2011

- January – Asda announces that it has met the UK Office of Fair Trading's requirement to agree purchasers for a number of Netto stores across the UK. Subject to final regulatory approval, Asda will operate 147 Netto stores in the UK, adding 1.2 million sq. ft of space to its portfolio. The stores will trade under the Asda Supermarket banner and will average 8,000 sq. ft in size.

- May – The South African Competition Tribunal announces that the Walmart and Massmart merger can proceed to finality and has accepted the conditions proposed by Walmart and Massmart, which include the set-up of a 100 million South African rand supplier development fund, no merger-related retrenchments for a period of two years and continued recognition of SACCAWU for three years after the merger.

- May – Asda announces that it is exploring opportunities to franchise its George at Asda range in markets overseas. It states that it expects to announce its first overseas franchising partner with the intention of establishing a small number of pilot stores in the Middle East in the first half of 2012.

- June – Target announces that Target Canada has reached an agreement to transfer to Walmart Canada the rights for leasehold interests in up to 39 sites, currently operated by Zellers (the Canadian discount chain acquired by Walmart's US rival Target).

FURTHER READING

Bergdahl, M (2004) *What I Learned from Sam Walton: How to compete and thrive in a Wal-Mart world*, John Wiley & Sons, Hoboken

Bianco, A (2006) *The Bully of Bentonville: How the high cost of Wal-Mart's Everyday Low Prices is hurting America*, Doubleday, New York

Dicker, J (2005) *The United States of Wal-Mart*, Penguin, New York

Lichtenstein, N *et al* (2006) *Wal-Mart: The face of twenty-first-century capitalism*, The New Press, New York

Moreton, B (2009) *To Serve God and Wal-Mart: The making of Christian free enterprise*, Harvard University Press, Cambridge, MA

Ortega, B (1999) *In Sam We Trust: The untold story of Sam Walton and how Wal-Mart is devouring the world*, Kogan Page, London

Quinn, B (2000) *How Wal-Mart is Destroying America (and the World) and What You Can Do About It*, Ten Speed Press, Berkeley, CA

Rosen, M (2009) *Boom-Town: How Wal-Mart Transformed an All-American Town into an International Community*, Chicago Review Press, Chicago

Slater, R (2004) *The Wal-Mart Triumph*, Penguin, London

Soderquist, D (2005) *The Wal-Mart Way: The inside story of the success of the world's largest company*, Thomas Nelson, Nashville, TN

Vedder, R and Cox, W (2006) *The Wal-Mart Revolution: How big-box stores benefit consumers, workers, and the economy*, The AEI Press, Washington, DC

Walton, S with Huey, J (1992) *Sam Walton: Made in America*, Doubleday, New York

INDEX

HF
5429.215
U6
R63
2012

Roberts, Bryan R.,
1939-

Walmart.

$39.95

DATE			

WITHDRAWN

Library & Media Ctr.
Carroll Community College
1601 Washington Rd.
Westminster, MD 21157

CEO Display

NOV 28 2012

BAKER & TAYLOR